Collins *gem*

Calorie
Counter

D0243949

This book has been compiled with the assistance
of hundreds of brand-name manufacturers.
Other sources are listed on page 39.

HarperCollins*Publishers*
Westerhill Road, Bishopbriggs, Glasgow G64 2QT

www.collins.co.uk

First published 1984
Seventh edition published 2000
This edition published 2003

Reprint 10 9 8 7 6 5 4 3 2 1

© HarperCollins*Publishers* 2003

ISBN 0-00-717847-6

Typeset by Davidson Pre-Press Graphics Ltd, Glasgow

Printed in Italy by Amadeus S.p.A.

PREFACE TO THE EIGHTH EDITION

Since its first publication in 1984, the *Collins Gem Calorie Counter* has firmly established itself as one of the most successful and popular reference guides available for weight watchers.

The text for this edition has been completely revised and updated. Included is data on the amount of Calories contained in a wide range of branded foods, as well as figures for the amount of protein, carbohydrate, fat and dietary fibre in the products covered. Doctors and nutritionists agree that combining these ingredients in the correct proportions is essential to ensure a healthy diet.

The inclusion of this information makes the *Collins Gem Calorie Counter* more than ever the ideal companion for the health-conscious shopper.

CONTENTS

INTRODUCTION

Doctors, nutrition experts and successful dieters have
long known that the healthiest and most effective way to
lose weight is to combine a calorie-controlled diet with
regular exercise. If you burn off more energy than you
consume in food, then your body will be forced to use
some of the energy it stores as fat and you will lose weight.
Conversely, if you consume more energy than you expend,
the excess will be stored as fat and you will put on weight.
A proportion of the energy provided by food is used to
keep the body functioning, while the other part is burned
up by activity. Active people tend to use more energy and
therefore need to eat more to fulfill their requirements.

The energy supplied by food is generally measured in
calories, also called kilocalories (Kcal). It has been
calculated that one kilogram of fat is equivalent to 7,700
calories, so for every kilogram that a dieter wants to lose,
7,700 calories must be burned up through exercise or cut
out of the diet over a period of several days. See the chart
on pages 22–3 for an indication of the number of calories
burned off by different types of exercise and activity.

However, the equation is not quite as straightforward
as it might sound. The rate at which the body uses up
energy varies from person to person and depends on
many factors, such as a person's age, sex and general
fitness, as well as the composition of their diet. We all

know people who seem to be able to eat what they like without putting on weight, while others complain that they have a 'sluggish metabolism'.

If you keep dieting and exercising without achieving your target, it may be that you are being unrealistic and trying to reach a weight that is unhealthy for your height, body frame and metabolism. The section below explains how to calculate the ideal weight for your particular body shape and your level of activity.

You should start to lose weight soon after you cut down the number of calories you consume each day, but in the long term you will make yourself ill if you don't ensure that you eat a balanced diet with all the recommended nutrients. The **Calorie Counter** doesn't just list the calorie content of each food, but also gives the nutritional composition. On pages 22–35 there is an explanation of the elements required in a healthy diet and you can use the **Food Pyramid** on page 35 as a quick reminder.

Anyone who is considering trying to lose a lot of weight should consult their doctor first. You should also talk to your doctor before starting a diet if you have any long-term health problems.

FINDING YOUR IDEAL BODY WEIGHT

We only have partial control over our weight. Height, bone structure, metabolism and the body's tendency to store fat are all influenced by genetic predisposition.

Some families seem to stay slim effortlessly while others have to work harder at maintaining a healthy weight.

Everyone is born with a 'natural weight range'. If you consistently eat too much and don't exercise, it is possible to reach a weight well above this natural range. It is much harder to maintain a weight that is below your natural range. Long-term dieters, especially 'crash dieters', can end up confusing their metabolism, so that they gain weight quickly as soon as they stop dieting.

Charts that give ideal weight ranges for your height, such as the one on pages 14–15, are just approximations that reflect cultural averages. Two people of the same height can have completely different weights and yet both be healthy. Muscle weighs more than fat, so someone who exercises regularly might weigh more than someone of the same height who is sedentary. Weight also depends on body frame, so you should calculate whether you are small, medium or large-framed before consulting **height and weight charts** (page 12).

> **Your ideal weight** is the one at which you feel healthy and most attractive, give or take a few kilos. This might vary naturally during the year – some people put on a little more weight in winter and lose it in summer – and it also tends to change with age. So long as you feel comfortable and are within the average category for your frame and height, then you are a healthy weight.

DETERMINING YOUR FRAME SIZE

The easiest way to do this is to measure around the narrowest part of your wrist with a tape measure and then refer to the list below to detemine whether you have a small, medium or large frame.

WOMEN
Height under 1.58m:
• Small frame = wrist size less than 14cm
• Medium frame = wrist size 14cm to 15cm
• Large frame = wrist size over 15cm
Height 1.58 to 1.65m:
• Small frame = wrist size less than 15cm
• Medium frame = wrist size 15cm to 16cm
• Large frame = wrist size over 16cm
Height over 1.65m:
• Small frame = wrist size less than 16cm
• Medium frame = wrist size 16 to 17cm
• Large frame = wrist size over 17cm
MEN
Height under 1.65m:
• Small frame = wrist size less than 16cm
• Medium frame = wrist size 16 to 17cm
• Large frame = wrist size over 17cm
Height over 1.65m:
• Small frame = wrist size less than 17cm
• Medium frame = wrist size 17cm to 19cm
• Large frame = wrist size over 19cm

BODY MASS INDEX

Body Mass Index is a height to weight formula that is used to calculate whether people are clinically underweight, overweight or obese. Weight in the average range is considered to be healthy. This formula is a good approximation of total body fat, but may not work for some individuals, such as heavily muscled athletes or pregnant women.

To find your body mass index, divide your weight in kilograms by the square of your height in metres, i.e. weight ÷ height^2. Check your total against the list below to see if you fall into an average range.

For example, if you are 1.75m tall and weigh 64kg,

$$1.75 \times 1.75 = 3.06$$
$$64 \div 3.06 = 20.91$$

BMI scale:

less than 15	emaciated
15–19	underweight
19–25	average
25–30	overweight
30–40	obese

If your BMI is in the emaciated or obese range in this scale, you should visit your doctor for advice, as you could be seriously endangering your health.

The ideal body weight chart (pages 14–15) gives standard body weights for people of around 30 years of age. You will need to check your frame size before using it.

TABLES FOR STANDARD BODY WEIGHT

MEN

Height m (ft)	Small Frame kg (lbs)	Medium Frame kg (lbs)	Large Frame kg (lbs)
1.55 (5'1")	49–59 (107–130)	51–61 (113–134)	55–64 (121–140)
1.57 (5'2")	50–60 (110–132)	53–63 (116–138)	56–65 (124–144)
1.60 (5'3")	51–61 (113–134)	54–64 (119–140)	58–68 (127–150)
1.63 (5'4")	53–61 (116–135)	55–65 (122–142)	59–70 (131–154)
1.65 (5'5")	54–62 (119–137)	57–66 (125–146)	60–72 (133–159)
1.68 (5'6")	56–64 (123–140)	59–68 (129–149)	62–74 (137–163)
1.70 (5'7")	58–65 (127–143)	60–69 (133–152)	64–76 (142–167)
1.73 (5'8")	60–66 (131–145)	62–71 (137–155)	66–78 (146–171)
1.75 (5'9")	61–68 (135–149)	64–72 (141–158)	68–80 (150–175)
1.78 (5'10")	63–69 (139–152)	66–73 (145–161)	70–81 (154–179)
1.80 (5'11")	65–70 (143–155)	68–75 (149–165)	72–83 (159–183)
1.83 (6")	67–72 (147–159)	70–77 (153–169)	74–85 (163–187)
1.85 (6'1")	69–75 (151–165)	71–80 (157–175)	76–86 (167–189)
1.88 (6'2')	70–76 (155–168)	73–81 (161–179)	78–89 (171–197)
1.90 (6'3")	72–79 (157–173)	75–84 (166–185)	80–92 (176–202)

WOMEN Height m (ft)	Small Frame kg (lbs)	Medium Frame kg (lbs)	Large Frame kg (lbs)
1.47 (4'10")	41–49 (91–108)	43–52 (95–115)	47–54 (103–119)
1.50 (4'11")	42–51 (93–112)	44–55 (98–121)	48–57 (106–125)
1.52 (5')	44–52 (96–115)	46–57 (101–124)	49–58 (109–128)
1.55 (5'1")	45–54 (99–118)	47–58 (104–127)	51–59 (112–131)
1.57 (5'2")	46–55 (102–121)	49–60 (107–132)	52–61 (115–135)
1.60 (5'3")	48–56 (105–124)	50–62 (110–135)	54–63 (118–138)
1.63 (5'4")	49–58 (108–127)	51–63 (113–138)	55–65 (122–142)
1.65 (5'5")	50–59 (111–130)	53–64 (117–141)	57–66 (126–145)
1.68 (5'6")	52–60 (115–133)	55–66 (121–144)	59–67 (130–148)
1.70 (5'7")	54–62 (119–136)	57–67 (125–147)	61–69 (134–151)
1.73 (5'8")	56–63 (123–139)	58–68 (128–150)	62–71 (137–155)
1.75 (5'9")	58–64 (127–142)	60–69 (133–153)	64–73 (141–159)
1.78 (5'10")	59–66 (131–145)	62–71 (137–156)	66–75 (146–165)
1.80 (5'11")	61–68 (135–148)	64–72 (141–159)	68–77 (150–170)
1.83 (6')	63–69 (138–151)	65–74 (143–163)	69–79 (153–173)

15

CHILDREN'S WEIGHT

Doctors use growth charts to compare a child's measurements with those of other children his or her age. These measurements include height for age, weight for age, weight for height and body mass index. Babies under 2 years will be measured for length for age, weight for age, weight for length and head circumference for age. Measurements should only be taken by your doctor or health professional. Don't try to do them yourself at home because they need to be interpreted in a particular way, and inaccurate measurements could cause unnecessary alarm.

If you look at the growth charts in your doctor's surgery, you will see seven curves that follow the same pattern. Each one represents a different percentile: 5th, 10th, 25th, 50th, 75th, 90th and 95th. The 50th percentile line represents the average value for the age. If your child's weight for height is on the 25th percentile, then 75% of children that height weigh more and 25% weigh less.

Children who fall below the 5th percentile on the weight for height chart are considered underweight; children at or above the 85th percentile are usually (but not always) considered overweight; and those at or above the 95th percentile are obese.

Doctors will chart these measurements over time to show the pattern of your child's development. High or low readings don't necessarily indicate a problem. A baby whose head circumference falls in the 90th percentile

may also fall in the 90th percentile for length and weight
and just be a normal child who is large overall. Doctors
look for steady growth and would only become alarmed if
a measurement is above the 95th percentile, below the 5th,
or if it crosses two percentile curves, which could indicate
the possibility of a health problem affecting growth.

Children develop at different rates and can have growth
spurts at different ages. The important thing is not to
panic and put your child on a diet if they look a bit
overweight at one stage. Make sure that the whole family
eats a healthy diet and guide them towards nutritious
snacks rather than junk food, and you may find that the
excess weight turns into a few centimetres added to their
height within the year. You should also encourage them
to take regular exercise. If you are concerned about a
child's weight, talk to your doctor before taking any action.

AVERAGE CHILDREN'S CALORIE NEEDS

0 to 3 months	515 calories
3 to 6 months	695 calories
6 to 9 months	845 calories
9 to 12 months	945 calories
1 to 5 years	½ as much as adults
6 to 9 years	⅔ as much as adults
10 years +	as much or more than adults

USING CALORIES

We have seen that weight management depends on a balance between the amount of energy you put into your body (food calories) versus the amount of energy you expend to burn off those calories. There are several criteria you have to take into account when calculating how many calories your body needs to reach or maintain a particular weight.

First of all, you have to find your basal metabolic rate. This is the amount of energy your body expends before exercise, on physiological processes like heartbeat, breathing and maintaining your body temperature. Use the box opposite to find your own basal metabolic rate (BMR).

The BMR is the number of food calories you burn off before taking any exercise. You can now add to this any calories you expend through physical activity; see the chart on pages 22–3.

Finally, the body requires a certain amount of energy to digest food; this is known as the thermic effect. It can be simply calculated by multiplying the number of kilocalories consumed by 10%. For example, if 2,000 kcals are consumed per day, 200 kcals of this will be expended on the thermic effect.

By adding together the basal metabolic rate, the number of calories burned during activity and the calories expended for thermic effect, you will get the total number of calories that you can consume in a day

CALCULATING BMR

For men of around 20 years of age, multiply your weight in kilograms x 26.4

For example, a 20-year-old man who weighs 80kg has a BMR of 80 x 26.4 = 2,112 cal/day

For women of around 20 years of age, multiply your weight in kilograms x 24.2

For example, a 20-year-old woman who weighs 60kg has a BMR of 60 x 24.2 = 1,452 cal/day.

However, our basal metabolic rate decreases as we get older, while our weight generally increases. If you are over 20, you have to make a further calculation to arrive at your BMR. For each decade over 20, subtract 2% from the total.

For an 80kg man in his 30s, the BMR would be 2112 – 2% = 2070 cal/day

For an 80kg man in his 40s, the BMR would be 2112 – 4% = 2028 cal/day, and so on.

without losing or putting on weight. Eat fewer calories and you will lose weight; eat more and you will gain weight.

If this calculation seems too complicated, there is a simpler way to make a quick estimate of how many calories you should be consuming:

For sedentary people:
Weight in kilograms x 31 = estimated calories per day

For moderately active people (those who get aerobic exercise roughly 3–4 times per week):
Weight in kilograms x 37 = estimated calories per day

For active people: (those who get aerobic exercise roughly 5–7 times per week):
Weight in kilograms x 44 = estimated calories per day

LOSING WEIGHT BY CALORIE COUNTING

To lose one kilogram a week, you must eat 7,700 calories less that you expend in energy – roughly 1,100 calories less per day. If you calculated that you need 2,400 kcal/day to maintain your present weight, then you would have to reduce your food intake to 1,300 kcal/day. Sensible, healthy weight loss is in the range of 0.5–0.8kg per week.

Don't expect weight loss to be steady. The first week of a diet tends to produce the most dramatic weight loss as you burn up glycogen stores in your muscles and liver and your body sheds water. Once the glycogen stores are depleted, your body begins to burn fat, and this can be a slower process. If you want to lose 20kg, give yourself at least 6 months to shed it gradually. Trying to lose weight quicker than this is counter-productive as crash diets can have unwanted side-effects:

• Your metabolism will slow down as your body tries to protect its fat stores, making it more difficult to shed

> If you combine a regular exercise programme with your calorie counting, you may help to speed up your metabolism and you will either be able to eat more calories, or lose weight more quickly.

weight. Once you stop dieting, this low metabolism will remain, and you are likely to pile the weight back on again.

- You will burn up muscle tissue rather than fat. Muscle tissue burns up calories, even at rest, while fat doesn't, so your rate of weight loss could slow down.

- Deprivation dieting or skipping meals can cause a drop in blood sugar levels, which leads to sugar cravings and an urge to binge.

- The more extreme your diet, the greater the likelihood that you will not be able to stick to it.

It is important that you make sure you are getting enough nutrition from your calorie-controlled diet. Read pages 22–35 to make sure you understand the elements of a healthy diet and use the **Food Pyramid** on page 35 as a quick reminder.

You will also have to weigh and measure serving sizes accurately (see the section on portion sizes, pages 36–7). Keep a food diary listing the calorie content of everything you eat and drink, and you might want to note the protein, carbohydrate, fibre and fat contents as well, to ensure you are getting balanced nutrition.

NUMBER OF CALORIES BURNED IN 30 MINUTES OF ACTIVITY (IN RELATION TO BODY WEIGHT)

Activity/exercise	50kg	55kg	60kg	65kg	70kg	75kg
Aerobics	155	170	185	200	225	250
Badminton	190	200	210	220	230	240
Basketball	310	350	390	430	470	500
Bowling	95	100	105	110	115	120
Canoeing	120	125	135	140	145	150
Carpentry	125	135	140	145	150	160
Cooking	70	75	80	85	90	95
Cycling	150	165	180	195	210	240
Dancing, moderate	115	120	130	135	140	150
Dancing, fast	300	310	320	330	340	350
Dish-washing	70	75	80	85	90	95
Dressing	40	40	45	45	50	50
Driving	50	55	60	65	70	75
Exercise, moderate	150	160	170	180	190	200
Exercise, fast	200	220	240	260	280	300
Football	275	300	325	350	375	400
Gardening	120	130	140	150	160	170
Golf, no cart	120	125	130	140	145	150
Golf, with cart	70	75	80	85	90	95
Handball	260	275	290	310	330	350
Hockey (field or ice)	300	310	320	330	340	350
Horseback-riding	130	140	150	160	170	180
Housework, active	100	105	110	120	125	135

Activity/exercise	50kg	55kg	60kg	65kg	70kg	75kg
Ironing	70	70	75	75	80	80
Jogging, light	225	235	245	255	265	275
Lacrosse	300	315	330	345	360	375
Office work	65	70	75	80	85	90
Painting (walls)	130	135	140	150	160	170
Piano playing	100	105	110	115	120	125
Reading	15	15	20	20	25	25
Rowing	325	350	375	400	425	450
Running, slow	290	315	345	375	405	435
Running, fast	375	415	450	490	525	550
Sewing	25	25	30	30	35	35
Singing	35	40	45	50	55	60
Sitting at rest	15	15	20	20	25	25
Skating, energetically	250	260	270	280	290	300
Skiing, energetically	250	260	270	280	290	300
Stair climbing	170	185	200	215	230	250
Sweeping floor	70	75	80	90	100	110
Swimming, slow	190	210	230	250	270	290
Swimming, fast	240	260	285	305	330	355
Tennis	165	180	195	215	230	245
Typing	85	90	95	100	105	110
Volleyball	170	185	200	215	230	250
Walking, moderately	105	115	125	135	145	155
Walking, fast	125	135	145	155	165	175
Writing	50	55	60	65	70	75

COMPONENTS OF A HEALTHY DIET

The food we eat is made up of three major kinds of nutrients: proteins, carbohydrates and fats. It also provides the body with vitamins and minerals; these are known as micro-nutrients, because they are required in much smaller quantities. A healthy diet supplies all the nutrients the body needs for it to grow, heal and undertake all the processes necessary to life.

As you'll see from the **Calorie Counter**, a single food can combine several different types of nutrients and micro-nutrients. If you eat a varied diet, with the correct number of servings from each food group (see the **Food Pyramid** on page 35), then you shouldn't need to add up exactly how much you are consuming of each micro-nutrient, but read the list on pages 31–34 and check that you regularly eat foods that supply each of the main vitamins and minerals listed there.

Recommended daily allowances (RDAs) are guidelines for the levels of nutrients and micro-nutrients believed to be adequate to meet the needs of an average person. Different countries recommend different levels. In the UK, we follow EU guidelines. The packaging on foods often indicates what percentage they contain of the daily RDA of specific nutrients.

PROTEIN

Proteins are the building blocks of the human body. The cells of our bones, muscles, skin, nails, hair and every other tissue are made up of proteins. Many vital fluids, such as blood, enzymes and hormones, also contain proteins. There is an enormous variety of different kinds of protein, each made up of a special combination of components called amino acids.

The protein in our food is broken down into its component amino acids by the digestive system, and new proteins are synthesized by the body. The best sources of protein in the diet are meat, fish, eggs, milk and other dairy products, corn, lentils and other pulses. Protein obtained from animal sources contains more amino acids than protein from plants. Vegans, therefore, have to eat a wide variety of foods in order to ensure that their diet includes the full complement of amino acids.

Nutritionists recommend that protein represents 10% of the body's daily energy intake. This means that if a person consumes 2,400 calories a day, 240 of them should be provided by the protein in their food. One gram of protein provides about 4 calories, so that person needs to consume about 60 g of protein a day.

In industrialized countries, protein often makes up nearly 40% of the caloric intake. There is little evidence to suggest that too much protein is a health risk, although if it is mainly animal protein, you should watch your cholesterol level (see page 28). However, too little protein is harmful, particularly to the young who are still growing. If you develop white spots on your nails, or brittle, lustreless hair, it could be that you are not eating enough protein.

CARBOHYDRATES

Carbohydrates are the body's main source of energy. They are found mostly in plant-based foods, such as fruits, vegetables, grains and pulses. Carbohydrates are made up of different kinds of simple sugars, such as glucose. Simple carbohydrates, such as the kind of sugar we stir into tea (sucrose) or the sugar found in fruit (fructose), go straight into the bloodstream and give the body a 'lift', but the energy they supply is used up quickly and can cause a feeling of depletion as the blood sugar level drops around 20 minutes later. Complex carbohydrates are broken down more slowly by the digestive system, giving a steadier blood sugar level and no sense of depletion.

Most nutritionists recommend that over 50% of the total daily caloric intake should come from complex carbohydrates. If a person eats 2,400 calories a day, at least 1,200 of them should come from complex carbohydrates. One gram of carbohydrate provides about 4 calories, so that person should eat about 300g of carbohydrate a day.

Try to opt for unrefined carbohydrates, such as whole grains, beans, pulses, fruits and vegetables. These are a good source of micronutrients: grains provide B vitamins, while fruit is an important source of vitamin C. Refined carbohydrates, such as white bread, cakes and biscuits, sweets and snack foods, have had much of the fibre and nutrient content processed out of them, so energy from these sources is often defined as 'empty calories'. Also, foods that are high in refined carbohydrates tend to be high in fats as well, and are loaded with calories.

Dietary fibre, found in complex carbohydrates, cannot be broken down by the digestive system. It adds bulk to food and contributes to the 'full' feeling after a meal. Although it does not provide any nutrients, it is an essential part of the diet and has a number of beneficial effects, especially assisting the regular and comfortable evacuation of the bowels. Certain kinds of dietary fibre, such as oat bran, are believed to lower levels of cholesterol in the blood.

The average UK diet provides only about 12g of dietary fibre a day. Nutritionists recommend that this figure should be nearer 30g. However, if the intake of dietary fibre is increased too rapidly, it may cause flatulence and diarrhoea, and a very high consumption of fibre may impede the absorption of certain vital minerals.

FATS

Fats in food are the perennial enemy of the dieter. Fat has a very high energy value: 1g of fat provides 9 calories, more than twice the calorific value of 1g of carbohydrate or protein. The fat obtained from food is only broken

down and used as energy when other sources of energy –
carbohydrate and protein – have been exhausted. If all
the fat in the diet is not converted into energy, it is
simply laid down in the body's fat stores. A high intake
of fats will, therefore, cause weight gain.

There are two categories of fats – *saturated* and
unsaturated. Most *saturated fats* are of animal origin,
although a few, such as coconut oil and palm oil, come
from plants. Dripping, lard, butter, cream and cheese all
contain saturated fats. Some meats have a high fat
content, although this can be reduced by trimming away
any visible areas of fat before or after cooking. The liver
uses saturated fats to manufacture cholesterol, and high
cholesterol can lead to heart disease when arteries become
blocked with cholesterol deposits. For information on
your cholesterol level and how your fat intake might
affect it, consult your doctor.

Unsaturated fats, found in many vegetable, nut and fish
oils, do not raise cholesterol levels and some are thought
to actively reduce the risk of heart disease. Olive oil and
oily fish, such as mackerel, are especially recommended.

Fat represents about 40% of the total energy intake of
the average UK diet. This figure is much higher than it
needs to be for the body's requirements. The body needs
some fat as an energy store and for the formation of cell
membranes and the protective sheath that surrounds
nerves, as well as the synthesis of certain hormones and
enzymes. Most fats can be synthesized from excess

Daily calorie intake	Recommended calories from fat	Recommended fat intake
1,500	300	33g
2,000	400	44g
2,500	500	55g

carbohydrate and protein, but there are special fats, called essential fatty acids, which must be obtained from the diet. In order to ensure that these substances appear in the diet, fat should represent at least 2% of the body's energy intake.

However, a diet this low in fat would be unpalatable and difficult to prepare, so *nutritionists recommend that fat provides around 20% of the daily intake*. This means that if a person consumes 2,400 calories a day, 480 of them should be provided by fat in their food. Since 1g of fat provides 9 calories, that person should eat about 53g of fat a day.

FATS IN COMMON FOODS

Note that some low-fat foods have extra sugar added to make them more palatable, so they may contain more calories than non-low-fat alternatives. Read labels carefully.

You might be surprised how easy it can be to exceed your recommended daily fat intake. If you have bacon and egg for breakfast along with a slice of buttered toast, you will already have exceeded the recommended fat intake for those on 1,500 calories per day. A hamburger and chips meal plus a Mars bar almost reaches the daily recommended fat intake for someone on 2,500 calories a day. Using low-fat dairy products and choosing cooking methods other than frying (see pages 34–5) will significantly reduce your intake of saturated fats.

Food	Calories	Fat (g)
Whole milk (250ml)	165	9.75
Semi-skimmed milk (250ml)	115	4.25
Skimmed milk (250ml)	80	0.5
Cheddar cheese (30g)	115	9
Feta cheese (30g)	75	6
Cottage cheese (30g)	30	1.29
Low-fat cottage cheese (30g)	24	0.45
Plain whole milk yoghurt (30g)	24	0.9
Plain low-fat yoghurt (30g)	17	0.3
Butter (10g)	74	8.2
Margarine, soft (10g)	73	8.1
1 medium fried egg	179	13.9
1 medium boiled egg	147	10.8
Chips, deep-fried (100g)	280	15.5
Chips, oven-baked (100g)	162	4.2
Mars bar	449	17.4
Doughnut	262	11.9
Hamburger (each)	253	7.7
Grilled bacon, 2 rashers	295	22

VITAMINS AND MINERALS

Vitamins and minerals (micronutrients) are needed by the body in small amounts to enable it to grow, develop and function. A diet that has plenty of fresh, unrefined foods should provide an adequate supply. Many of the processes used to preserve food, such as freezing and canning, can result in loss of nutrients, though, and fruits and vegetables lose some of their goodness every extra day they sit in a fruit bowl or vegetable basket.

Here are the main vitamins and minerals and the foods that are good sources of each. Before you embark on a diet, make sure it will include items from each of these or you may risk suffering from a deficiency.

Vitamin A
- Eggs, butter, fish oils, dark green and yellow fruits and vegetables, liver.
- *Essential for:* strong bones, good eyesight, healthy skin, healing.

Vitamin B1 (Thiamine)
- Plant and animal foods, especially wholegrain products, brown rice, seafood and beans.
- *Essential for:* growth, nerve function, convertion of blood sugar into energy.

Vitamin B2 (Riboflavin)
- Milk and dairy produce, green leafy vegetables, liver, kidneys, yeast.
- *Essential for:* cell growth and reproduction, production of energy.

Vitamin B3 (Niacin)
- Meats, fish and poultry, wholegrains, peanuts and avocados.
- *Essential for:* digestion, energy, the nervous system.

Vitamin B5 (Pantothenic acid)
- Organ meats, fish, eggs, chicken, nuts and wholegrain cereals.
- *Essential for:* strengthening immunity to disease and fighting infections, healing wounds.

Vitamin B6 (Pyridoxine)
- Meat, eggs, wholegrains, yeast, cabbage, melon, molasses.
- *Essential for:* the production of new cells, a healthy immune system, production of antibodies and white blood cells.

Vitamin B12 (Cyanocolbalamin)
- Fish, dairy produce, beef, pork, lamb, organ meats, eggs and milk.
- *Essential for:* energy and concentration, production of red blood cells, growth in children.

Vitamin C
- Fresh fruit and vegetables, potatoes, leafy herbs and berries.
- *Essential for:* healthy skin, bones, muscles, healing, eyesight and protection from viruses.

Vitamin D
- Milk and dairy produce, eggs, fatty fish.
- *Essential for:* healthy teeth and bones, vital for growth.

If you are unable to get fresh food, look out for foods that have extra vitamins or minerals added. Packaged foods often state the quantity of micro-nutrients they contain, and the percentage they supply of the recommended daily allowance (RDA).

Vitamin E
- Nuts, seeds, eggs, milk, wholegrains, leafy vegetables, avocados and soya.
- *Essential for:* absorption of iron and essential fatty acids, slowing ageing, increasing fertility.

Vitamin K
- Green vegetables, milk products, apricots, wholegrains, cod liver oil.
- *Essential for:* blood clotting.

Calcium
- Dairy produce, leafy green vegetables, salmon, nuts, root vegetables, tofu.
- *Essential for:* strong bones and teeth, hormones and muscles, blood clotting and the regulation of blood pressure.

Iron
- Liver, kidney, cocoa powder, dark chocolate, shellfish, pulses, dark green vegetables, egg yolks, red meat, beans, molasses.
- *Essential for:* supply of oxygen to the cells and healthy immune system.

Magnesium
- Brown rice, soya beans, nuts, wholegrains, bitter chocolate, legumes.
- *Essential for:* transmission of nerve impulses, development of bones, growth and repair of cells.

Potassium
- Avocados, leafy green vegetables, bananas, fruit and vegetable juices, potatoes and nuts.
- *Essential for:* maintaining water balance, nerve and muscle function.

COOKING METHODS

The way you cook food will affect its calorie content and its nutritional value.

- Any fats added during cooking, such as oil for frying or a knob of butter on top, will add to the calories in the prepared dish. Young boiled carrots contain 22 calories per 100g. A small knob of 5g butter on top would add another 37 calories.

- Sugar added during cooking will increase calorie and carbohydrate content. 100g of apples stewed without sugar have just 35 calories, while 100g stewed with sugar have more than double the amount, at 74 calories.

- Grilling meat on a grill tray that allows fat to drip through will reduce the fat content. A fried rump steak has 190 calories per 100g, while grilled rump steak has only 168 calories per 100g.

- If you boil vegetables, vitamins and minerals leach out into the cooking water; steaming, stir-frying or cooking briefly in a microwave retains more of them.

- Soups, stews and casseroles preserve more of the nutritional value of foods, as vitamins and minerals will be retained in the broth.

- In general, the shorter the cooking time, the more nutrients will be retained.

FOOD PYRAMID

Fats, oils and sweets
use sparingly

Meat, poultry, fish, dry beans, eggs and nuts
2–3 servings a day

Milk, yoghurt and cheese
2–4 servings a day

Fruits 2–4 servings a day

Vegetables 3–5 servings a day

Bread, cereal, rice and pasta 6–11 servings a day

Portion Sizes

When following the **Food Pyramid** as a guide to healthy eating, it is not necessary to weigh and measure every last crumb but you should bear in mind the following guidelines to portion sizes. A single serving is not a bowl heaped full of pasta, or a steak the size of a dinnerplate.

Remember that every component of a meal or snack must be included in your calculations. For example, a tuna fish sandwich made with two slices of buttered bread would consist of 2 servings of bread, 1 of fish and one of fat.

A serving of bread, cereal, rice or pasta is:
- 1 slice of bread
- ½ bagel or roll
- 30g of cereal (this will go about halfway up a standard-sized cereal bowl)
- 50g of cooked rice or pasta (a pile about the size of a child's clenched fist); see the note about pasta and rice on page 38.

A serving of vegetables is:
- a cup of raw, leafy greens (a pile about the size of a woman's clenched fist)
- a large piece of broccoli (about the size of a lightbulb)
- a half cup of chopped vegetables (about as much as you can fit in the palm of your hand)
- ¾-full cup of vegetable juice
- 1 baked potato (about the size of a computer mouse).

A serving of fruit is:
- a medium apple or orange (200g; about the size of a tennis ball)
- a medium banana (150g peeled; it should fit on the average side plate)
- a half cup (100g) of chopped fruit or berries
- ¾-full cup of fruit juice.

A serving of milk, yoghurt or cheese is:
- 1 cup (236ml) of milk
- 1 cup (236ml) of yoghurt
- 28g of cheese (the volume of four stacked dice, or about the size of your thumb)
- a slice of cheese (about the size of a floppy computer disk)
- a half cup (57g) of cottage cheese.

A serving of meat, poultry, fish, dry beans, eggs, nuts is:
- 85g lean cooked meat, poultry or fish (the size of a deck of playing cards – or this book)
- 1 medium pork chop
- 1 small hamburger
- 1 fish fillet
- ½ of a whole chicken breast
- a medium chicken leg
- 1 medium egg
- ½ cup cooked beans (about the size of a tennis ball)
- 2 tablespoons of peanut butter (the size of a golf ball)
- a handful of nuts or seeds

HOW TO USE THE CALORIE COUNTER

The foods in this book are grouped into categories –
Bakery, Biscuits, Burgers, etc – and listed in bold type in
alphabetical order in the left-hand column of each page
together with the name of the manufacturer of branded
foods. The energy value in calories, the protein,
carbohydrate, fat and dietary fibre contents per 100 grams
or 100 millilitres are given in the third, fourth, fifth, sixth
and seventh columns respectively. This figure has been
chosen for convenience but please note that it does not
necessarily correspond to the portion sizes described on
pages 36–7. To find the values for a 28g portion of cheese,
you would have to divide the figures given by 100 and
multiply by 28. Where we have been unable to obtain
the information per 100g/100ml, it has been specified.

Note that pasta, rice and pulses swell to up to
approx. three times their weight when cooked.
The **Calorie Counter** gives values for cooked
items, while food packaging may often give values
for their dry weight. Therefore, 100g of boiled white
rice has 138 calories, but 100g of dry uncooked rice
has 343 calories. 100g of standard cooked pasta
has 89 calories, while 100g of dried, uncooked pasta
has 362 calories.

Values for unbranded foods have been obtained from *The Composition of Foods* (5th edition, 1991 and 6th summary edition, 2002) and *Vegetables, Herbs and Spices* (supplement, 1991), and have been reproduced by permission of Controller of Her Majesty's Stationery Office. Where we had gaps, Asda kindly supplied information.

The recipes in the Family Favourites have been reproduced from *The Composition of Foods 6th Summary Edition* by permission of Controller of Her Majesty's Stationery Office. The aim of including the recipes in *The Composition of Foods 6th Summary Edition* was to allow readers to see where the information was derived from. They were not intended for use as recipes.

The publishers are grateful to all the manufacturers who gave information on their products. The list of foods included is as up-to-date as it was possible to make it, but it should be remembered that new food products are frequently put on the market and existing ones withdrawn, so it has not been possible to include everything. If you cannot find a particular food here, you can still, however, obtain guideline figures by finding an equivalent product from one of the other manufacturers listed in the book.

We have included a few pages at the end of the book where you can record nutritional information for any products that you use regularly and which we have not included.

CONVERSION CHART

Metric to imperial
100 grams (g) = 3.53 ounces (oz)
1 kilogram (kg) = 2.2 pounds (lb)
100 millilitres (ml) = 3.38 fluid ounces (fl oz)
1 litre = 1.76 pints

Imperial to metric
1 ounce (oz) = 28.35 grams (g)
1 pound (lb) = 453.60 grams (g)
1 stone (st) = 6.35 kilograms (kg)
1 fluid ounce (fl oz) = 29.57 millilitres (ml)
1 pint = 0.568 litres

KEY TO READING TABLES

g	gram
kcal	kilocalorie
ml	millilitre
N	the nutrient is present in significant quantities but there is no accurate information on the amount
n/a	not available
Tr	trace (less than 0.1g present)
as sold	usually refers to mixes, granules, etc, which need to have milk or water added
recipe	indicates that the recipe used to obtain the nutritional information per 100g can be found at the back of the book

BAKERY

All amounts per 100g/100ml unless otherwise stated	Cal kcal	Pro g	Carb g	Fat g	Fibre g
NON-BRANDED BREAD AND ROLLS					
Bread					
brown	218	8.5	44.3	2	5.9
brown, toasted	272	10.4	56.5	2.1	7.1
ciabatta	271	10.2	52	3.9	2.3
currant	289	7.5	50.7	7.6	3.8
currant, toasted	323	8.4	56.8	8.5	4.2
French stick	270	9.6	55.4	2.7	5.1
garlic bread, pre-packed, frozen	365	7.8	45	18.3	n/a
granary	235	9.3	46.3	2.7	6.5
malt	268	8.3	56.8	2.4	6.5
pitta, white	265	9.2	57.9	1.2	2.2
rye	219	8.3	45.8	1.7	5.8
wheatgerm	212	9.5	41.5	2	5.1
wheatgerm, toasted	271	12.1	53.2	2.6	6.5
white	235	8.4	49.3	1.9	3.8
white, fried in oil/lard	503	7.9	48.5	32	3.8
white, toasted	265	9.3	57.1	1.6	4.5
wholemeal	215	9.2	41.6	2.5	7.4
wholemeal, toasted	252	10.8	48.7	2.9	8.7
Rolls					
brown, crusty	255	10.3	50.4	2.8	7.1
brown, soft	268	10	51.8	3.8	6.4
hamburger buns	264	9.1	48.8	5	1.5
white, crusty	280	10.9	57.6	2.3	4.3
white, soft	268	9.2	51.6	4.2	3.9
wholemeal	241	9	48.3	2.9	8.8

Calorie Counter

All amounts per 100g/100ml unless otherwise stated	Cal kcal	Pro g	Carb g	Fat g	Fibre g
BRANDED BREAD AND ROLLS					
Bagels NEW YORK BAGELS	271	11.2	53.2	1.5	2.2
onion	274	11.1	53.9	1.6	2.1
sesame	272	11.4	52.7	1.8	2.2
Baps, white, sliced WARBURTONS	235	9.8	43.6	4.4	2.7
Bread					
Amazing Grain Malted NIMBLE	222	10.5	44.1	1.5	5.6
Best of Both HOVIS	219	9	40.8	2.3	4.5
brown SUNBLEST	221	7.5	43.8	1.7	4.6
Burgen Soya & Linseed ALLIED BAKERIES	278	17.6	28.6	10	6.1
Country Gold Malted Wheat KINGSMILL	234	9.4	43.4	2.5	2.7
Country Grain Wholemeal HOVIS	222	11.2	37.4	3.1	5.7
Danish brown HEINZ WEIGHT WATCHERS	200	8.6	37.7	1.6	9.6
Danish malted HEINZ WEIGHT WATCHERS	218	10.2	41.3	1.4	6.9
Danish toaster SUNBLEST	232	8.9	45.4	1.6	2.1
Danish white HEINZ WEIGHT WATCHERS	222	8.7	43.9	1.3	2.8
Danish white SUNBLEST	232	8.9	45.4	1.6	2.1
Danish white WARBURTONS	243	10.7	46.9	1.4	2.7
Danish wholemeal WARBURTONS	229	13.1	38.6	2.5	7.2
Farmhouse White HOVIS	228	9	44.6	1.5	2.3

All amounts per 100g/100ml unless otherwise stated	Cal kcal	Pro g	Carb g	Fat g	Fibre g
Farmhouse Wholemeal HOVIS	206	10.2	36.6	2.1	5.3
Gold White KINGSMILL	237	8.8	44.2	2.8	2.3
Good Health White WARBURTONS	220	9.4	41.6	1.8	4.1
Good Health Wholegrain WARBURTONS	234	10.7	41.7	2.7	6.1
Good Health Wholemeal WARBURTONS	226	10.3	39.6	2.9	7.2
granary brown HOVIS	225	9.1	42.7	2	3.3
Great Tasting Wholemeal WARBURTONS	231	10.6	40.9	2.8	6.3
HiBran ALLINSON	212	13.2	33.6	2.8	8
Malted Batch WARBURTONS	262	10.9	48.8	2.6	5.1
Mighty White MIGHTY WHITE	224	7.2	45.5	1.5	3.7
Oat Batch WARBURTONS	262	10.9	45.7	3.9	6.7
Oat Danish HEINZ WEIGHT WATCHERS	227	10.7	38.6	3.3	7.7
Oatmeal CROFTERS KITCHEN	234	8.1	41.6	3.9	3.7
Premium Brown WARBURTONS	244	10.3	42.7	3.6	5.1
Premium White HOVIS	235	9	44.4	2.3	2.1
Rye, German style KELDERMAN	155	5.6	30.2	1.4	7.7
Scottish Plain White SUNBLEST	232	9.7	42.8	2.4	3
Seeded Batch WARBURTONS	289	12.3	39.8	8.9	3.2
Square Cut White HOVIS	234	9.5	44.3	2.1	2.4
Stoneground Wholemeal WARBURTONS	217	9.8	39.3	2.3	7.2
Tasty Crust White KINGSMILL	259	9.4	48.8	2.9	2.4

Calorie Counter

All amounts per 100g/100ml unless otherwise stated	Cal kcal	Pro g	Carb g	Fat g	Fibre g
Tasty Crust Wholemeal KINGSMILL	251	11.2	42.2	4.2	5.9
Tasty Wholemeal KINGSMILL	228	10.1	39.2	3.4	5.2
Wheatgerm VITBE	232	10.4	39.6	3.6	4.2
white HEINZ WEIGHT WATCHERS	231	10.6	43.6	1.6	3.6
white HOVIS	233	10.8	40.1	3.3	3.7
white MOTHERS PRIDE	229	8	45.6	1.6	3
white NIMBLE	249	10.3	46.3	2.6	2.2
white SUNBLEST	232	7.4	46.4	1.9	2.1
white KINGSMILL	232	8.8	43.8	2.4	2.8
White Farmhouse WARBURTONS	237	9.9	43.6	2.6	2.7
White Rice ENER-G BREAD	258	1.7	36.7	12	1.4
White Toastie WARBURTONS	235	10.1	44.6	1.8	2.7
white, medium slice WARBURTONS	235	10.1	44.6	1.8	2.7
white, organic WARBURTONS	228	9.6	42.1	2.4	2.7
white, sliced crusty HOVIS	233	8.8	44.3	2.2	2.1
Whole White KINGSMILL	228	9	42.3	2.5	4
wholemeal HOVIS	220	10.8	37.7	2.9	5.9
wholemeal ALLINSON	213	10.1	37.3	2.6	7.5
wholemeal NIMBLE	216	11.2	36.9	2.7	6.9
Wholemeal Gold KINGSMILL	221	10.9	37.8	2.9	6
wholemeal, medium slice WARBURTONS	234	10.3	40.1	3.6	7.2
wholemeal, organic ALLINSON	217	9.5	39.6	2.3	6.5
wholemeal, organic WARBURTONS	219	11	36.4	3.3	7.2

All amounts per 100g/100ml unless otherwise stated	Cal kcal	Pro g	Carb g	Fat g	Fibre g
Chapatis					
made with fat	328	8.1	48.3	13	N
made without fat	202	7.3	43.7	1	N
PATAK'S	310	11.2	44.9	9.5	n/a
Milk Roll WARBURTONS					
White	251	10.8	45.3	3	2.8
Wholemeal	231	12.5	38.1	3.2	7
Naan Bread	336	8.9	50.1	13	1.9
garlic & coriander SHARWOOD	244	7.1	46.2	3.4	2
garlic & corinader PATAK'S	323	9.03	47.5	11	n/a
onion bhaji SHARWOOD	291	7.3	48.4	7.6	2.2
plain feast SHARWOOD	272	8.5	42.9	7.4	2.4
tandoori SHARWOOD	244	7.2	46.3	3.3	2
Pitta Bread					
toasted sesame					
INTERNATIONAL HARVEST	263	9.7	48	3.6	3
white SUNBLEST	251	8.6	50	1.8	2.3
wholewheat SUNBLEST	227	10.6	41	2.3	6.2
Rolls					
brown MORTONS	249	11.6	48.9	0.8	5.6
brown HEINZ WEIGHT WATCHERS	212	12.1	36.8	1.9	6.3
cobble style HOVIS	235	10.4	46.4	3.8	3
Country Choice Harvester, each KINGSMILL	148	6.4	28.5	0.9	2.1
Good Health White WARBURTONS	225	9.7	42.1	2	4.1

Calorie Counter

All amounts per 100g/100ml unless otherwise stated	Cal kcal	Pro g	Carb g	Fat g	Fibre g
Seeded WARBURTONS	310	13.2	41.3	10	n/a
Tasty Wholemeal WARBURTONS	231	10.2	39.1	3.8	n/a
traditional hand made					
MORTONS	274	11.6	55.3	0.7	1.4
well fired MORTONS	272	11.6	54.2	1	1.7
white MORTONS	272	11.6	54.2	1	1.7
white HEINZ WEIGHT WATCHERS	231	10.6	43.6	1.6	3.6
white WARBURTONS	249	9.7	42.9	4.3	n/a
White Farmhouse					
WARBURTONS	250	9.7	43	4.4	n/a
white, each KINGSMILL	151	5.6	26.7	2.5	1.4
Whole White KINGSMILL	251	9.5	43.7	4.2	3.5
wholemeal, each ALLINSON	151	5.5	26.6	2.5	3.7
Taco Shells OLD EL PASO	**485**	7.4	60.8	23	n/a
Tortillas					
corn OLD EL PASO	315	10	44	11	n/a
flour OLD EL PASO	342	10	60	6.6	n/a
flour DISCOVERY FOODS	313	8.6	53.9	7	2.5
flour, garlic & coriander					
DISCOVERY FOODS	313	8.6	53.9	7	2.5
flour, organic DISCOVERY FOODS	310	9.1	52	7.9	1.3

BREAKFAST AND TEATIME BREADS/CAKES

Bagels, cinnamon & raisin
NEW YORK BAGELS | 282 | 10.5 | 56 | 1.8 | 2.2

All amounts per 100g/100ml unless otherwise stated	Cal kcal	Pro g	Carb g	Fat g	Fibre g
Brioche CONTINENTAL CLASSICS	349	8.2	58.3	9.3	n/a
Chelsea Buns	366	7.8	56.1	14	1.7
Cranberry Loaf with Orange WARBURTONS	273	7.3	49.9	4.9	2.7
Croissants	360	8.3	38.3	20	2.5
INTERNATIONAL HARVEST	459	8.5	36.9	31	1.2
Crumpets					
WARBURTONS	178	7.1	35.8	0.7	n/a
each SUNBLEST	91	2.5	19.4	0.4	0.8
Currant Buns	296	7.6	52.7	7.5	N
SUNBLEST	298	7.2	52.6	6.5	2
Danish Pastries	374	5.8	51.3	18	1.6
Doughnuts					
jam	336	5.7	48.8	15	N
ring	397	6.1	47.2	22	N
Eccles Cakes	475	3.9	59.3	26	1.6
Fruit Loaf					
banana SOREEN	313	6.8	60.9	4.7	n/a
Lincolnshire Plum SOREEN	297	7.9	56.3	4.5	n/a
Rich SOREEN	310	7.4	60.7	4.1	n/a
with Orange WARBURTONS	271	8.1	51.9	3.4	3.4
Hot Cross Buns	310	7.4	58.5	6.8	1.7

Calorie Counter

All amounts per 100g/100ml unless otherwise stated	Cal kcal	Pro g	Carb g	Fat g	Fibre g
Malt Loaf					
cherry SUNBLEST	297	8.5	63.6	0.9	2.4
fruit, original SOREEN	312	7.6	66.5	1.7	n/a
fruity, organic DOVES FARM	315	7.3	61.5	4.1	4.3
Sunmalt SUNBLEST	280	9.2	56.9	1.7	5.4
Muffins					
SUNBLEST	239	9	46.8	1.7	2.3
blueberry MCVITIE'S	429	4.3	49.9	24	1.1
Pancakes					
WARBURTONS	329	9	53.4	8.8	n/a
sultana & syrup SUNBLEST	270	5.3	53	4.1	1.2
Pikelets SUNBLEST	193	5.8	40.9	0.7	1.7
Potato Scones					
MOTHER'S PRIDE	207	4.7	42	2.2	4.3
SUNBLEST	222	3.4	39.5	5.6	1.7
Raisin Loaf with Cinnamon					
WARBURTONS	276	7.5	52.9	3.8	4.2
Scones					
fruit	316	7.3	52.9	9.8	N
plain, recipe	364	7.2	53.7	14.8	1.8
wholemeal	326	8.7	43.1	14	5.2
Scotch Pancakes	292	5.8	43.6	12	1.4
SUNBLEST	375	6	51.6	4.9	1.2

All amounts per 100g/100ml unless otherwise stated	Cal kcal	Pro g	Carb g	Fat g	Fibre g
Soda Scones MOTHER'S PRIDE	**158**	4.2	25.4	4.3	3.1
Teacakes					
fruited WARBURTONS	**263**	9.8	48.2	3.4	2.7
fruited, each SUNBLEST	**210**	4.8	37.7	4.5	1.5

CAKES AND CREAM CAKES

	Cal kcal	Pro g	Carb g	Fat g	Fibre g
Almond Slice MR KIPLING	**383**	6.8	58.6	13	1.6
Angel Slice MR KIPLING	**362**	2.6	49.8	17	0.4
Apple Sauce Spice Cake CALIFORNIA CAKE COMPANY LTD	**343**	2.9	58.1	10	0.8
Apricot Cake Bar JACOB'S VITALINEA	**377**	4.1	66.5	11	0.9
Bakewell Slice MR KIPLING	**436**	3.7	59.5	20	1
Banana Cake CALIFORNIA CAKE COMPANY LTD	**347**	3.2	55.9	12	0.7
Battenburg Cake					
LYONS CAKES	**431**	6.9	70.3	14	1.3
MR KIPLING	**429**	7.1	70.6	13	1.4
Bramley Apple Danish Bar SARA LEE	**241**	4.2	42.7	24	1
Bramley Apple Fruit Pie Bars MR KIPLING	**361**	3.5	54.7	14	1.3

Calorie Counter

All amounts per 100g/100ml unless otherwise stated	Cal kcal	Pro g	Carb g	Fat g	Fibre g
Brownies, Luxury CALIFORNIA CAKE COMPANY LTD	415	5.2	48.9	21	1.4
Butterfly Cakes MR KIPLING	392	4.4	43.4	22.2	0.6
Caramel Cake Bars CADBURY	411	6.4	57	17	0.5
Caramel Shortcake Bars MR KIPLING	495	4.1	55.2	29	1
Caramel Shortcakes MR KIPLING	495	4.1	55.2	29	1
Carrot Cake CALIFORNIA CAKE COMPANY LTD	377	3.5	52.8	16	1.2
Light & Moist	277	3	56.4	2.7	1.9
Cherry Cake LYONS CAKES	343	4.6	44.1	16.4	0.7
Chocolate Chip Bar Cake MCVITIE'S	392	5.8	528	19	1
Chocolate Chip Cake Bars MR KIPLING	448	6.1	45.2	27	0.6
Chocolate Cup Cakes LYONS CAKES	324	2.6	67.2	4.9	0.8
Chocolate Fudge Cake ENTENMANN'S	316	5.3	56.9	7.8	0.9
Chocolate Orange Cake Bar JACOB'S VITALINEA	382	3.3	70.4	9.7	2.2
Chocolate Roll, Rich CADBURY	360	4.6	51.6	15	1.8

All amounts per 100g/100ml unless otherwise stated	Cal kcal	Pro g	Carb g	Fat g	Fibre g
Chocolate Sandwich LYONS CAKES	378	5.7	46.7	19	1.2
Christmas Slices MR KIPLING	327	2.5	62.5	7.4	0.9
Coconut Sandwich LYONS CAKES	390	3.9	46.8	21	0.9
Country Slices MR KIPLING	361	3.3	52.8	15	1.1
Crunchie Cake Bars CADBURY	460	5.9	58.3	22.6	0.4
Date and Walnut Loaf Cake LYONS CAKES	382	6.3	43.2	20.5	1.5
Eclairs, frozen	396	5.6	26.1	31	0.8
Fancy Iced Cakes	407	3.8	68.8	15	N
Farmhouse Slices LYONS CAKES	358	3.8	53.3	14	1.2
Flake Cake CADBURY	445	6.3	54.5	22	0.9
Flapjack	484	4.5	60.4	27	2.7
apple & sultana, organic DOVES FARM	430	5	62.2	19	4.1
apricot & sultana MR KIPLING	456	4.6	59	22	3.6
fruit HOLLAND & BARRETT	468	4.8	58	24	1.8
Homebake Berry MCVITIE'S	484	6.3	57.4	26	3.5
plain, wholewheat HOLLAND & BARRETT	490	5.3	54.9	28	2.1
traditional butter, organic DOVES FARM	437	5.6	62.2	20	4.1

Calorie Counter

All amounts per 100g/100ml unless otherwise stated	Cal kcal	Pro g	Carb g	Fat g	Fibre g
French Fancies MR KIPLING	356	2.3	65.1	9.6	0.4
French Sandwich Cake LYONS CAKES	355	4.1	46.5	17	0.7
Fruit Cake					
plain, retail	354	5.1	57.9	13	N
rich, iced	356	4.1	62.7	11	1.7
rich, recipe	343	3.9	59.9	11.4	1.5
wholemeal	363	6	52.8	16	2.4
Fry's Turkish Delight Cakes CADBURY	349	4.6	58	11	0.7
Galaxy Cake Bar MCVITIE'S	496	5.1	55.5	28	0.4
Gateau	337	5.7	43.4	17	0.4
Go Ahead Cake Bar, chocolate dream MCVITIE'S	394	4.7	63.9	13.3	0.9
Go Ahead Mini Cake Bars, chocolate chip MCVITIE'S	356	6.4	56.9	12.4	1
Golden Syrup Bar Cake MCVITIE'S	385	3.6	60.2	14	1.2
Grannies Cake LYONS CAKES	389	4.9	46.9	20	1.3
Greek Pastries (sweet)	322	4.7	40	17	N

All amounts per 100g/100ml unless otherwise stated	Cal kcal	Pro g	Carb g	Fat g	Fibre g
Homebake Cake McVitie's					
chocolate	357	5.7	56.5	14	1.4
lemon	385	4.5	55.5	18	1.1
marble	371	5.2	55.4	14	1.2
Jaffa Cake Bar McVitie's	408	3.9	59	17.4	2.9
Jaffa Fingers Lyons Cakes	476	3.6	62.7	23	1
Jamaica Ginger Bar Cake McVitie's	388	3.5	60.2	15	1.2
Lemon Cake, Light & Moist California Cake Company Ltd	329	3.4	69.1	2.6	3
Lemon Loaf Cake Lyons Cakes	380	4.8	48.1	18.7	0.9
Lemon Slices					
Lyons Cakes	356	3.8	55.8	13	0.5
Mr Kipling	397	4.1	58.5	16	0.6
Madeira Cake	393	5.4	58.4	17	0.9
Mandarin Chocolate Roll Lyons Cakes	378	4.5	55.2	16	0.5
Manor House Cake Mr Kipling	402	5.1	49.1	21	1.4
Maple Walnut Cake California Cake Company Ltd	412	4.3	51.7	22	0.6
Milk Chocolate Cake Bar Cadbury	401	6.8	48.8	19.8	0.8

Calorie Counter

All amounts per 100g/100ml unless otherwise stated	Cal kcal	Pro g	Carb g	Fat g	Fibre g
Milky Way Cake Bar McVitie's	**518**	5.2	53.5	31.4	0.3
Mince Slices Mr Kipling	**367**	3.5	55.9	14	1.5
Mini Rolls Cadbury					
chocolate	**420**	5.4	53.2	21	0.9
orange	**390**	5	55	16.8	0.8
strawberry	**390**	4.9	54.4	17	0.5
Penguin Snack Cake McVitie's	**504**	5.2	54.6	29.5	1.3
Sponge Cake					
recipe	**467**	6.3	52.4	27.2	0.9
fatless	**294**	10.1	53	6.1	0.9
jam filled	**302**	4.2	64.2	4.9	1.8
with butter icing	**490**	4.5	52.4	31	0.6
Stollen Slices Mr Kipling	**348**	5.2	51.7	13	1.4
Strawberry Starburst Cake Bar McVitie's	**352**	4.3	59	12.2	0.8
Strawberry Sundaes Mr Kipling	**357**	2.7	53	15	0.9
Swiss Gateau Cadbury	**379**	5	52.3	17	1.3
Swiss Roll					
chocolate, individual	**337**	4.3	58.1	11	N
chocolate Lyons Cakes	**366**	5.4	48.1	17	1.4
raspberry Lyons Cakes	**292**	5.2	60.5	3.2	1.2
Trifle Sponge Lyons Cakes	**324**	5.2	67.1	3.9	1
Viennese Fingers Mr Kipling	**523**	4.3	54.9	32	1.3

All amounts per 100g/100ml unless otherwise stated	Cal kcal	Pro g	Carb g	Fat g	Fibre g
PIES AND FLANS					
Apple & Blackcurrant Pies					
MR KIPLING	334	3.4	51	13	1.6
individual	331	3.1	52.7	12	1.5
Apple Pies McVITIE'S	235	2.8	35.3	9.6	0.9
Bakewell Tart					
LYONS CAKES	397	3.8	56.7	17	0.9
McVITIE'S	396	5	48.9	20	0.7
Bakewells, Cherry MR KIPLING	412	3.9	58.5	18	1.2
Bramley Apple & Custard Pies					
MR KIPLING	335	3.2	47.8	15	1.1
Bramley Apple Pies MR KIPLING	334	3.4	51	13	1.3
individual	329	3	52	12	1.2
Custard Tarts	277	6.3	32.4	15	1.2
Dutch Apple Tart McVITIE'S	237	3.2	34.4	9.9	0.6
Easter Lemon Bakewells					
MR KIPLING	417	4	59.8	18	1
Fruit Pie					
individual	369	4.3	56.7	16	N
one crust	186	2	28.7	7.9	1.7
pastry top & bottom, recipe	260	3	34	13	1.8
wholemeal, one crust	183	2.6	26.6	8.1	2.7

Calorie Counter

All amounts per 100g/100ml unless otherwise stated	Cal kcal	Pro g	Carb g	Fat g	Fibre g
Jam Tarts					
retail	368	3.3	63.4	13	N
real fruit LYONS CAKES	351	3.5	52.9	14	1.3
Lemon Curd Tarts LYONS CAKES	406	3.7	59.3	17	1
Lemon Meringue Pie	319	4.5	45.9	14	0.7
SARA LEE	272	2.4	46.1	8.9	0.9
Lemon Mousse Tarts MR KIPLING	379	2.8	46.6	20	0.8
Mince Pies MR KIPLING	372	3.8	56.8	14	1.5
luxury	387	3.7	55.7	14	1.5
Mince Tartlets, glazed MR KIPLING	363	3.9	53.5	15	1.5
Orchards Pie MCVITIE'S	272	3.8	38.4	12	1.1
Santa Bakewells MR KIPLING	412	3.8	59.5	18	1
Treacle Lattice Tart LYONS CAKES	364	4.4	59.3	12	1.1
Treacle Tart	368	3.7	60.4	14	1.1

BEANS, LENTILS AND CEREAL PRODUCTS

All amounts per 100g/100ml unless otherwise stated	Cal kcal	Pro g	Carb g	Fat g	Fibre g

BAKED BEANS AND BAKED BEAN PRODUCTS

Baked Beans

in tomato sauce	84	5.2	15.3	0.6	6.9
in tomato sauce HEINZ	75	4.7	13.6	0.2	3.7
in tomato sauce HP	85	4.7	15	0.7	3.7
in tomato sauce, no added sugar					
HEINZ WEIGHT WATCHERS	56	4.7	8.6	0.2	3.7
Healthy HP	63	4.4	11	0.2	3.7
Healthy Balance, in tomato					
sauce HEINZ	67	4.6	11.7	0.2	3.7

Baked Beans & Vegetable Sausages, Healthy Balance HEINZ	96	5.8	10.2	3.6	2.9
Baked Beans with Bacon HEINZ	91	6	12.9	1.7	3
Baked Beans with Chicken Nuggets HEINZ	104	6.6	12.4	3.1	3.2
Baked Beans with Pork Sausages HEINZ	89	5.5	11.2	2.5	2.6
Baked Beans, curried HEINZ	103	4.9	17.9	1.3	4
Barbecue Beans HEINZ	82	4.9	14.9	0.3	4

Calorie Counter

All amounts per 100g/100ml unless otherwise stated	Cal kcal	Pro g	Carb g	Fat g	Fibre g
Beef Chilli Baked Bean Cuisine HEINZ	85	4.6	10.8	2.6	1.7
Beef Lasagne Baked Bean Cuisine HEINZ	90	5.1	11.5	2.6	1.2
Bolognese Beanfeast, as sold BATCHELORS	302	23.9	39	5.6	13.5
Cheesy Pasta Bake Baked Bean Cuisine HEINZ	106	5	14.3	3.2	1.4
Chilli Beanfeast, as sold BATCHELORS	312	24.3	42.7	4.9	13.6
Curry Beanfeast, as sold BATCHELORS	328	21.1	44.1	7.5	12.5
Lamb Hotpot Baked Bean Cuisine HEINZ	99	5.4	12.1	3.2	2.1
Ocean Pie Baked Bean Cuisine HEINZ	91	5.9	10.1	3	1.3
Sausage Hotpot Baked Bean Cuisine HEINZ	99	5.2	13.3	2.7	2.5
Savoury Mince Beanfeast, as sold BATCHELORS	316	24.7	39.5	6.6	12.7

Beans, Lentils and Cereal Products

All amounts per 100g/100ml unless otherwise stated	Cal kcal	Pro g	Carb g	Fat g	Fibre g
Shepherd's Pie Baked Bean Cuisine HEINZ	88	4.1	11.6	2.8	1.5
Tuna Pasta Bake Baked Bean Cuisine HEINZ	103	6.6	12.8	2.8	1.2
BEANS AND LENTILS					
Aduki Beans					
dried	272	19.9	50.1	0.5	11.1
dried, boiled	123	9.3	22.5	0.2	5.5
Blackeye Beans					
dried	311	23.5	54.1	1.6	8.2
dried, boiled	116	8.8	19.9	0.7	3.5
Broad Beans, canned	64	6.7	8.5	0.3	4.2
Butter Beans					
canned	77	5.9	13	0.5	4.6
canned BATCHELORS	83	6	13.9	0.4	4.8
dried, boiled	103	7.1	18.4	0.6	5.2
dried HOLLAND & BARRETT	273	19.1	49.8	1.1	16
Cannellini Beans, canned	84	6.8	13.5	0.3	6
Chick Peas					
canned	115	7.2	16.1	2.9	4.1
dried	320	21.3	49.6	5.4	10.7
dried, boiled	121	8.4	18.2	2.1	4.3

Calorie Counter

All amounts per 100g/100ml unless otherwise stated	Cal kcal	Pro g	Carb g	Fat g	Fibre g
Chilli Beans					
canned	79	4.8	13.8	0.5	3.7
dried	70	4.9	12.2	0.5	3.9
Haricot Beans					
dried	286	21.4	49.7	1.6	17
dried, boiled	95	6.6	17.2	0.5	6.1
Lentils					
green/brown, dried	297	24.3	48.8	1.9	8.9
green/brown, dried, boiled	105	8.8	16.9	0.7	3.8
red, split, dried	318	23.8	56.3	1.3	4.9
red, split, dried, boiled	100	7.6	17.5	0.4	1.9
Marrowfat Peas BATCHELORS					
Farrow's Giant, canned	77	5.9	12.3	0.5	4.9
quick-soak, dried	290	25.3	41.9	2.4	14
Bigga, canned	66	5.6	10.1	0.3	4
Bigga, dried	262	23.1	37.6	2.1	20.2
Mung Beans					
dried	279	23.9	46.3	1.1	10
dried, boiled	91	7.6	15.3	0.4	3
Pinto Beans					
dried	327	21.1	57.1	1.6	N
dried, boiled	137	8.9	23.9	0.7	N
refried	107	6.2	15.3	1.1	N

Beans, Lentils and Cereal Products

All amounts per 100g/100ml unless otherwise stated	Cal kcal	Pro g	Carb g	Fat g	Fibre g
Red Kidney Beans					
canned	100	6.9	17.8	0.6	8.5
canned BATCHELORS	91	8.1	13.5	0.5	6.4
canned HOLLAND & BARRETT	262	22.1	40.2	1.4	15.7
dried, boiled	103	8.4	17.4	0.5	9
Refried Beans OLD EL PASO	83	5.8	13.5	1	n/a
Soya Beans					
dried	370	35.9	15.8	18.6	15.7
dried, boiled	141	14	5.1	7.3	6.1
Split Peas					
dried, boiled	126	8.3	22.7	0.9	2.7
yellow, dried WHITWORTHS	310	22.1	56.6	1	5.9
Tofu (soya bean curd)					
steamed	73	8.1	0.7	4.2	N
steamed, fried	261	23.5	2	17.7	N

Fresh beans & peas: *see* FRUIT AND VEGETABLES

CEREAL PRODUCTS

Barley, pearl, as sold WHITWORTHS	360	7.9	83.6	1.7	7.3
Bran					
wheat	206	14.1	26.8	5.5	39.6
wheat HOLLAND & BARRETT	171	12.5	25	3	43
soya, cooked ITONA	169	16	15	5	55

Calorie Counter

All amounts per 100g/100ml unless otherwise stated	Cal kcal	Pro g	Carb g	Fat g	Fibre g
Bulgur Wheat, as sold HOLLAND & BARRETT	**354**	11	75	1.5	1.8
Couscous, as sold HOLLAND & BARRETT	**355**	13.5	72.5	1.9	2
Cracked Wheat: *see* **Bulgur Wheat**					
Polenta, ready-made ITALFRESCO	**71.9**	1.6	15.7	0.3	n/a
Wheatgerm	**302**	26.7	44.7	9.2	15.6

BISCUITS

All amounts per 100g/100ml unless otherwise stated	Cal kcal	Pro g	Carb g	Fat g	Fibre g
SWEET BISCUITS					
Abbey Crunch Biscuits MCVITIE'S	**477**	6	72.8	17.9	2.5
Boasters MCVITIE'S					
chocolate chunk	**522**	5.9	61.9	27.8	1.8
hazelnut & chocolate chunk	**548**	7.1	55.2	33.3	2.3
Bourbon Creams JACOB'S	**467**	n/a	70.4	19.1	n/a
Caramel Log TUNNOCK'S	**472**	4.2	64.3	24	n/a
Caramel Wafers TUNNOCK'S	**454**	4.6	68	20.1	n/a
Chocolate Biscuit Cakes, gluten-free ITONA	**494**	10.9	51.7	27.1	n/a
Chocolate Chip & Orange Biscuits, gluten-free ITONA	**467**	10.5	57.6	21.6	n/a
Chocolate Chip Cookies					
CADBURY	**495**	6.5	66.2	22.5	2.6
Real HEINZ WEIGHT WATCHERS	**427**	5.3	66.1	15.7	1.6
Chocolate Digestive: *see* **Digestive Bisuits**					
Chocolate Farls TUNNOCK'S	**521**	5.5	62.8	27.5	n/a
Chocolate Mallow JACOB'S	**420**	4.5	65.9	15.4	1.5
Chocolate Oliver Biscuits FORTTS	**359**	6.5	69.5	23.9	3.9

Calorie Counter

All amounts per 100g/100ml unless otherwise stated	Cal kcal	Pro g	Carb g	Fat g	Fibre g
Chocolate Wafer Cream					
Tunnock's	513	6.6	63.2	28	n/a
Club Biscuits Jacob's					
fruit	497	5.7	61.6	25.3	2.1
milk chocolate	511	5.8	62.6	26.4	2
mint	517	5.6	62.5	27.2	1.7
orange	519	5.6	62.2	27.6	1.7
Cocoa Swirls, organic					
Doves Farm	491	5.5	59.2	25.8	5.5
Coconut Snowballs Tunnock's	388	3.9	47	21.8	n/a
Custard Creams					
Crawford's	514	6.1	69.7	23.4	1.6
Jacob's	498	5.3	68.3	22.6	1.4
Dark Treacle Cookies					
Heinz Weight Watchers	423	5.2	66.7	15.1	1.7
Date Syrup Biscuits, high-fibre Itona	387	10.3	48.2	18.5	12
Digestive Biscuits	471	6.3	68.6	20.9	4.6
Holland & Barrett	477	5.4	66.3	21.2	Tr
McVitie's	496	7	67.5	21.9	2.9
organic Doves Farm	390	5.6	54.2	16.8	5.1
chocolate (milk & plain)	493	6.8	66.5	24.1	3.1
milk chocolate McVitie's	503	6.8	66.3	23.3	2.3

All amounts per 100g/100ml unless otherwise stated	Cal kcal	Pro g	Carb g	Fat g	Fibre g
milk chocolate, organic					
DOVES FARM	439	5.8	53.4	22.5	4.3
plain chocolate MCVITIE'S	506	6.1	66	24.2	2.8
plain chocolate, organic					
DOVES FARM	428	5.8	51.4	22.1	6.4
Fig Rolls					
JACOB'S	357	3.5	67.7	8	3.9
Vitalinea JACOB'S	339	3.7	68.2	5.8	3.8
Finger Shortcake MCVITIE'S	483	5.9	69.6	20.1	2.1
Fingers CADBURY					
milk chocolate	526	6.9	64.3	26.8	1.8
white chocolate	532	7.1	62.5	28.2	1.5
Florida Orange TUNNOCK'S	519	5.1	64	29	n/a
Fruit & Nut Biscuits, gluten-free ITONA	461	11.1	57	20.9	n/a
Fruity Oat Biscuit, organic DOVES FARM	471	7.6	62.7	21.1	4
Garibaldi JACOB'S	397	5.6	67.2	11.7	3.3
Gingernut Biscuits	456	5.6	79.1	15.2	1.4
MCVITIE'S	473	5.6	75.3	16.6	1.7
Gipsy Creams MCVITIE'S	515	4.8	66	25.7	2.7
Hob Nobs MCVITIE'S	485	7.7	63.6	22.1	4.7
milk chocolate	497	7	63.5	23.9	3.7

Calorie Counter

All amounts per 100g/100ml unless otherwise stated	Cal kcal	Pro g	Carb g	Fat g	Fibre g
Jaffa Cakes McVitie's	381	4	73.8	7.7	1.3
Jam & Cream Sandwich Jacob's	492	5	67.7	22.3	1.5
Lemon Puff Jacob's	535	5.6	57.5	31.4	1.5
Lincoln Biscuits McVitie's	514	6.3	69	23.6	2
Nice Biscuits Jacob's	455	7.2	68.5	16.9	4.1
Original Biscuit Cakes, gluten-free Itona	496	12.1	52.2	26.3	n/a
Penguin Biscuit McVitie's	532	5.4	65.2	27.7	1.5
Plain Biscuits, gluten-free Itona	464	11.5	58.6	20.4	n/a
Rich Tea Biscuits McVitie's	475	7.3	76.5	15.5	2.3
Shortbread, recipe	498	5.9	63.9	26.1	1.9
Shortbread Biscuit Holland & Barrett	518	4.5	64.3	27	Tr
Shortcake Jacob's	485	6.7	65.6	21.8	2
Snack Cadbury					
orange, Sandwich	525	7.2	62.6	27.2	n/a
Shortcake	525	6.9	64.6	26.6	n/a
Shortcake, breakpack	525	7	64.2	26.8	n/a
Wafer	555	4.3	57.3	33.7	n/a
Stem Ginger Cookies Heinz Weight Watchers	399	5	64.5	13.4	1.4

All amounts per 100g/100ml unless otherwise stated	Cal kcal	Pro g	Carb g	Fat g	Fibre g
Sultana & Cinnamon Cookies HEINZ WEIGHT WATCHERS	398	5	67.1	12.1	1.8
Tea Cakes TUNNOCK'S	413	5.2	61	18.1	n/a
Viennese Whirls MR KIPLING	497	4.1	51.5	30.5	1.2
Wafer Biscuits, filled	535	4.7	66	29.9	N
YoYo, mint MCVITIE'S	545	3.9	63.1	30.8	1.1

See also: **KIDS' FOOD**

SAVOURY BISCUITS AND CRISPBREADS

Allison Wholemeal Light Crispbread RYVITA	349	11.7	69.7	2.6	11
Bath Oliver					
JACOB'S	432	9.6	67.5	13.7	2.6
FORTTS	412	8.4	65.5	2.7	n/a
Bran Cracker JACOB'S	454	9.7	62.8	18.2	3.2
Cheddars JACOB'S	542	10	55.1	31.3	2.6
Cheeselet JACOB'S	491	9.5	55.1	25.8	2.3
Choice Grain Cracker JACOB'S	435	9.2	65.4	15.2	4.7
Cinnamon Toast Crunch NESTLÉ	416	4.6	75.1	10.9	4.2
Cornish Wafers JACOB'S	530	8	54.4	31.2	2.4

Calorie Counter

All amounts per 100g/100ml unless otherwise stated	Cal kcal	Pro g	Carb g	Fat g	Fibre g
Crackerbread RYVITA					
original	383	9.8	79.3	3	2.6
cheesy	379	12.7	75	3.1	3.2
high fibre	318	12.6	60.5	2.8	16.8
Cream Crackers	440	9.5	68.3	16.3	2.2
JACOB'S	438	10.2	66.9	14.4	2.9
Vitalinea JACOB'S	400	10.9	71.7	7.7	3.1
Croutons KNORR					
cracked black pepper	487	8.6	62.8	25	2.6
garlic & herb	479	8.4	62.4	25	2.5
slightly sea salted	491	8.4	62.2	25	2.7
Five Grain Crispbread PRIMULA	322	12	62.9	2.5	16.2
Garlic & Black Pepper Petal JACOB'S	394	11.5	72.9	6.3	4.6
High Fibre Biscuits ITONA	406	8.6	59.4	15	10
Hilo Crackers RAKUSEN	349	11	74	1	8
Hovis Cracker JACOB'S	447	10.2	60	18.5	4.4
Hovis Digestive JACOB'S	469	7.8	66	19.3	2.9
Krackawheat MCVITIE'S	515	9.1	62.4	25.4	4.8
Krispen Crispbread Crackers KAVLI					
light	371	10.7	71.8	4.6	5
rye	272	10.5	53	2	21
wholemeal light	366	9.7	71.2	4.7	7.9

All amounts per 100g/100ml unless otherwise stated	Cal kcal	Pro g	Carb g	Fat g	Fibre g
Matzo Crackers RAKUSEN	335	10.8	76.7	0.4	5.7
Oat Fingers, each PATERSON'S	45	n/a	n/a	1.9	n/a
Oatcakes NAIRN					
cheese	474	13.8	55.4	24.7	6.2
fine	435	10.5	65.7	18.9	8.6
organic	428	10.9	65.3	17.0	7.6
rough	430	10.7	65.3	16.9	6.6
traditional	439	11.7	63.5	17.8	7.8
Ritz Crackers JACOB'S					
cheese	490	10.4	55.5	25.2	2.2
original	509	6.9	55.6	28.8	2
Rye Crispbread	321	9.4	70.6	2.1	11.7
Ryvita, per slice RYVITA					
currant crunch	48	1.3	10.1	0.3	1.9
dark rye	27	0.9	5.6	0.2	1.7
multigrain	37	1.3	6.4	0.7	1.8
original	27	0.8	5.7	0.2	1.6
sesame	31	0.9	5.3	0.6	1.4
Tuc Biscuits JACOB'S	512	7.8	57.7	27.8	2.1
Tuc Sandwich Biscuits JACOB'S	546	8	50.5	34.7	1.5
Water Biscuits					
High Bake JACOB'S	414	10.5	76.4	7.4	3
Table, small CARR'S	438	10.4	82	7.7	3.3

Calorie Counter

All amounts per 100g/100ml unless otherwise stated	Cal kcal	Pro g	Carb g	Fat g	Fibre g
Wholegrain Crispbread KAVLI					
original	**335**	9.8	70.2	1.7	12.6
garlic	**363**	9.5	69.3	5.2	10.3
onion	**368**	10	67.4	6.5	11.3
Wholemeal Crackers	**413**	10.1	72.1	11.3	4.4

BREAKFAST CEREALS

All amounts per 100g/100ml unless otherwise stated	Cal kcal	Pro g	Carb g	Fat g	Fibre g
BREAKFAST CEREALS					
All-Bran KELLOGG'S	280	14	46	4.5	27
Alpen Wheat Flakes WEETABIX	350	10.2	72	2.4	9
Apricot Bites KELLOGG'S	290	10	57	3	18
Bio-biz Organic Breakfast Biscuits DOVES FARM	335	11	65	2.8	11
Bran Flakes KELLOGG'S	330	10	67	2	15
Cheerios NESTLÉ	369	7.9	75.9	3.8	6.2
Cheerios, Honey Nut NESTLÉ	372	7	78.3	3.7	5.8
Cinnamon Grahams NESTLÉ	410	4.6	75.9	9.8	4.2
Coco Pops KELLOGG'S	380	4.5	85	2.5	2
Coco Pops Crunchers KELLOGG'S	380	7	81	3.5	3
Corn Flakes KELLOGG'S	370	7	84	0.8	2.5
Choco KELLOGG'S	380	5	84	3	2.5
organic DOVES FARM	362	7	81.1	0.7	4.5
Corn Pops KELLOGG'S	380	4.5	87	1.5	1
Crunchy Bran WEETABIX	299	11.8	52.3	4.7	24.8
Crunchy Nut Cornflakes KELLOGG'S	390	6	83	3.5	2.5

Calorie Counter

All amounts per 100g/100ml unless otherwise stated	Cal kcal	Pro g	Carb g	Fat g	Fibre g
Crunchy Nut Red Cornflakes KELLOGG'S	410	7	74	10	3
Crunchy Oatbran MORNFLAKE	345	14.8	49.7	9.7	15.2
Farmhouse Wheatbran MORNFLAKE	174	13	21.7	3.9	45.8
Fibre 1 NESTLÉ	264	10.8	49.2	2.6	31.3
Force NESTLÉ	344	10.6	70.3	2.3	9.2
Frosted Wheats KELLOGG'S	350	10	72	2	9
Frosties KELLOGG'S	370	4.5	87	0.5	2
Frosties, Chocolate KELLOGG'S	390	4.5	82	4.5	3
Fruit 'n' Fibre KELLOGG'S	350	8	70	5	9
Golden Grahams NESTLÉ	374	6	80.8	3	3.4
Golden Nuggets NESTLÉ	381	6.2	87.4	0.7	1.5
Grape Nuts KRAFT	345	10.5	72.5	1.9	8.6
Honey B's KELLOGG'S	380	6	83	2.5	3
Honey Crispix KELLOGG'S	380	5	87	1.5	1.5
Honey Loops KELLOGG'S	360	9	75	3	7
Just Right KELLOGG'S	360	7	77	3	5
Malt Wheats, organic WEETABIX	360	10.8	78.4	5	5.6

Breakfast Cereals

All amounts per 100g/100ml unless otherwise stated	Cal kcal	Pro g	Carb g	Fat g	Fibre g
Multiflakes, organic DOVES FARM	354	11.8	69.5	3.2	7.9
Multi-Grain Start KELLOGG'S	370	7	82	2	4
Nesquik Breakfast Cereal NESTLÉ	394	5	83.6	4.4	2.4
Nutty Oatios MORNFLAKE	441	9.9	60.2	17.8	7.3
Oat Bran Crispies QUAKER	383	11	69	6.5	9
Oat Bran Flakes KELLOGG'S	330	10	67	2	15
Oat Krunchies QUAKER	361	10.5	63	7	11
Puffed Wheat QUAKER	328	15.3	62.4	1.3	5.6
Raisin Wheats KELLOGG'S	320	9	69	2	9
Rice Krispies KELLOGG'S	380	6	87	1	1
Rice Pops, organic DOVES FARM	362	6.6	80.6	1.5	1.7
Ricicles KELLOGG'S	380	4	90	0.7	0.9
Shredded Wheat NESTLÉ	330	11.2	66.1	2.1	11.5
Bitesize	335	11.5	67.7	2.2	11.6
Fruitful	354	8.3	68.7	5.1	8.9
Honey Nut	379	10.9	69.2	6.6	10.3
Shreddies NESTLÉ	343	9.8	71.7	1.9	11.2
Coco	363	7.3	79.4	1.8	7.1
Frosted	363	6.7	81.1	1.3	6.8
Special K KELLOGG'S	370	16	74	1	3
Red Berries	370	14	75	1	4

Calorie Counter

All amounts per 100g/100ml unless otherwise stated	Cal kcal	Pro g	Carb g	Fat g	Fibre g
Sporties NESTLÉ	**356**	8.5	76.9	1.6	8.4
Sugar Puffs QUAKER	**387**	6.5	86.5	1	3
Sultana Bran KELLOGG'S	**320**	8	68	2	12
Sustain KELLOGG'S	**350**	8	74	3.5	7
Weetabix WEETABIX	**340**	11.2	67.6	2.7	10.5
Weetos WEETABIX	**384**	6.2	78.4	5	5.6

HOT CEREALS

	Cal kcal	Pro g	Carb g	Fat g	Fibre g
Oat Sensations, sultana, apple & cinnamon JORDANS	**363**	8.4	69.4	5.7	6.9
Oatbran MORNFLAKE	**345**	14.8	49.7	9.7	15.2
Oatmeal (Medium or Fine) MORNFLAKE	**359**	11	60.4	8.1	8.5
Oats					
jumbo MORNFLAKE	**359**	11	60.4	8.1	8.5
organic MORNFLAKE	**359**	11	60.4	8.1	8.5
porridge WHITWORTHS	**401**	12.4	72.8	8.7	7
Quaker QUAKER	**368**	11	62	8	7
Scott's Porage QUAKER	**368**	11	62	8	7
Scott's Piper QUAKER	**368**	11	62	8	7
Superfast MORNFLAKE	**359**	11	60.4	8.1	8.5

Breakfast Cereals

All amounts per 100g/100ml unless otherwise stated	Cal kcal	Pro g	Carb g	Fat g	Fibre g
Oatso Simple QUAKER					
baked apple	374	8	71	6	5.5
berry burst	374	8	71	6	5.5
golden syrup	376	7.5	72	6	5
original	372	11	62	8.5	7
Porridge					
made with water	49	1.5	9	1	0.8
made with whole milk	116	4.8	13.7	5.1	0.8
Ready Brek WEETABIX	356	11.6	58.8	8.3	8.9
chocolate	360	9.6	63.7	7.4	8.1
Scott's So-easy QUAKER	372	11	62	8.5	7
demerara sugar & cream	385	9	66	9	5.5

MUESLI AND GRANOLA

	Cal kcal	Pro g	Carb g	Fat g	Fibre g
Alpen WEETABIX	365	10	66	6.8	7.7
no added sugar	357	12.1	61.3	7.1	9
Alpen, Caribbean Crunch WEETABIX	403	9.1	68.7	10.2	5.2
Banana and Toffee Crisp MORNFLAKE	443	5.7	68.8	16.1	5.4
Chocolate Fruit & Nut Crunch MORNFLAKE	408	7.7	66.7	12.3	8.3
Clusters NESTLÉ	387	10.3	67.3	8.5	8.9

Calorie Counter

All amounts per 100g/100ml unless otherwise stated	Cal kcal	Pro g	Carb g	Fat g	Fibre g
Country Crisp JORDANS					
four nut	**480**	8.8	54.2	25	7.2
raisin	**410**	6.2	66.7	13.3	5.9
raspberry	**438**	7.3	64.6	16.7	6
strawberry	**440**	7.3	65.3	16.6	6.9
wild about berries	**443**	7.5	68	15.7	3.1
Country Store KELLOGG'S	**350**	9	68	5	7
Crispy Crunch MORNFLAKE	**430**	6.3	70.3	13.7	6
Crunchy Cereal, organic JORDANS	**419**	8.1	66.3	13.5	6.4
Four Berry Crisp, organic JORDANS	**442**	7.7	67.1	15.8	5.4
Fruit & Nut Crunch HOLLAND & BARRETT	**372**	10.1	61.1	11.2	6.7
Golden Honey & Nut Crunchy JORDANS	**446**	8.1	68.2	15.6	4.9
Harvest Crunch QUAKER					
with honeycombe caramel	**454**	6.5	67	17.5	4
with nuts	**470**	8	60	22	4.5
with real red berries	**447**	7	66	17	4.5
with soft juicy raisins	**442**	6	67	16	4
Hawaiian Crunch MORNFLAKE	**423**	7.8	66.2	14.1	6.5

All amounts per 100g/100ml unless otherwise stated	Cal kcal	Pro g	Carb g	Fat g	Fibre g
Mini Crunch WEETABIX					
banana	370	8.8	73	5	8.1
chocolate	383	9.5	71.2	6.7	7
fruit & nut	353	8.8	71.2	3.8	8.1
honey	358	9.8	74.8	2.2	7.5
Muesli					
apricot HOLLAND & BARRETT	285	7.7	59.2	3.5	5.6
deluxe DORSET CEREALS	343	10.8	56.2	9.9	11.7
high fibre HOLLAND & BARRETT	317	10.3	70.9	1.8	5.9
natural JORDANS	346	9.6	63	6.2	8.6
organic JORDANS	381	9.9	62.3	10.2	9.3
Rich HOLLAND & BARRETT	381	11	60.5	12.2	7.7
Special JORDANS	378	7.3	60.6	11.8	6.7
Super Cranberry, Cherry & Almond DORSET CEREALS	355	9.2	60.5	8.5	8.4
Swiss style	363	9.8	72.2	5.9	6.4
Swiss style, organic JORDANS	359	9.7	62.9	7.6	7.4
with no added sugar	366	10.5	67.1	7.8	7.6
Oat Crunch QUAKER	445	8	66.5	16	5
Original Crunchy JORDANS					
maple & pecan	448	9.9	59.9	18.7	6.5
raisin & almond	410	8.4	66	12.5	5
tropical	424	9	66	13.8	5
Pecan and Maple Crisp MORNFLAKE	437	6.6	67.2	15.7	5.7

Calorie Counter

All amounts per 100g/100ml unless otherwise stated	Cal kcal	Pro g	Carb g	Fat g	Fibre g
Raspberry Crisp MORNFLAKE	**428**	6.5	68.2	14.3	6.8
Strawberry Crisp MORNFLAKE	**436**	6.5	68.9	14.9	6.3
Sultana & Apple Crunch MORNFLAKE	**378**	7.6	59.3	12.2	12.5
Traditional Crunch MORNFLAKE	**400**	8	65.4	11.8	9.6
Treasure Crunch MORNFLAKE	**377**	7.7	60.2	11.7	10.7
Triple Chocolate Crisp MORNFLAKE	**435**	7.1	67.7	15.1	4.9

CEREAL BARS

	Cal kcal	Pro g	Carb g	Fat g	Fibre g
Alpen Apple & Blackberry Cereal Bar, with yoghurt WEETABIX	**421**	5.7	73	11.8	3
Alpen Fruit & Nut Cereal Bar WEETABIX	**394**	6.5	71.2	9.2	3.4
with chocolate	**431**	7	68	14.5	2.6
Alpen Strawberry Cereal Bar, with yoghurt WEETABIX	**418**	5.6	74.1	11	3.2
Banana Break, each JORDANS	**152**	2.3	27.6	3.6	2
Brunch Bar, each CADBURY					
hazelnut	**165**	2.5	21.4	7.6	n/a
raisin	**150**	2	23.4	5.5	n/a

All amounts per 100g/100ml unless otherwise stated	Cal kcal	Pro g	Carb g	Fat g	Fibre g
Chewy Fruity Corn Flake Cakes, organic, each DOVES FARM	155	2.3	25.8	5.6	1.8
Chewy Rice Pop & Chocolate Cakes, organic, each DOVES FARM	156	1.4	24.5	7.1	0.8
Coco Pops Cereal & Milk Bar KELLOGG'S	450	7	69	16	1.5
Corn Flakes Cereal & Milk Bar KELLOGG'S	440	9	66	16	2
Crunchy Bar, each JORDANS					
honey & almond	155	2.9	18.7	7.6	1.9
maple & pecan	155	2.6	18.9	7.6	2.2
organic	151	2.7	18.9	7.2	2.6
Frosties Cereal & Milk Bar KELLOGG'S	440	8	69	15	1.5
Fruit & Nut Break, each JORDANS	137	2.6	23.2	3.8	3
Frusli Bar, each JORDANS					
absolutely apricot	122	1.7	21.3	3.3	2.1
blueberry burst	134	1.6	22.9	4	1.5
raisin & hazelnut	142	2.1	20.4	5.8	1.3
tangy citrus	131	1.4	23.5	3.5	1.4
wild berries	132	2	22.4	3.8	1.6
Harvest Chewy Bar, each QUAKER					
apple & raisin	89	1.2	15	2.6	0.7
banana blast	93	1.4	14.3	3.3	0.7

Calorie Counter

All amounts per 100g/100ml unless otherwise stated	Cal kcal	Pro g	Carb g	Fat g	Fibre g
berry burst	89	1.2	14.5	2.9	0.7
chocolate chip	94	1.3	14.1	3.5	0.7
white chocolate chip	94	1.3	14.5	3.3	0.7
Muesli Break, each JORDANS	178	2.7	30.6	5	2
Nutri-grain Bar KELLOGG'S					
apple	360	3.5	68	9	3
cappucino	370	4.5	66	10	2.5
cherry	360	4	68	9	3
chocolate	380	4.5	66	11	3.5
orange	370	5	68	9	4
strawberry	360	4	68	9	3
Elevenses	360	5	67	8	3.5
Rice Krispies Cereal & Milk Bar KELLOGG'S	460	9	66	18	1
Rice Krispies Squares KELLOGG'S	410	3	76	11	1.5
chocolate & caramel	430	4.5	71	14	2
Special K Cereal & Milk Bar KELLOGG'S	390	7	75	7	2
Sultana & Honey Break, each JORDANS	133	2.2	24.2	3	3.4
Tracker Bar MARS					
chocolate chip	531	8.1	59.5	29	n/a
roast nut	490	6.3	64.2	23.2	n/a

BURGERS

All amounts per 100g/100ml unless otherwise stated	Cal kcal	Pro g	Carb g	Fat g	Fibre g
Beefburgers					
fried	**329**	28.5	0.1	23.9	0
grilled	**326**	26.5	0.1	24.4	0
100%, each BIRDS EYE	**125**	6.5	0.3	11	0
100% ROSS	**293**	17	0	25	0
economy ROSS	**255**	13.6	9.9	18.1	0.4
original, each BIRDS EYE	**115**	8.7	2	8	0.1
quarter-pounders, each BIRDS EYE	**200**	17.5	4	12.7	0.2
Chicken Burgers, each BIRDS EYE	**150**	7.8	9.6	8.7	0.2
Veggie Burgers					
flame-grilled LINDA MCCARTNEY FOODS	**134**	22.6	2.9	3.6	1.6
vegetable burgers LINDA MCCARTNEY FOODS	**238**	3.1	27.7	12.7	2.3
Vegetable Quarter Pounders, each BIRDS EYE	**190**	4.3	23	9.1	1.8

See also: **FAST FOOD**

CHIPS, FRIES AND SHAPED POTATO PRODUCTS

All amounts per 100g/100ml unless otherwise stated	Cal kcal	Pro g	Carb g	Fat g	Fibre g
Non-branded Chips					
crinkle cut, frozen, fried	**290**	3.6	33.4	16.7	2.2
French fries, retail	**280**	3.3	34	15.5	2.1
homemade, fried	**189**	3.9	30.1	6.7	2.2
microwave	**221**	3.6	32.1	9.6	2.9
oven	**162**	3.2	29.8	4.2	2
retail	**239**	3.2	30.5	12.4	2.2
straight cut, frozen, fried	**273**	4.1	36	13.5	2.4
Beefeater Fast Fry Chips McCAIN	**132**	2.2	23	3.5	n/a
Beefeater Oven Ready Chips McCAIN	**115**	2	27.5	4.1	n/a
Chips, Chip Shop ROSS	**75**	2	17.6	0.2	1.3
Chips, Chunky ROSS	**118**	2.4	21.9	3	1.6
Chips, Crinkle Cut McCAIN	**139**	2.4	21.7	4.7	n/a
Croquettes, Potato					
fried in oil	**214**	3.7	21.6	13.1	1.3
each BIRDS EYE	**45**	1	6.5	1.5	0.3
Croquette Royales, Cheesey ROSS	**228**	4.2	23.7	13.4	1.6
Hash Browns McCAIN	**190**	3	24	9.8	n/a
Lattice Fries, spicy McCAIN	**183**	2.6	22.8	9	n/a

Chips, Fries and Shaped Potato Products

All amounts per 100g/100ml unless otherwise stated	Cal kcal	Pro g	Carb g	Fat g	Fibre g
Micro Chips McCAIN	193	2.5	27.4	8.2	n/a
straight	207	3.5	24.7	10.5	n/a
Oven Chips					
McCAIN	154	1.9	26.9	4.3	n/a
ROSS	131	2.4	20.6	5.1	1.6
crinkle cut McCAIN	157	1.9	26.7	4.7	n/a
Stringfellows McCAIN	164	2.3	23.2	6.9	n/a
Potato Fritters, Crispy BIRDS EYE	174	2.2	17.2	10.7	1.3
Potato Pancakes ROSS	239	3.2	18.8	17.4	1.3
with Onion	228	2.9	22	15.2	2.2
Potato Waffles					
frozen, cooked	200	3.2	30.3	8.2	2.3
frozen, cooked BIRDS EYE	168	2	20.7	8.6	2
frozen, cooked ROSS	225	2.3	22	12.3	2
Southern Fries McCAIN					
savoury herb ranch	164	2.1	25.3	6	n/a
savoury herb slice	158	2.1	22.4	6.7	n/a
Southern Style Skins McCAIN	147	2.2	17.8	7.4	n/a
Wedge Fries, Spicy McCAIN	157	2.7	24.8	5.2	n/a

CONDIMENTS AND SAUCES

All amounts per 100g/100ml unless otherwise stated	Cal kcal	Pro g	Carb g	Fat g	Fibre g
TABLE SAUCES					
Apple Sauce, Bramley COLMAN'S	105	0.2	25.5	Tr	1.3
Barbecue Sauce, bottled					
HP	145	0.4	34.5	Tr	n/a
HEINZ	123	1.3	28.5	0.4	0.4
classic HEINZ	89	1.2	20.5	0.2	0.7
original HP	143	0.8	33.1	0.2	n/a
smokey HEINZ	121	1.3	27.9	0.4	0.4
Beetroot in Redcurrant Jelly BAXTERS	167	0.7	43.9	Tr	0.9
Branston Fruity Sauce CROSSE & BLACKWELL	110	0.5	24.3	0.1	1.1
Brown Sauce					
bottled	99	1.1	25.2	0	0.7
bottled BURGESS	102	0.8	22	0.2	1.1
bottled DADDIES	102	0.9	24.3	0.6	n/a
organic MERIDIAN FOOD LTD	133	1.6	28.4	0.6	0.6
Burger Sauce BURGESS	594	2.2	10.7	59.9	0
Chilli Sauce HP	134	1.2	32.3	Tr	n/a
Cranberry Jelly BAXTERS	268	0	67	0	0

All amounts per 100g/100ml unless otherwise stated	Cal kcal	Pro g	Carb g	Fat g	Fibre g
Cranberry Sauce					
BAXTERS	180	0.1	45	0	0.5
BURGESS	126	0.1	33.3	0	1.4
Fruity Sauce HP	141	1.2	35.1	0.1	n/a
Garlic Sauce					
LEA & PERRINS	337	1.8	17.8	29	n/a
creamed BURGESS	424	2.5	20.9	36.1	1.6
Ginger Sauce LEA & PERRINS	116	0.3	28.8	Tr	n/a
Horseradish, creamed BURGESS	184	2.4	19.6	9.8	2.3
Horseradish Relish COLMAN'S	110	1.9	9.6	6.2	2.6
Horseradish Sauce	153	2.5	17.9	8.4	2.5
BAXTERS	345	2.9	10	32.6	0
hot BURGESS	131	2.2	14.1	6.7	2
HP Sauce HP	119	0.9	27.5	0.2	n/a
Mint Jelly					
BAXTERS	264	0	66	0	0
BURGESS	165	0.4	37.6	0.7	0.5
Mint Sauce					
BAXTERS	62	1.7	13.2	0.3	0
BURGESS	68	1.6	12	0	2
classic COLMAN'S	114	1	24.3	0.2	1.6
garden fresh COLMAN'S	21	1.8	3.1	0.2	1.9

Calorie Counter

All amounts per 100g/100ml unless otherwise stated	Cal kcal	Pro g	Carb g	Fat g	Fibre g
Mushroom Ketchup BURGESS	27	0.5	5.5	0.1	Tr
Redcurrant Jelly					
BAXTERS	260	0	65	0	0
BURGESS	129	0.6	31	0	0
Soy Sauce, (light & dark)	43	8.3	8.2	Tr	0
Tabasco, per serving (1 tsp)	0	0	0	0	0
Tartare Sauce					
BAXTERS	515	1	8	53.3	0.3
BURGESS	268	1.5	18.7	20	0.7
COLMAN'S	281	1.2	16.1	23	0.6
Tomato Ketchup	98	2.1	24	Tr	0.9
HEINZ	107	1	24.7	0.1	0.6
DADDIES	110	0.9	26.5	0.3	n/a
organic MERIDIAN FOOD LTD	114	1.8	28.4	0.1	1.1
Tomato Sauce BURGESS	156	1.3	34.4	0.8	0.7
Wild Rowan Jelly BAXTERS	268	0	67	0	0
Worcestershire Sauce LEA & PERRINS	88	1.1	22	Tr	n/a

MUSTARDS

	Cal kcal	Pro g	Carb g	Fat g	Fibre g
Dijon Mustard COLMAN'S	129	6.4	5.5	9.1	3.6

All amounts per 100g/100ml unless otherwise stated	Cal kcal	Pro g	Carb g	Fat g	Fibre g
English Mustard COLMAN'S	188	7	19	9.3	1.6
French Mustard BURGESS	145	7.5	14.9	4.9	0.6
Honey Mustard COLMAN'S	170	6.3	23.4	5.5	5
Horseradish Mustard COLMAN'S	159	6.4	23.1	4.6	3.8
Peppercorn Mustard COLMAN'S	143	8.4	15.1	5.3	5.4
Wholegrain Mustard COLMAN'S	131	8.5	16.6	3.4	3.8
hot	149	7.7	12.5	7.6	3.6

VINEGARS

Balsamic Vinegar CARAPELLI	100	Tr	21	0	0
Cider Vinegar DUFRAIS	20	0.1	1.2	0	0
Cyder Vinegar HOLLAND & BARRETT	18	0	0.4	0	0.4
Garlic Vinegar DUFRAIS	20	0.1	0.8	0	0
Raspberry Vinegar DUFRAIS	20	0.1	1	0	0
Red Wine Vinegar DUFRAIS	25	0.2	0.8	0	0
Sherry Vinegar DUFRAIS	25	0.4	1.7	0	0
Tarragon Vinegar DUFRAIS	20	0.1	0.8	0	0
White Wine Vinegar DUFRAIS	20	0.1	0.8	0	0

Calorie Counter

All amounts per 100g/100ml unless otherwise stated	Cal kcal	Pro g	Carb g	Fat g	Fibre g
STOCK CUBES, GRANULES AND PURÉES					
Aromat KNORR	165	13.1	20.8	3.6	1
Basil Herb Cube KNORR	472	6.1	35.9	33.8	0.6
Beef Gravy & Horseradish Granules, as sold OXO	315	10.6	56.5	5.2	1
Beef Gravy & Mustard Granules, as sold OXO	332	10.6	56.5	7.1	1
Beef Oxo Cubes, original OXO	265	17.3	38.4	4.7	1.5
Beef Stock Cubes					
KNORR	326	11.1	21	22	0.2
BOVRIL	173	9.1	24.8	4.1	Tr
Bisto Original, as sold BISTO	248	1.7	59.8	0.2	1.3
Chicken Granulated Stock KNORR	232	13.1	36.5	3.7	0.4
Chicken Gravy & Sage & Onion Granules, as sold OXO	316	11.1	54.2	6.1	0.7
Chicken Gravy Granules, as sold OXO	305	11.1	54.2	4.9	0.7
Chicken Oxo Cubes OXO	224	11.1	37.1	3.5	1.4
Chicken Stock Cubes KNORR	301	10.1	23.6	18.5	0.2

All amounts per 100g/100ml unless otherwise stated	Cal kcal	Pro g	Carb g	Fat g	Fibre g
Chicken Stock Cubes, organic KNORR	232	13.1	36.5	3.7	0.4
Chinese Herb & Spice Cubes OXO	263	11	40.9	6.1	3.6
Fish Stock Cubes KNORR	323	19.2	16.2	20.2	0.7
Garlic Herb & Spice Cubes OXO	297	13.4	48.5	5.5	3.6
Garlic Purée	423	2.7	13	40	6
Gravy Browning BURGESS	72	3.3	14.7	0	0
Gravy Granules with Onion, as sold BISTO	365	2.9	56.1	14.3	1.8
Gravy Granules, as sold					
BISTO	384	3.1	56.4	16.2	1.5
OXO	313	10.2	57.2	4.8	1
chicken BISTO	385	3.2	57.9	15.6	1.4
Gravy Instant Granules	462	4.4	40.6	32.5	Tr
made up with water	33	0.3	2.9	2.4	Tr
Ham Stock Cubes KNORR	313	11.8	24.4	18.7	0
Indian Herb & Spice Cubes OXO	291	11.5	43.9	7.7	6.7
Italian Herb & Stock Cubes OXO	309	11.9	48.9	7.3	4.6
Lamb Gravy & Mint Granules, as sold OXO	410	9.6	60.3	7.7	1

Calorie Counter

All amounts per 100g/100ml unless otherwise stated	Cal kcal	Pro g	Carb g	Fat g	Fibre g
Lamb Oxo Cubes Oxo	**289**	15	44	5.9	2.1
Lamb Stock Cubes KNORR	**301**	14.7	12.9	22	0.2
Marmite Stock Cubes BESTFOODS	**247**	25	25.5	5	n/a
Mexican Herb & Spice Cubes Oxo	**243**	8.5	38.7	6	3.7
Onion Gravy Granules, as sold Oxo	**328**	8.2	62.3	4.8	0.8
Perfect Cubes KNORR					
Mince Beef & Herbs	**431**	12.2	4.2	40.7	0.4
Pasta Garlic & Basil	**395**	7.4	31.3	26.7	2.2
Pasta Mushroom	**365**	10.3	21.3	26.5	1.7
Potato Garlic & Parsley	**547**	6	21.8	48.4	1.6
Rice Pilau	**290**	11.3	11.8	22.1	3.6
Rice Saffron	**290**	14.1	13.1	20	3.2
Pork Stock Cubes KNORR	**339**	12.1	17.6	24.5	0.2
Roast Vegetable Flavour Gravy Granules, as sold BISTO	**309**	2.1	64.9	4.5	1.1
Tomato Purée	**86**	4.5	15	0.2	Tr
NAPOLINA	**90**	4.8	18	Tr	n/a
SHARWOOD	**72**	5.3	12.3	0.5	3

All amounts per 100g/100ml unless otherwise stated	Cal kcal	Pro g	Carb g	Fat g	Fibre g
Vegetable Granulated Stock KNORR	199	8.4	39.8	1	0.9
Vegetable Gravy Granules, as sold OXO	316	8.4	59.5	4.9	0.9
Vegetable Oxo Cubes OXO	253	11.2	41.9	4.5	1.7
Vegetable Stock Cubes					
KNORR	308	11.9	21.7	19.3	1.3
organic KNORR	284	6.4	19.8	19.9	1
White Sauce Granules, as sold BISTO	510	5.7	50.7	31.6	1

STUFFINGS

Apple, Mustard & Herb Stuffing Mix PAXO	159	3.8	31.9	1.8	2.5
Chestnut & Cranberry Stuffing Mix PAXO	141	4	26.7	2	2.4
Chestnut Stuffing Mix, traditional PAXO	136	3.9	24.8	2.3	4.2
Golden Crumbs PAXO	351	11	72.5	1.9	5.1
Parsley, Thyme & Lemon Stuffing Mix PAXO	150	4.3	28.4	2.1	2.4

Calorie Counter

All amounts per 100g/100ml unless otherwise stated	Cal kcal	Pro g	Carb g	Fat g	Fibre g
Sage & Onion Stuffing	231	5.2	20.4	14.8	1.7
WHITWORTHS	398	5.7	73.6	9	1.9
Sage & Onion Stuffing Mix PAXO	123	3.6	23	1.8	1.7

DRESSINGS

	Cal kcal	Pro g	Carb g	Fat g	Fibre g
Basil & Oregano Salad Dressing with Olive Oil HELLMANN'S	437	Tr	0.8	48.9	0.1
Blue Cheese Dressing	457	2	8.7	46.3	0
Blue Cheese Flavoured Low Fat Dressing HEINZ WEIGHT WATCHERS	59	1.5	5.8	3.4	0
Caesar Dressing					
Creamy KRAFT	335	3	7.9	32	0.2
Creamy (only 4% Fat) KRAFT	102	2.1	15	3.5	0.1
organic MERIDIAN FOOD LTD	438	2.4	4.3	45.4	0.3
Caesar Style Low Fat Dressing HEINZ WEIGHT WATCHERS	60	1.6	5.8	3.4	0
Creamy Dressing, 93% fat free CROSSE & BLACKWELL	120	1	14.4	6.4	0.2
Dijonnaise HELLMANN'S	210	2.9	5.1	19.7	Tr
French Dressing					
recipe	462	0.1	4.5	49.4	0
Classic KRAFT	159	0.9	7.3	13.5	0.1
Classic Fat Free KRAFT	37	0.1	8.3	Tr	0.5
organic MERIDIAN FOOD LTD	371	0.4	3.9	39.3	0.3

Condiments and Sauces

All amounts per 100g/100ml unless otherwise stated	Cal kcal	Pro g	Carb g	Fat g	Fibre g
Garlic & Herb Light Reduced					
Calorie Salad Dressing HELLMANN'S	**233**	0.7	13.1	19.3	0.4
Herb 'n' Garlic Dressing KRAFT	**380**	1.1	7.7	38	0.3
(only 5% Fat)	**108**	1.2	14.5	4.8	0.2
Honey & Mustard Dressing KRAFT	**230**	1.1	17	17	1.1
(only 5% Fat)	**124**	1.2	18	4.7	1.2
Italian Dressing KRAFT					
Classic	**117**	0.1	5.4	10	0.5
Classic Fat Free	**30**	0.1	6.4	Tr	0.6
Low Fat Dressing					
HEINZ WEIGHT WATCHERS	**107**	1.4	16	4.2	0
Mayonnaise	**691**	1.1	1.7	75.6	0
HEINZ	**734**	1.5	0.4	80.7	0
light HEINZ WEIGHT WATCHERS	**131**	1.6	9.7	9.5	0
light, reduced calorie					
HELLMANN'S	**299**	0.7	6.7	29.8	Tr
organic MERIDIAN FOOD LTD	**660**	0.9	3.6	71.3	n/a
Real BURGESS	**717**	1.4	3	77.5	0.4
Real HELLMANN'S	**722**	1.1	1.3	79.1	0
Salad BURGESS	**579**	2.4	8.1	59.2	0
Mustard, Mild, Low Fat Dressing					
HEINZ WEIGHT WATCHERS	**63**	2	5.7	3.6	0
Miracle Whip Dressing KRAFT	**380**	0.3	12.5	36	0.1

Calorie Counter

All amounts per 100g/100ml unless otherwise stated	Cal kcal	Pro g	Carb g	Fat g	Fibre g
Salad Cream	**348**	1.5	16.7	31	N
HEINZ	**327**	1.4	19.8	26.8	0
economy BURGESS	**283**	1.2	7.5	27.3	0
light HEINZ	**234**	1.4	12.5	19.8	0
organic MERIDIAN FOOD LTD	**346**	1.9	11.6	32.1	0.2
reduced calorie	**194**	1	9.4	17.2	N
Seafood Sauce					
BAXTERS	**533**	1.5	9.9	54.2	0.7
COLMAN'S	**340**	0.8	23.8	26.6	0.5
Thousand Island Dressing					
KRAFT	**360**	0.9	19.5	30.5	0.4
fat free KRAFT	**83**	0.5	19	0.1	2.6
organic MERIDIAN FOOD LTD	**352**	1.1	12.2	33.2	0.5
Tomato/Basil Dressing, organic MERIDIAN FOOD LTD	**188**	0.9	5.8	17.6	0.8

CHUTNEYS AND PICKLES

Albert's Victorian Chutney BAXTERS	**151**	0.9	36.2	0.3	1
Apple Chutney	**201**	0.9	52.2	0.2	1.2
Barbecue Relish BURGESS	**136**	1.8	29.3	0.7	1
Branston Original CROSSE & BLACKWELL	**140**	0.7	34.2	0.3	1.3

All amounts per 100g/100ml unless otherwise stated	Cal kcal	Pro g	Carb g	Fat g	Fibre g
Branston Small Chunk CROSSE & BLACKWELL	140	0.7	0.3	0.1	1.3
Branston Spicy Pickle CROSSE & BLACKWELL	140	0.7	34.2	0.3	1.3
Chutney Sauce, Green Label SHARWOOD	185	0.4	16.8	0.2	1.6
Lime Pickle SHARWOOD	152	2.2	15	9.3	2.9
Mango Chutney					
BURGESS	279	0.2	61	3.1	0.8
Bengal Spice SHARWOOD	236	0.5	58	0.2	1.2
Green Label SHARWOOD	234	0.3	57.8	0.2	0.9
Major Grey Sweet SHARWOOD	215	0.4	52.9	0.2	1
Tropical Lime SHARWOOD	206	0.4	50.5	0.3	0.8
Mango with Ginger Chutney BAXTERS	187	0.5	45.7	0.2	0.9
Mediterranean Chutney BAXTERS	119	1.8	26	0.9	1.3
Mustard Pickle, mild HEINZ SPECIALITY	128	2.4	26.7	1.3	1
Piccalilli HEINZ SPECIALITY	89	1.2	20.5	0.3	0.5
Ploughman's Pickle HEINZ	114	0.8	27.3	0.2	1
Sandwich Pickle, tangy HEINZ SPECIALITY	133	0.9	31.8	0.2	1.1

Calorie Counter

All amounts per 100g/100ml unless otherwise stated	Cal kcal	Pro g	Carb g	Fat g	Fibre g
Sauerkraut	9	1.1	1.1	Tr	2.2
Spiced Fruit Chutney BAXTERS	143	0.6	34.8	0.1	0.8
Spreadable Chutney, Green Label SHARWOOD	203	0.5	49.8	0.2	1.2
Sweet Pickle	134	0.6	34.4	0.3	1.2
BURGESS	167	1	39.3	Tr	2
Tomato Chutney	161	1.2	40.9	0.4	1.4
Tomato Pickle, tangy HEINZ SPECIALITY	106	2.3	23.5	0.3	1.8
Tomato with Red Pepper Chutney BAXTERS	164	2	38	0.4	1.5

COOKING SAUCES AND MARINADES

All amounts per 100g/100ml unless otherwise stated	Cal kcal	Pro g	Carb g	Fat g	Fibre g
TRADITIONAL					
Barbecue Cook-In-Sauce HOMEPRIDE	83	0.8	16.2	1.7	n/a
Barbecue 'Marinade in Minutes' KNORR	306	6.2	66.4	1.3	3.4
Barbecue Sauce, Texas Hot KNORR	306	6.2	66.4	1.3	3.4
Bechamel Sauce Mix, Bonne Cuisine, as sold CROSSE & BLACKWELL	320	12	59.9	8.3	1.6
Beef Casserole Dry Casserole Mix, as sold COLMAN'S	279	6.3	61.9	0.7	4.6
Bread Sauce					
made with semi-skimmed milk	128	4.2	11.1	7.8	0.6
made with whole milk	150	4.1	10.9	10.3	0.6
Bread Sauce Mix, as sold					
COLMAN'S	315	13.4	63.1	1	3.5
KNORR	442	7.9	49.9	23.3	2.1
Caramelised Onion & Red Wine Sauce BAXTERS	51	1.1	8.6	1.4	1
Casserole Mix ROSS	22	0.9	6.2	0.2	1.8

Calorie Counter

All amounts per 100g/100ml unless otherwise stated	Cal kcal	Pro g	Carb g	Fat g	Fibre g
Cheese & Bacon Pasta Bake Sauce HOMEPRIDE	100	2.2	2.6	9	n/a
Cheese & Bacon Potato Bake Sauce HOMEPRIDE	132	1.6	3.2	12.5	n/a
Cheese & Onion Potato Bake Sauce HOMEPRIDE	141	2.1	5.1	12.4	n/a
Cheese Sauce, recipe					
made with semi-skimmed milk	181	8.2	8.8	12.8	0.2
made with whole milk	198	8.1	8.7	14.8	0.2
Cheese Sauce Packet Mix					
made with semi-skimmed milk	90	5.4	9.5	3.8	N
made with whole milk	110	5.3	9.3	6.1	N
Cheese Dry Sauce Mix, as sold COLMAN'S	394	19.7	45.2	14.9	1.5
Cheese Sauce Granules, as sold BISTO	495	7.3	45.3	31.6	0.8
Cheese Sauce Mix, as sold KNORR	469	7.8	38	31.8	0.3
Chicken & Mushroom Create-a-Stir FINDUS	140	7.9	20.2	2.8	1.6
Chicken Supreme Dry Casserole Mix, as sold COLMAN'S	362	12.1	53.2	11.2	6.5

Cooking Sauces and Marinades

All amounts per 100g/100ml unless otherwise stated	Cal kcal	Pro g	Carb g	Fat g	Fibre g
Classic White Sauce Dry Mix, as sold COLMAN'S	343	12.1	53.3	9	6
Coronation Sauce HEINZ	334	0.8	13.1	31	0.9
Cranberry & Red Onion Sizzling Sauce HOMEPRIDE	83	0.5	17.7	1	n/a
Creamy Cheese & Bacon Pasta Bake Dry Casserole Mix, as sold COLMAN'S	394	16.6	44.6	16.6	5.7
Creamy Ham Pour Over Sauce, as sold KNORR	670	162	2	5	4
Creamy Ham & Mushroom Pasta Bake Sauce HOMEPRIDE	115	1.8	2.8	10.7	n/a
Creamy Leek & Wholegrain Mustard Simply Sausages Sauce KNORR	117	1.3	6.6	10.6	1.4
Creamy Mushroom Chicken Tonight Sauce KNORR	87	0.4	5.5	7	0.5
Creamy Mushroom & Garlic Cook-In-Sauce HOMEPRIDE	77	0.9	5.1	6	n/a
Creamy Mushroom & Herb Sauce BAXTERS	168	1.7	6.2	15.2	0.3
Creamy Tomato & Bacon Pasta Bake Sauce HOMEPRIDE	91	1.9	6.4	6.4	n/a

Calorie Counter

All amounts per 100g/100ml unless otherwise stated	Cal kcal	Pro g	Carb g	Fat g	Fibre g
Creamy Tomato & Herb Pasta Bake Sauce HOMEPRIDE	102	2	7.5	7.1	n/a
Creamy Tomato & Herb Potato Bake Sauce HOMEPRIDE	197	2.2	5.6	18.4	n/a
Creamy White Wine & Herb Deliciously Good Sauce HOMEPRIDE	68	0.6	6.3	4.5	0.3
Four Cheese Dry Sauce Mix, as sold COLMAN'S	414	17.8	40.5	20.1	3.8
Garlic & Herb 'Bake & Crunch' Mix, as sold COLMAN'S	371	9.6	60.2	13	3.2
Garlic & Herb Chicken Marinade BIRDS EYE	190	15.1	10.7	9.6	0.3
Garlic & Herb Potato Bake Sauce HOMEPRIDE	153	1	4.6	14.5	n/a
Garlic & Herb Potato Roasters COLMAN'S	330	8.9	52.7	11.1	3.8
Hearty Cumberland Simply Sausages Sauce KNORR	34	0.7	7.4	0.2	0.8
Herby Garlic Marinade, organic MERIDIAN FOODS LTD	242	0.7	5.3	23.8	0.2
Hollandaise Pour Over Sauce, as sold KNORR	158	Tr	7	14	Tr

Cooking Sauces and Marinades

All amounts per 100g/100ml unless otherwise stated	Cal kcal	Pro g	Carb g	Fat g	Fibre g
Hollandaise Sauce Mix, Bonne Cuisine, as sold CROSSE & BLACKWELL	390	10	50.3	16.8	1.6
Honey & Mustard Chicken Tonight Sauce KNORR	106	0.8	15.1	4.7	0.6
Honey Rich Baste 'n' Grill Sauce LEA & PERRINS	177	2.1	40.6	0.9	n/a
Lamb Hotpot Dry Casserole Mix, as sold COLMAN'S	282	7.3	59.8	1.5	2.7
Lamb Ragout Classic Creations Mix, as sold CROSSE & BLACKWELL	340	9.5	59.9	6.9	1.9
Lemon & Dill Marinade LEA & PERRINS	122	0.5	19.1	4.3	n/a
Liver & Bacon Dry Casserole Mix, as sold COLMAN'S	282	9.7	58	1.2	6.1
Madeira Wine Gravy Sauce Mix, Bonne Cuisine, as sold CROSSE & BLACKWELL	335	8.4	59.1	7.2	1.2
Mushroom & Garlic Deliciously Good Sauce HOMEPRIDE	74	0.9	6.9	4.8	0.3
Mushroom & White Wine Pour Over Sauce, as sold KNORR	98	1	4	8	Tr

Calorie Counter

All amounts per 100g/100ml unless otherwise stated	Cal kcal	Pro g	Carb g	Fat g	Fibre g
Onion Sauce					
made with semi-skimmed milk	86	2.9	8.4	5	0.4
made with whole milk	99	2.8	8.3	6.5	0.4
Onion Dry Sauce Mix, as sold					
COLMAN'S	318	9.8	67.7	0.9	4
KNORR	385	6.2	44.7	20.2	3.3
Parsley Dry Sauce Mix, as sold					
COLMAN'S	307	8.1	65.3	1.5	3.7
Parsley Sauce Granules, as sold					
BISTO	500	5.4	49.1	31.4	0.7
Parsley Sauce Mix, as sold KNORR	437	4.2	50.6	24.2	0.8
Pepper & Brandy Pour Over Sauce, as sold KNORR	104	1	4	9	Tr
Peppercorn & Whisky Sauce BAXTERS	132	1.9	6.7	10.8	0.2
Pork Dry Casserole Mix, as sold COLMAN'S	293	5.3	65.5	1.1	3.4
Potato Bake Cheddar Mix BATCHELORS	386	11.4	46.7	17	8.3
Potato Bake Cheese & Onion Mix BATCHELORS	360	9.6	48	14.4	9.7
Prawn Cocktail Sauce BURGESS	336	2.3	20.1	26.6	0.8

Cooking Sauces and Marinades

All amounts per 100g/100ml unless otherwise stated	Cal kcal	Pro g	Carb g	Fat g	Fibre g
Red Wine & Herbs RAGU	62	2.1	8.8	2	1.1
Red Wine Cook-In-Sauce HOMEPRIDE	46	0.4	9.8	0.6	n/a
Rich & Spicy Baste 'n' Grill Sauce LEA & PERRINS	176	1.5	43.7	0.8	n/a
Rich Red Wine & Onion Simply Sausages Sauce KNORR	39	0.9	8.5	0.2	1.3
Roaster Garlic & Herb Coating Mix BATCHELORS	316	9.5	47.1	11.4	7.8
Sauce au Poivre Mix, Bonne Cuisine, as sold CROSSE & BLACKWELL	410	7.1	48.9	20.7	0.7
Sauce de Paris Mix, Bonne Cuisine, as sold CROSSE & BLACKWELL	335	11.6	48.6	10.1	2.4
Sausage & Tomato Classic Creations Mix, as sold CROSSE & BLACKWELL	375	11.7	61.1	8.4	2.4
Sausage Casserole Cook-In-Sauce HOMEPRIDE	68	0.8	15.8	0.2	n/a
Shepherd's Pie Classic Creations Mix, as sold CROSSE & BLACKWELL	300	12.1	48	6.2	1.6

Calorie Counter

All amounts per 100g/100ml unless otherwise stated	Cal kcal	Pro g	Carb g	Fat g	Fibre g
Spicy Tomato & Pepperoni Pasta Bake Sauce HOMEPRIDE	71	1.6	8.1	3.6	n/a
Sweet Barbecue Deliciously Good Sauce HOMEPRIDE	74	1.4	12	2.2	1.2
Tomato & Herb Marinade LEA & PERRINS	100	1.2	24.1	0.5	n/a
Tomato & Onion Cook-In-Sauce HOMEPRIDE	48	1	9.9	0.5	n/a
Tomato & Tarragon Deliciously Good Sauce HOMEPRIDE	43	1	7.6	1.3	n/a
Traditional Chicken Dry Casserole Mix, as sold COLMAN'S	278	5	63.1	0.6	3.1
Traditional Sausage Dry Casserole Mix, as sold COLMAN'S	304	8.1	65.7	1	5.4
Tuna Pasta Bake Dry Casserole Mix, as sold COLMAN'S	319	10.4	57.1	5.4	5.2
White Sauce, savoury, recipe					
made with semi-skimmed milk	130	4.4	10.7	8	0.2
made with whole milk	151	4.2	10.6	10.3	0.2
White Sauce Granules, as sold BISTO	510	5.7	50.7	31.6	1
White Sauce Mix, savoury, as sold KNORR	410	4.4	50.5	21.1	0.2

Cooking Sauces and Marinades

All amounts per 100g/100ml unless otherwise stated	Cal kcal	Pro g	Carb g	Fat g	Fibre g
White Wine & Cream Cook-in-Sauce HOMEPRIDE	79	1.1	8.5	4.5	n/a
White Wine Gravy Sauce Mix, Bonne Cuisine, as sold CROSSE & BLACKWELL	350	7.8	66.7	5.6	1.2
White Wine, Garlic & Pepper Marinade LEA & PERRINS	99	0.5	23.7	0.7	n/a

CHINESE

	Cal kcal	Pro g	Carb g	Fat g	Fibre g
Black Bean & Pepper Chinatown Cook-in-Sauce KNORR	56	1.4	12.2	0.2	1.3
Black Bean & Roasted Red Pepper Chinese Noodle Sauce SHARWOOD	125	2.9	21.3	4.4	1.2
Black Bean & Vegetable Chinese Stir Fry Sauce UNCLE BEN'S	50	1.8	9	0.7	n/a
Black Bean Chicken Tonight Sizzle & Stir KNORR	174	1.7	10.1	14.1	2.9
Black Bean Sauce AMOY	150	10.3	22.7	2	n/a
Black Bean Sauce, Straight to Wok AMOY	139	2	32	0.3	n/a
Black Bean Stir Fry Creations, as sold CROSSE & BLACKWELL	375	10.8	65.3	7.6	2.8

Calorie Counter

All amounts per 100g/100ml unless otherwise stated	Cal kcal	Pro g	Carb g	Fat g	Fibre g
Black Bean Stir Fry Sauce SHARWOOD	90	0.3	19.9	1.3	1.2
Black Pepper Sauce, Hong Kong AMOY	142	2.2	20.5	5.7	n/a
Chilli & Garlic Sauce					
AMOY	112	12	27	n/a	n/a
LEA & PERRINS	60	1	14.9	Tr	n/a
Chilli & Lime Chinatown Cook in Sauce KNORR	121	0.6	2.2	3.3	0.5
Chinese 'Marinades in Minutes' KNORR	313	6	68.4	1.6	5
Chinese 5 Spice Chicken Tonight Stir it Up KNORR	597	2.4	34.1	50.1	6.6
Chinese Szechuan Cooking Sauce HEINZ WEIGHT WATCHERS	48	1.2	7.7	1.4	0.8
Chow Mein Mix ROSS	58	2.2	13.3	0.4	1.8
Hoi Sin Chinese Spare Rib Sauce SHARWOOD	186	2.8	38.3	2.4	1.9
Hoi Sin & Plum Chinatown Cook in Sauce KNORR	73	0.8	15.8	0.7	1.2
Hot Chilli Chinese Pouring Sauce SHARWOOD	120	0.5	29.4	0.6	1.3

Cooking Sauces and Marinades

All amounts per 100g/100ml unless otherwise stated	Cal kcal	Pro g	Carb g	Fat g	Fibre g
Lemon Sauce, Straight to Wok AMOY	162	0.1	40	0.2	n/a
Light Soy Chinese Pouring Sauce SHARWOOD	18	4.4	0.2	Tr	0.3
Oriental Beef Stir Fry Creations, as sold CROSSE & BLACKWELL	350	9	66	5.3	1.1
Oriental Chicken Stir Fry Creations, as sold CROSSE & BLACKWELL	335	6.1	70.9	2.8	0.4
Oriental Sweet & Sour Chicken Tonight Sauce KNORR	92	0.6	20.9	0.7	0.9
Oriental Sweet & Sour Cooking Sauce HEINZ WEIGHT WATCHERS	51	0.8	11.7	0.1	0.8
Peking Chicken Tonight Sizzle & Stir KNORR	121	0.8	9.4	8.9	1.6
Plum Chinese Spare Rib Sauce SHARWOOD	241	0.5	59.4	0.2	0.6
Plum Sauce AMOY	211	0.5	51.9	0.2	n/a
Plum Sauce, Straight to Wok AMOY	246	0.2	61	0.2	n/a
Real Oyster Chinese Pouring Sauce SHARWOOD	77	1.2	17.6	0.2	0.1

Calorie Counter

All amounts per 100g/100ml unless otherwise stated	Cal kcal	Pro g	Carb g	Fat g	Fibre g
Rich Soy Chinese Pouring Sauce SHARWOOD	48	4.6	7.5	Tr	0.3
Spicy Sweet & Sour Chicken Tonight Sizzle & Stir KNORR	142	0.6	15.5	8.5	2.1
Sweet & Sour Barbecue Sauce HEINZ	125	1	26.3	1.7	0.4
Sweet & Sour Chinatown Cook in Sauce KNORR	84	0.4	20.4	0.1	0.6
Sweet & Sour Chinese Stir Fry Sauce SHARWOOD	100	0.8	18.6	0.1	1
Sweet & Sour Cooking Sauce, organic MERIDIAN FOOD LTD	102	0.6	24.3	0.3	0.7
Sweet & Sour Cook-In-Sauce HOMEPRIDE	92	0.3	22.5	0.1	n/a
Sweet & Sour Pineapple Chinatown Cook in Sauce KNORR	83	0.3	20.3	0.1	1
Sweet & Sour Sauce					
AMOY	171	Tr	33.7	3.9	n/a
BURGESS	150	0.6	35.2	Tr	0.2
Sweet & Sour Sauce, Straight to Wok AMOY	186	0.3	45.5	0.3	n/a

Cooking Sauces and Marinades

All amounts per 100g/100ml unless otherwise stated	Cal kcal	Pro g	Carb g	Fat g	Fibre g
Sweet & Sour Sizzling Sauce HOMEPRIDE	70	0.4	16.8	0.1	n/a
Sweet & Sour Stir Fry Sauce UNCLE BEN'S	104	0.3	25.7	Tr	n/a
Sweet 'n' Sour Dry Sauce Mix, as sold COLMAN'S	333	2.6	79.9	0.4	2.2
Sweet and Sour Chicken Tonight Sizzle & Stir KNORR	149	0.6	19.5	7.7	1.6
Sweet Chilli & Garlic Stir-in Noodle Sauce SHARWOOD	94	0.8	18.2	3.1	0.5
Sweet Chilli Chinese Pouring Sauce SHARWOOD	187	0.6	44.4	0.8	1.5
Szechuan Chilli Sauce & Vegetable Stir Fry UNCLE BEN'S	88	1.2	11.1	4.4	n/a
Szechuan Pepper Chinatown Cook in Sauce KNORR	83	0.7	11.6	3.8	1.2
Yellow Bean Chinese Stir Fry Sauce SHARWOOD	132	0.3	28.8	1.7	1.5
Yellow Bean Sauce AMOY	155	3.3	33.1	1 ·	n/a
Yellow Bean Stir Fry Sauce, Straight to Wok AMOY	159	1.6	36.9	0.5	n/a

Calorie Counter

All amounts per 100g/100ml unless otherwise stated	Cal kcal	Pro g	Carb g	Fat g	Fibre g
ITALIAN					
Basil & Oregano Sauce RAGU	38	2	7.6	Tr	0.8
Bolognese Sauce					
recipe	161	11.8	2.5	11.6	0.6
DOLMIO	91	7.2	7.1	3.8	n/a
RAGU	51	1.7	10.7	0.1	1
Bolognese with Extra Mushrooms Deliciously Good Sauce HOMEPRIDE	40	1.3	8	0.3	0.7
Bolognese with Onions & Garlic Deliciously Good Sauce HOMEPRIDE	41	1.3	7.7	0.5	0.7
Bolognese with Spicy Peppers Deliciously Good Sauce HOMEPRIDE	38	1	8.2	0.2	0.8
Carbonara Creamy Pasta Bake NAPOLINA	101	3.8	9.6	5.3	0.1
Carbonara Pasta Sauce DOLMIO					
chilled	180	3.6	4.6	16.4	n/a
jar	131	1.6	4.5	11.8	n/a
Country Mushroom Sauce RAGU	68	2	9.5	2.1	1.2
Creamy Ham & Mushroom Pasta Stir & Serve HOMEPRIDE	135	1.8	5.5	11.7	n/a

Cooking Sauces and Marinades

All amounts per 100g/100ml unless otherwise stated	Cal kcal	Pro g	Carb g	Fat g	Fibre g
Creamy Tomato & Pesto Premium Pasta Sauce NAPOLINA	87	2.2	9.3	4.6	0.8
Extra Basil Pasta Sauce DOLMIO	58	0.8	7.8	2.7	n/a
Extra Chunky Vegetables Pasta Sauce DOLMIO	35	1.9	6.9	Tr	n/a
Extra Garlic Pasta Sauce DOLMIO	38	1.1	7.3	0.5	n/a
Four Cheese, organic MERIDIAN FOODS LTD	105	2.9	4.1	8.5	0.1
Italian Cheese & Ham Sauce BAXTERS	149	6.7	7	10.5	0.1
Italian Pasta Cooking Sauce HEINZ WEIGHT WATCHERS	38	1.5	7.6	0.2	0.9
Italian Tomato Feast Chicken Tonight Sauce KNORR	39	1.3	7	0.6	1.5
Italienne Tomato & Herbs Chicken Tonight Stir it Up KNORR	632	4.8	18.3	60	4.4
Lasagne Creamy Pasta Bake NAPOLINA	85	2.9	9.4	4	0.1
Lombardy Port Regional Recipe RAGU	32	0.6	7	0.2	0.7

Calorie Counter

All amounts per 100g/100ml unless otherwise stated	Cal kcal	Pro g	Carb g	Fat g	Fibre g
Milanese Chicken Regional Recipe RAGU	48.8	0.9	4.9	2.9	0.9
Mushroom & Mascarpone, organic MERIDIAN FOODS LTD	91	1.2	4.1	7.7	0.1
Mushroom Pasta Sauce DOLMIO	36	0.9	8.2	Tr	n/a
Mushroom Sauce, organic MERIDIAN FOODS LTD	65	1.8	8	2.8	1
Napoletana Pasta Sauce DOLMIO					
chilled	49	1.3	7	1.8	n/a
with red wine & herbs	30	0.8	6.6	Tr	n/a
Olive Sauce, organic MERIDIAN FOODS LTD	64	1.5	7.3	3.2	1.1
Onion & Garlic Sauce RAGU	64	2.2	11.4	1.1	1.2
Original Bolognese Deliciously Good Sauce HOMEPRIDE	35	1.3	7.1	0.2	0.8
Original Pasta Sauce DOLMIO	37	0.9	8.4	Tr	n/a
lite	24	0.8	5.2	Tr	n/a
with mushrooms	36	0.9	7.9	Tr	n/a
with spicy peppers	36	0.9	8.2	Tr	n/a
Pasta 'n' Sauce BATCHELORS					
cheese, leek & ham	379	14.1	68.3	5.5	2.3
chicken & mushroom	361	12.4	73.5	2	2.7
macaroni cheese	378	17.2	63.6	6.1	2.8

Cooking Sauces and Marinades

All amounts per 100g/100ml unless otherwise stated	Cal kcal	Pro g	Carb g	Fat g	Fibre g
mild cheese & broccoli	371	13.5	69	4.5	2.8
mushroom & wine	377	12	71.3	4.9	2.5
tomato, onion & herb	348	13.2	64.5	4.1	5.8
Pasta Sauce, tomato based	47	2	6.9	1.5	N
Red Pepper & Chilli, organic MERIDIAN FOODS LTD	99	1.5	10.6	5.5	1.1
Risotto Create-a-Stir FINDUS	130	6.2	22.4	1.9	1.4
Sicilian Pork Regional Recipes RAGU	35	1	6	0.8	0.7
Spaghetti Bolognese Classic Creations Mix, as sold CROSSE & BLACKWELL	275	11.4	42.1	6.3	2.7
Spicy Arabbiata Premium Pasta Sauce NAPOLINA	62	1.3	7.2	3.1	0.9
Spicy Bolognese Sauce RAGU	64	1.6	9.3	2.3	1.2
Spinach & Ricotta, organic MERIDIAN FOODS LTD	70	2.2	4.1	4.9	0.3
Sun-Dried Tomato Pasta Stir & Serve HOMEPRIDE	62	1	7.6	3	n/a
Tomato & Bacon Pasta Stir & Serve HOMEPRIDE	84	2.7	8.1	4.5	n/a
Tomato & Basil Pasta Stir & Serve HOMEPRIDE	58	1.2	6.7	2.9	n/a

Calorie Counter

All amounts per 100g/100ml unless otherwise stated	Cal kcal	Pro g	Carb g	Fat g	Fibre g
Tomato & Prawn Premium Pasta Sauce NAPOLINA	76	3	8	3.5	0.5
Tomato Lasagne Sauce RAGU	37	1.5	7.4	0.2	1
Tomato Sauce, Classic Mediterranean BAXTERS	114	3.2	10.7	6.5	2.1
Tomato, Salmon & Marscapone Premium Pasta Sauce NAPOLINA	95	3.1	8.5	5.4	0.6
Tomato/Herb Sauce, organic MERIDIAN FOODS LTD	64	1.6	8.1	2.8	1.1
Traditional Sauce for Pasta RAGU	67	2	9.9	2.1	1.2
White Lasagne Sauce RAGU	167	0.5	4.7	16.3	0.3

INDIAN

Balti Chicken Tonight Sizzle & Stir KNORR	102	0.7	6.8	9.5	2.9
Balti Cooking Sauce					
SHARWOOD	88	1.1	9.1	5.2	0.5
organic MERIDIAN FOOD LTD	82	0.9	8.7	4.8	0.7
Balti Cook-In-Sauce HOMEPRIDE	68	1.2	9.2	2.9	n/a
Balti Deliciously Good Sauce HOMEPRIDE	58	1.1	9.1	1.9	0.6

Cooking Sauces and Marinades

All amounts per 100g/100ml unless otherwise stated	Cal kcal	Pro g	Carb g	Fat g	Fibre g
Chicken Byriani Create-a-Stir FINDUS	110	5	18	2.5	2.1
Chicken Curry Indian Creations Mix, as sold CROSSE & BLACKWELL	305	8.1	50.1	7.3	4.8
Chicken Korma Dry Casserole Mix, as sold COLMAN'S	459	6.6	38.8	30.8	13.2
Creamy Curry Chicken Tonight Sauce KNORR	85	1.5	4.6	6.7	0.8
Curry Cook-In-Sauce HOMEPRIDE	108	0.7	9.1	7.6	n/a
Curry Deliciously Good Sauce HOMEPRIDE	61	1.1	10	1.8	0.5
Curry Paste SHARWOOD					
hot	332	4.3	12.6	29.4	5.3
medium	369	4.3	14	32.8	6.9
mild	356	4.8	4.8	35.3	7.1
Curry Sauce					
canned	78	1.5	7.1	5	N
HP	124	1.4	26.3	2.4	n/a
Curry Sauce Dry Mix, Mild, as sold COLMAN'S	439	4.6	70.5	5.4	6.2
Dansak Curry Sauce UNCLE BEN'S	108	1.9	10.8	6.2	n/a
Dhansak Chicken Tonight Sizzle & Stir KNORR	131	3.8	7.6	9.5	6.6

Calorie Counter

All amounts per 100g/100ml unless otherwise stated	Cal kcal	Pro g	Carb g	Fat g	Fibre g
Dhansak Cooking Sauce SHARWOOD	91	2.8	9.7	4.6	1.8
Dopiaza Cooking Sauce SHARWOOD	92	1.4	10.2	5.1	0.6
Indian Curry & Vegetables Stir Fry Sauce UNCLE BEN'S	74	1	13.3	1.9	n/a
Indian Tandoor Chicken Tonight Stir it Up KNORR	641	5.2	23.2	58.6	4.9
Indian Tikka Masala Cooking Sauce HEINZ WEIGHT WATCHERS	55	1.4	8.6	1.7	0.8
Indian Tikka with Yoghurt Chicken Tonight Sauce KNORR	128	1.3	10	9.2	1.2
Indian Tomato Sizzling Sauce HOMEPRIDE	34	0.9	7	0.2	n/a
Jalfrezi Chicken Tonight Sizzle & Stir KNORR	113	1.1	4.4	10.1	2.4
Jalfrezi Cooking Sauce SHARWOOD	75	1.1	8.1	4.2	1.2
Korma Chicken Tonight Sizzle & Stir KNORR	240	1.2	11.2	21.2	2.7
Korma Cooking Sauce SHARWOOD	88	2.2	8.5	5	2.3
Korma Deliciously Good Sauce HOMEPRIDE	88	1.4	10.6	4.4	1.4

Cooking Sauces and Marinades

All amounts per 100g/100ml unless otherwise stated	Cal kcal	Pro g	Carb g	Fat g	Fibre g
Korma Sauce HOMEPRIDE	68	1.1	11.3	2	n/a
Madras Cooking Sauce SHARWOOD	100	1.7	6.9	7.3	1.6
Rogan Josh Chicken Tonight Sizzle & Stir KNORR	93	2	6.2	6.7	2.8
Rogan Josh Cooking Sauce					
SHARWOOD	90	2.8	7.3	5.6	2.6
organic MERIDIAN FOOD LTD	57	1.4	11	0.8	0.9
Rogan Josh Deliciously Good Sauce HOMEPRIDE	60	1.8	11.6	0.7	1.5
Rogan Josh Sauce HOMEPRIDE	61	2.1	11.3	0.8	n/a
Sweet Chilli & Coriander Sizzling Sauce HOMEPRIDE	51	0.7	11.5	0.2	n/a
Tandoori Chicken Marinade BIRDS EYE	187	14.2	6.7	11.5	0.4
Tandoori Marinade LEA & PERRINS	133	1.4	31.7	0.7	n/a
Tenghai Cooking Sauce SHARWOOD	116	1.2	9.6	7.8	1.8
Tikka 'Marinade in Minutes' KNORR	305	6.6	63.8	2.5	4.8
Tikka Korai Chicken Tonight Sizzle & Stir KNORR	112	1.3	7	8.8	2.5

Calorie Counter

All amounts per 100g/100ml unless otherwise stated	Cal kcal	Pro g	Carb g	Fat g	Fibre g
Tikka Masala Chicken Tonight Sizzle & Stir KNORR	187	1.2	8.3	16.5	3.9
Tikka Masala Cooking Sauce					
SHARWOOD	99	3	8.4	5.8	2.3
organic MERIDIAN FOOD LTD	126	2.3	11.3	7.8	1.6
spicy SHARWOOD	107	1.2	9.6	7.1	0.9
Tikka Masala Deliciously Good Sauce HOMEPRIDE	81	2.1	10	3.6	1.5
Tikka Masala Sauce HOMEPRIDE	112	1.5	13	6	n/a

MEXICAN AND US

	Cal kcal	Pro g	Carb g	Fat g	Fibre g
Beef Taco Sauce Dry Casserole Mix, as sold COLMAN'S	252	9.1	26.9	12	14
Burrito Cooking Sauce OLD EL PASO	75	3.4	14.4	0.5	n/a
Burrito Seasoning Mix OLD EL PASO	304	13	54	4	n/a
Cajun 'Marinade in Minutes' KNORR	252	6	53.9	1.2	4.5
Cajun Chicken Marinade BIRDS EYE	172	15.2	8.7	8.5	0.9
Cajun Chicken Tonight Sizzle & Stir KNORR	126	0.8	12	8.3	1.7

Cooking Sauces and Marinades

All amounts per 100g/100ml unless otherwise stated	Cal kcal	Pro g	Carb g	Fat g	Fibre g
Californian Lemon Pepper Chicken Tonight Stir it Up KNORR	659	5.2	26.1	59.3	2.7
Chicken Fahitas Mexican Creations Mix, as sold CROSSE & BLACKWELL	310	11.4	48.4	7.1	3.5
Chicken Fajita Dry Casserole Mix, as sold COLMAN'S	373	10.8	13.3	30.7	13.8
Chili Seasoning Mix OLD EL PASO	301	7	57	5	n/a
Chilli con Carne Cook-In-Sauce HOMEPRIDE	60	2.5	11.2	0.6	n/a
Chilli con Carne Dry Casserole Mix, as sold COLMAN'S	305	7.5	58.4	4.6	7.7
Chilli con Carne Mexican Creations Mix, as sold CROSSE & BLACKWELL	320	14	32.3	14.6	8.8
Chilli con Carne Sauce UNCLE BEN'S					
hot	81	4.54	14.8	0.6	n/a
medium	79	4.5	14.6	0.6	n/a
mild	75	4.4	13.5	0.6	n/a
Chilli Deliciously Good Sauce HOMEPRIDE	52	1.3	10.6	0.5	1.1
Enchilada Cooking Sauce OLD EL PASO	79	2.7	8.6	3.8	n/a

Calorie Counter

All amounts per 100g/100ml unless otherwise stated	Cal kcal	Pro g	Carb g	Fat g	Fibre g
Enchilada Seasoning Mix OLD EL PASO	299	8	52	6.5	n/a
Fajita Cooking Sauce OLD EL PASO	42	0.9	9.3	0.2	n/a
Fajita Seasoning Mix OLD EL PASO	313	11	56	5	n/a
Medium Chilli Con Carne Chicken Tonight Sizzle & Stir KNORR	111	2.7	9.1	7.1	2.7
Medium Chilli Deliciously Good Sauce HOMEPRIDE	56	2.3	10.4	0.5	1.2
Mexican Chilli Cooking Sauce HEINZ WEIGHT WATCHERS	37	1.5	7	0.3	1.2
Mexican Fajita Chicken Tonight Stir it Up KNORR	596	4.4	22.6	54.2	7.8
Ranch Barbecue Simply Sausages Sauce KNORR	74	1.8	17.3	0.1	1.1
Sizzling Fajita OLD EL PASO					
sour cream & red onion	60	1.9	13.4	5.2	n/a
spicy cheese	160	5.7	12.2	9.9	n/a
sweet sun-dried tomato	150	2	14.1	9.8	n/a
Spicy Chilli Marinade, organic MERIDIAN FOODS LTD	278	0.6	2.6	29.2	0.3
Taco Seasoning Mix OLD EL PASO	334	5.5	69	4	n/a

Cooking Sauces and Marinades

All amounts per 100g/100ml unless otherwise stated	Cal kcal	Pro g	Carb g	Fat g	Fibre g
EUROPEAN					
Beef Bourguignon Dry Casserole Mix, as sold COLMAN'S	283	4.1	65.9	0.4	2.9
Beef Stroganoff Dry Casserole Mix, as sold COLMAN'S	399	12.4	48.4	17.3	6.4
Chasseur Cook-In-Sauce Classic HOMEPRIDE	40	0.7	9.2	0.1	n/a
Chicken Chasseur Dry Casserole Mix, as sold COLMAN'S	276	12.1	54.1	1.2	4.8
Coq au Vin Dry Casserole Mix, as sold COLMAN'S	287	7.2	60.1	2	4.9
Country French Chicken Tonight Sauce KNORR	94	0.4	5.7	7.7	0.2
Mediterranean Sizzling Sauce HOMEPRIDE	86	0.9	6.3	6.4	n/a
Paella Create-a-Stir FINDUS	130	6.2	22.4	1.9	1.4
Spanish Chicken Chicken Tonight Sauce KNORR	49	1.2	8	1.3	1
WORLD					
Authentic Red Thai Curry Sauce BAXTERS	175	2.3	7.1	15.3	0.7

Calorie Counter

All amounts per 100g/100ml unless otherwise stated	Cal kcal	Pro g	Carb g	Fat g	Fibre g
Fruity Moroccan Curry Sizzling Sauce HOMEPRIDE	79	1.1	18.1	0.2	n/a
Indonesian Satay Sauce SHARWOOD	140	3.8	13.8	7.7	1
Jamaican Jerk Chicken Tonight Stir it Up KNORR	633	3.9	20.9	59.3	5.4
Japanese Teryaki Chicken Tonight Stir it Up KNORR	618	5	18.1	58.4	2.6
Malaysian Stir-in Noodle Sauce SHARWOOD	133	1.1	14.1	8.6	0.5
Moroccan Chicken Chicken Tonight Sauce KNORR	73	0.4	14.7	1.3	1.4
Satay Sauce AMOY	198	10.2	11.6	12.3	n/a
Thai Coconut, Coriander & Lime Marinade LEA & PERRINS	159	1.3	25.7	6.1	n/a
Thai Curry Sauce & Vegetables Stir Fry UNCLE BEN'S	91	1.3	11.7	4.4	n/a
Thai Red Curry Sauce SHARWOOD	106	1.2	7.9	8	0.2
Thai Red Curry Sizzle & Stir Sauce KNORR	182	1	5	17.5	2.4
Thai Sweet Chilli Sizzle & Stir Sauce KNORR	136	0.6	7.5	11.4	2.9

CRISPS AND NIBBLES

All amounts per 100g/100ml unless otherwise stated	Cal kcal	Pro g	Carb g	Fat g	Fibre g
CRISPS					
Barbecue Beef Wotsits, per pack (21g) GOLDEN WONDER	110	1.5	11.7	6.3	0.3
Cheese & Onion Crisps, per pack					
(34.5g) GOLDEN WONDER	181	1.5	12.3	8.4	1.2
(34.5g) WALKERS	181	2.2	17.3	11.4	1.4
Lites (28g) WALKERS	130	2.1	17.1	5.9	1.4
Cheesy Wotsits, per pack, (21g) GOLDEN WONDER	114	1.8	10.6	7.1	0.2
Crispy Bacon Wheat Crunchies, per pack (31g) GOLDEN WONDER	152	3.4	17.3	7.7	0.8
Hula Hoops KP SNACKS	517	3.2	55.3	31.4	2.2
Kettle Chips KETTLE FOODS					
Lightly Salted	465	6.4	51.5	25.9	6
Mature Cheddar with Chives	478	8.1	54.4	25.4	5
Salsa with Mesquite	458	6.1	54	24.2	5.7
Sea Salt with Balsamic Vinegar	468	5.8	60.9	24.4	4.4
Lightly Salted Golden Lights, per pack (21g) GOLDEN WONDER	95	1.1	13.8	3.9	0.8

Calorie Counter

All amounts per 100g/100ml unless otherwise stated	Cal kcal	Pro g	Carb g	Fat g	Fibre g
Pickled Onion Crisps, per pack					
(34.5g) GOLDEN WONDER	181	1.9	16.9	11.7	1.5
Potato Crisps	546	5.6	49.3	37.6	4.9
low fat	483	6.6	63	21.5	6.3
Prawn Cocktail Crisps, per pack					
(34.5g) GOLDEN WONDER	180	2	16.9	11.6	1.5
Prawn Cocktail Wotsits, per pack					
(21g) GOLDEN WONDER	111	1.4	11.8	6.4	0.2
Quavers, original, per pack, (20g)					
WALKERS	103	0.6	12.1	5.8	0.2
Ready Salted Crisps, per pack					
(34.5g) GOLDEN WONDER	186	1.9	17.2	12.2	1.6
(34.5g) WALKERS	183	2.2	16.9	11.7	1.4
Lites (28g) WALKERS	132	2.1	16.8	6.2	1.4
Roast Chicken Crisps, per pack					
(34.5g) GOLDEN WONDER	180	2.1	16.8	11.6	1.5
Salt & Vinegar Crisps, per pack					
(34.5g) GOLDEN WONDER	180	1.9	16.7	11.7	1.5
(34.5g) WALKERS	181	2.2	17.3	11.4	1.4
Golden Lights (21g)					
GOLDEN WONDER	94	1	13.8	3.8	0.8
Lites (28g) WALKERS	130	2.1	17.1	5.9	1.4

Crisps and Nibbles

All amounts per 100g/100ml unless otherwise stated	Cal kcal	Pro g	Carb g	Fat g	Fibre g
Salt & Vinegar Wheat Crunchies, per pack, (35g) GOLDEN WONDER	170	3.7	19.1	8.7	0.9
Smokey Bacon Crisps, per pack, (34.5g) GOLDEN WONDER	181	2	16.9	11.6	1.5
Sour Cream & Onion Golden Lights, per pack, (21g) GOLDEN WONDER	94	1.1	13.9	3.7	0.8
Spicy Tomato Wheat Crunchies, per pack, (35g) GOLDEN WONDER	151	3.3	17.2	7.7	0.8
Spring Onion Crisps, per pack, (34.5g) GOLDEN WONDER	180	2	17	11.6	1.5
Steak & Onion Crisps, per pack, (34.5g) GOLDEN WONDER	179	2.1	16.7	11.6	1.4
Tomato Sauce Crisps, per pack, (34.5g) GOLDEN WONDER	180	2	17	11.6	1.5
Worcester Sauce Crisps, per pack, (34.5g) GOLDEN WONDER	180	2	16.7	11.7	1.5
Worcester Sauce Wheat Crunchies, per pack, (35g) GOLDEN WONDER	170	3.8	19.2	8.7	0.8

See also: **KIDS' FOODS**

Calorie Counter

All amounts per 100g/100ml unless otherwise stated	Cal kcal	Pro g	Carb g	Fat g	Fibre g
NIBBLES					
Bites, Italian JACOB'S	504	8.4	53.4	28.5	4.2
Bites, rib 'n saucy JACOB'S	511	8.2	56	28.2	2.3
Bombay Mix					
HOLLAND & BARRETT	524	16.4	38.4	33.9	6.2
SHARWOOD	502	19.1	35.5	32.5	8.4
Cashews					
kernel only, roasted, salted	611	20.5	18.8	50.9	3.2
roasted & salted HOLLAND & BARRETT	624	24.2	17.3	50.9	3.2
Doritos, per pack, (40g) WALKERS					
cool original	204	3	25	10.5	1.4
pizza pizza	202	3	23	11	1.4
tangy cheese	204	3.2	23	11	1.2
Japanese Rice Crackers HOLLAND & BARRETT	397	9	79.7	4.7	0.3
Macadamia Nuts, salted	748	7.9	4.8	77.6	5.3
Nachos Kit OLD EL PASO	230	4	31	10	n/a
Nik Naks, per pack, (34g) GOLDEN WONDER					
cream 'n' cheesy	186	1.7	19.1	11.4	0.4
nice 'n' spicy	185	1.6	18.9	11.4	0.3
rib 'n' saucy	185	1.7	18.9	11.4	0.4

Crisps and Nibbles

All amounts per 100g/100ml unless otherwise stated	Cal kcal	Pro g	Carb g	Fat g	Fibre g
Paprika Savoury Snack JORDAN'S	404	7.4	72.6	9.3	3.2
Peanuts					
dry roasted	589	25.5	10.3	49.8	6.4
roasted and salted	602	24.5	7.1	53	6
Peanuts & Raisins	435	15.3	37.5	26	4.4
HOLLAND & BARRETT	473	17.8	31.8	30.6	4.8
yogurt coated HOLLAND & BARRETT	490	9.7	49.8	27.5	1.7
Popcorn					
candied	480	2.1	77.6	20	N
plain	592	6.2	48.6	42.8	N
plain HOLLAND & BARRETT	592	6.2	42.8	42.8	Tr
Poppadums					
SHARWOOD	279	21.3	44.7	1.7	10.3
fried in veg. oil	369	17.5	39.1	16.9	N
spiced SHARWOOD	281	20.4	45.6	1.9	10.3
Prawn Crackers SHARWOOD	527	0.5	62	30.8	1.2
Scooples KAVLI					
garlic	341	11.5	76.8	1.9	7.4
original	380	13.9	77.9	1.4	3
tomato	352	11.5	75.6	2.5	4.5
wholemeal	386	11.9	83.2	0.6	7.7
Snack-a-Jacks QUAKER					
caramel flavour	392	5	86	2.5	1
cheese flavour	399	8	82	3	1

Calorie Counter

All amounts per 100g/100ml unless otherwise stated	Cal kcal	Pro g	Carb g	Fat g	Fibre g
Sour Cream & Chives Savoury Snack JORDAN'S	**411**	7.5	70	11.2	3.2
Sundried Tomato & Herb Savoury Snack JORDAN'S	**403**	6.6	71.3	10.1	3.5
Thai Bites JACOB'S					
herb	**372**	7.1	78.8	3.2	0.2
salted	**375**	6.9	79.7	3.2	0.1
spice	**373**	7.1	78	3.6	0.2
Tortilla Chips	**459**	7.6	60.1	22.6	4.9
chili flavour OLD EL PASO	**496**	7	62	26	n/a
jalapeño cheese flavour OLD EL PASO	**520**	7	61	27	n/a
salsa flavour OLD EL PASO	**494**	7	65	26	n/a
Trail Mix	**432**	9.1	37.2	28.5	4.3
Twiglets JACOB'S	**401**	11.8	60.1	12.6	6.7
curry	**450**	8	56	21.5	6.1
tangy	**454**	8.1	56	21.9	5.5

DAIRY PRODUCTS

All amounts per 100g/100ml unless otherwise stated	Cal kcal	Pro g	Carb g	Fat g	Fibre g
MILK AND CREAM					
Buttermilk, cultured RAINES	40	4.3	5.5	0.1	0
Cream					
extra thick, organic YEO VALLEY	295	2.3	3.6	30	n/a
fresh, clotted	586	1.6	2.3	63.5	0
fresh, double	496	1.6	1.7	53.7	0
fresh, half	162	2.7	4.4	15	0
fresh, single	193	3.3	2.2	19.1	0
fresh, soured	205	2.9	3.8	19.9	0
fresh, whipping	381	2	2.7	40.3	0
sterilised, canned	239	2.5	3.7	23.9	0
UHT, aerosol spray	252	1.9	7.2	24.2	0
UHT, double ELMLEA	349	2.4	3.9	36	0.3
UHT, single ELMLEA	148	3.1	4.6	13	0.2
UHT, Squirty (aerosol) ELMLEA	254	1.5	6.3	24.8	Tr
UHT, whipping ELMLEA	285	2.4	3.5	29	0.2
Crème fraiche					
full fat	378	1.6	63.5	2.3	0
half fat	162	2.7	15	4.4	0
half fat, organic YEO VALLEY	185	2.3	3.5	18.5	n/a
Milk, fresh					
cows', whole, average	66	3.3	4.5	3.9	0
cows', semi-skimmed, average	46	3.4	4.7	1.7	0
cows', skimmed, average	32	3.4	4.4	0.2	0

Calorie Counter

All amounts per 100g/100ml unless otherwise stated	Cal kcal	Pro g	Carb g	Fat g	Fibre g
cows', Channel Island	78	3.6	5.1	4.8	0
goats', pasteurised	62	3.1	4.4	3.7	0
sheep's	60	3.1	3.7	4.4	0
Milk, evaporated NESTLÉ					
original	330	8.3	54.3	9.1	0
light	107	7.8	10.3	4.1	0
Carnation	160	8.2	11.5	9	0
Carnation Light	110	7.5	10.5	4	0
Ideal	160	8.2	11.5	9	0
Milk, dried					
skimmed	348	36.1	52.9	0.6	0
skimmed MARVEL	361	52.9	36.1	0.6	0
Milk, condensed					
wholemilk, sweetened	333	8.5	55.5	10.1	0
skimmed milk, sweetened	267	10	60	0.2	0
condensed Fussells NESTLÉ	280	10.5	59.2	0.2	0
Soya Milk					
unsweetened	26	2.4	0.5	1.6	0.2
unsweetened, organic PROVAMEL	36	3.7	0.4	2.1	0.3
sweetened	43	3.1	2.5	2.4	Tr
sweetened, organic PROVAMEL	45	3.7	2.8	2.1	0.3
Rice Drink PROVAMEL					
calcium enriched	50	0.1	10	1.1	0
vanilla, organic	49	0.1	10	1	0

All amounts per 100g/100ml unless otherwise stated	Cal kcal	Pro g	Carb g	Fat g	Fibre g

YOGURT AND FROMAGE FRAIS

Non-branded Yogurt

Greek-style, cows, fruit	137	4.8	11.2	8.4	Tr
Greek-style, cows, plain	133	5.7	4.8	10.2	0
Greek-style, sheep	92	4.8	5	6	0
low fat, fruit	78	4.2	13.7	1.1	0.2
low fat, plain	56	4.8	7.4	1	N
soya, fruit	73	2.1	12.9	1.8	0.3
virtually fat free, fruit	47	4.8	7	0.2	Tr
virtually fat free, plain	54	5.4	8.2	0.2	0
whole milk, fruit	109	4	17.7	3	N
whole milk, plain	79	5.7	7.8	3	N

Non-branded Fromage Frais

fruit	124	5.3	13.9	5.6	Tr
plain	113	6.8	5.7	7.1	0
vitually fat free, fruit	50	6.8	5.6	0.2	0.4
vitually fat free, plain	49	7.7	4.6	0.1	0

Apple & Banana Bio Yogurt
HOLLAND & BARRETT

	54	4.4	5.6	1.5	0

Apple & Prune Virtually Fat Free Yogurt, organic YEO VALLEY

	78	5.1	14.1	0.1	n/a

Apricot & Mango Extrafruit Yogurt SKI

	94	4.9	17.5	0.7	1

Calorie Counter

All amounts per 100g/100ml unless otherwise stated	Cal kcal	Pro g	Carb g	Fat g	Fibre g
Apricot Fruit Yogurt, organic YEO VALLEY	96	4	12.6	3.2	n/a
Apricot Virtually Fat Free Yogurt, organic YEO VALLEY	78	5.1	14.1	0.1	n/a
Black Cherry Yogurt SKI	95	5.1	17.3	1.1	0
Blackberry & Raspberry Fat Free Bio Yogurt, each ST IVEL SHAPE	53	5.5	6.7	0.2	0.3
Blackcurrant Bio Stirred Yogurt SKI	109	5.8	16	2.9	0
Cherry Bio Split Yogurt SKI	124	4.5	8.3	4	0
Cherry Low Fat Yogurt MÜLLER	104	4.8	10.9	1.9	n/a
Chocolate Low Fat Bio Yogurt ST IVEL SHAPE	111	4.9	17.4	2	0.2
Cranberry & Blackcurrant Fat Free Bio Yogurt, each ST IVEL SHAPE	54	5.4	6.8	0.2	0.3
Devon Toffee Low Fat Bio Yogurt ST IVEL SHAPE	99	4.6	15.4	1.8	0
Fruit Corner MÜLLER					
blackberry & raspberry	110	3.7	15	3.9	n/a
blueberry	112	3.7	15.1	3.9	n/a
cherry	110	3.7	15	3.9	n/a
peach & apricot	110	3.7	15	3.9	n/a
strawberry	118	3.7	17.1	3.9	n/a

All amounts per 100g/100ml unless otherwise stated	Cal kcal	Pro g	Carb g	Fat g	Fibre g
Goats' Milk Yogurt HOLLAND & BARRETT	60	3.3	4.4	3.5	Tr
Lemon & Lime Fat Free Bio Yogurt, each ST IVEL SHAPE	54	5.4	6.8	0.2	Tr
Lemon Greek-style Yogurt, each ST IVEL SHAPE	108	7.1	12.7	2.7	Tr
Mango & Passionfruit Smoothie, per bottle ST IVEL SHAPE	203	7.3	39.3	1.8	2.3
Müllerlight MÜLLER					
banana yogurt	53	4.4	8.7	0.1	n/a
cherry yogurt	50	4.4	7.9	0.1	n/a
country berries yogurt	52	4.4	8.3	0.1	n/a
strawberry yogurt	53	4.4	8.7	0.1	n/a
toffee yogurt	53	4.4	8.5	0.1	n/a
vanilla yogurt	53	4.6	8.3	0.1	n/a
Natural Bio Yogurt HOLLAND & BARRETT	54	4.4	5.6	1.5	0
Natural Yogurt, organic YEO VALLEY	80	4.7	6.9	3.7	n/a
Nectarine Bio Stirred Yogurt SKI	112	5.8	16.7	2.9	0
Orange & Banana Smoothie, per bottle ST IVEL SHAPE	183	7	35.5	1.5	2

Calorie Counter

All amounts per 100g/100ml unless otherwise stated	Cal kcal	Pro g	Carb g	Fat g	Fibre g
Orange Fat Free Bio Yogurt, each ST IVEL SHAPE	61	5.4	8.7	0.2	0.1
Orange Greek-style Yogurt, each ST IVEL SHAPE	102	7.2	11.3	2.8	0.1
Orange Yogurt SKI	88	5	16.4	0.7	0
Original Thick & Creamy Yogurt MÜLLER	109	4.8	11.3	5	n/a
Peach & Apricot Fat Free Bio Yogurt, each ST IVEL SHAPE	55	5.5	7	0.2	0.1
Peach Fromage Frais SKI	124	6.2	14.2	4.8	n/a
Peach Low Fat Yogurt MÜLLER	101	4.8	16.1	1.9	n/a
Peach Yogurt SKI	94	5.1	17	1.1	0
Pineapple Fat Free Bio Yogurt, each ST IVEL SHAPE	61	5.4	8.7	0.2	0.1
Pineapple Yogurt SKI	96	5	17.4	1.1	0
Raspberry & Cranberry Smoothie, per bottle ST IVEL SHAPE	190	7	37.3	1.5	2.3
Raspberry & White Chocolate Low Fat Bio Yogurt ST IVEL SHAPE	101	4.7	15.6	1.8	0.1
Raspberry Drinking Yogurt, per bottle ST IVEL	78	2.9	12.5	1.8	0.1

All amounts per 100g/100ml unless otherwise stated	Cal kcal	Pro g	Carb g	Fat g	Fibre g
Raspberry Fat Free Bio Yogurt, each ST IVEL SHAPE	59	5.5	8	0.2	0.2
Raspberry Fruit Yogurt, organic YEO VALLEY	96	4	12.6	3.2	n/a
Raspberry Low Fat Yogurt MÜLLER	101	4.8	10.1	1.9	n/a
Raspberry Wholemilk Yogurt, each ST IVEL	99	4.1	14	2.6	0
Raspberry Yogurt SKI	94	5.1	17	1.1	0
Red Cherry Fat Free Bio Yogurt, each ST IVEL SHAPE	57	5.5	7.7	0.2	0.1
Strawberry Bio Yogurt HOLLAND & BARRETT	54	4.4	5.6	1.5	0
Strawberry Drinking Yogurt, per bottle ST IVEL	78	2.9	12.6	1.8	0.1
Strawberry Fat Free Bio Yogurt, each ST IVEL SHAPE	56	5.4	7.4	0.2	0.1
Strawberry Fromage Frais SKI	123	6.1	14	4.8	n/a
Strawberry Fruit Yogurt, organic YEO VALLEY	96	4	12.6	3.2	n/a
Strawberry Low Fat Yogurt MÜLLER	99	4.8	15.7	1.9	n/a

Calorie Counter

All amounts per 100g/100ml unless otherwise stated	Cal kcal	Pro g	Carb g	Fat g	Fibre g
Strawberry Thick & Creamy Yogurt MÜLLER	112	4.1	16.8	3.2	n/a
Strawberry Virtually Fat Free Yogurt, organic YEO VALLEY	78	5.1	14.1	0.1	n/a
Strawberry Wholemilk Yogurt, each ST IVEL	99	4.1	14	2.6	0
Summer Berries Fat Free Bio Yogurt, each ST IVEL SHAPE	55	5.5	7.1	0.2	0.2
Vanilla Virtually Fat Free Yogurt, organic YEO VALLEY	78	5.1	14.1	0.1	n/a
Vitality MÜLLER					
apricot	98	4.7	15.8	1.8	n/a
raspberry	97	4.8	15.4	1.8	n/a
strawberry	97	4.7	15.8	1.8	n/a
Vitality Drink MÜLLER					
natural yogurt	67	5.5	6.9	1.9	n/a
peach	75	2.6	13	1.4	n/a
raspberry	74	2.6	12.8	1.4	n/a
Yoplait DAIRY CREST					
apricot & banana	87	3.7	14.5	1.6	n/a
black cherry	110	4.9	15.8	1.6	n/a
mango & guava	88	3.7	14.6	1.6	n/a
peach & apricot	108	4.8	15.8	1.6	n/a
peach & passionfruit	84	3.8	13.7	1.6	n/a

All amounts per 100g/100ml unless otherwise stated	Cal kcal	Pro g	Carb g	Fat g	Fibre g
pineapple	**86**	3.6	14.2	1.6	n/a
strawberry	**108**	4.8	15.8	1.6	n/a
summer fruits	**108**	4.9	15.3	1.6	n/a
Yoplait Fruit on the Bottom DAIRY CREST					
apricot & mango	**109**	4.7	18.5	1.6	n/a
blackberry & apple	**111**	4.7	19	1.6	n/a
nectarine & orange	**111**	4.7	19	1.6	n/a
strawberry	**109**	4.7	18.6	1.6	n/a

BUTTER AND MARGARINES

Butter

	Cal kcal	Pro g	Carb g	Fat g	Fibre g
lightly salted KERRYGOLD	**720**	n/a	Tr	80	0
lightly salted LURPAK	**719**	0.1	0.6	81	0
lightly salted, organic					
YEO VALLEY	**737**	0.5	Tr	81.7	n/a
spreadable	**745**	0.5	82.5	Tr	0
spreadable LURPAK	**724**	0.5	0.5	80	0
Lighter spreadable LURPAK	**540**	0.5	0.5	60	0
salted and unsalted	**744**	0.6	0.6	82.2	0
unsalted LURPAK	**719**	0.1	0.6	82	0

Margarine, hard

	Cal kcal	Pro g	Carb g	Fat g	Fibre g
animal & vegetable fat,					
over 80% fat	**718**	0.2	1	79.3	0
Stork, block STORK	**720**	Tr	0.1	80	0

Calorie Counter

All amounts per 100g/100ml unless otherwise stated	Cal kcal	Pro g	Carb g	Fat g	Fibre g
Margarine, soft					
polyunsaturated, over 80% fat	746	Tr	0.2	82.8	0
Stork, tub STORK	658	Tr	Tr	73	0
SPREADS					
Benecol BENECOL	571	0	0	64.3	0
Light	321	0	0	35.7	0
Carapelli, olive oil spread ST IVEL	536	0.5	0.8	59	0
Clover DAIRY CREST	654	0.6	0.9	72	0
reduced salt	654	0.6	0.9	72	0
Flora FLORA					
Buttery	634	0.4	0.5	70	0
Light	357	0.1	3.7	38	0.6
Low Salt	630	0.1	0.1	70	0
Pro.active	328	0.1	3.2	35	0.3
Sunflower Spread	630	0.1	0.1	70	0
Gold Light Margarine ST IVEL	359	0.9	3.3	38	Tr
unsalted	360	0.7	3.9	38	Tr
Golden Churn ST IVEL	615	1.1	1.6	67	0
I Can't Believe It's Not Butter BESTFOODS	625	0.4	0.7	69	0
Olivio OLIVIO					
with olive oil	536	0.2	1	59	Tr

All amounts per 100g/100ml unless otherwise stated	Cal kcal	Pro g	Carb g	Fat g	Fibre g
Spread, blended, 70–80% fat	680	0.6	1.1	74.8	0
Spread, dairy, 40% fat	388	7	0.1	40	0
Spread, very low fat, 20–25% fat	262	5.9	2.5	25.5	0
Utterly Butterly ST IVEL	615	1.1	1.6	67	0
Scandinavian style	606	0.3	0.5	67	0
Vitalite ST IVEL	578	0.4	1.2	63	0
Willow DAIRY CREST	708	0.6	0.9	78	n/a

CHEESES

	Cal kcal	Pro g	Carb g	Fat g	Fibre g
Babybel, mini FROMAGERIES BEL	308	23	0	24	n/a
Bavarian Smoked	277	17	0.4	23	0
Boursin BOURSIN					
ail & fines herbs	414	7	2	42	Tr
au naturel	423	7	2	43	n/a
au poivre	414	7	2	42	Tr
Brie	343	20.3	Tr	29.1	0
Caerphilly	375	23.2	0.1	31.3	0
Cambozola	430	13.5	0.5	41.5	0
Camembert	290	21.5	Tr	22.7	0

Calorie Counter

All amounts per 100g/100ml unless otherwise stated	Cal kcal	Pro g	Carb g	Fat g	Fibre g
Cathedral City DAIRY CREST	410	25	0.1	34.4	0
Cheddar					
English	416	25.4	0.1	34.9	0
vegetarian	390	25.5	Tr	32	0
with garlic & herbs DAIRY CREST	410	25	0.1	34.4	0
Cheddar-type, half fat	273	32.7	Tr	15.8	0
Cheshire	379	24	0.1	31.4	0
Cottage Cheese					
plain	101	12.6	3.1	4.3	0
reduced fat	79	13.3	3.3	1.5	0
with additions	95	12.8	2.6	3.8	Tr
Bodyline, natural EDEN VALE	85	14	4.4	1.5	0
Bodyline, onion & chive					
EDEN VALE	105	12.7	4.3	4	0
Bodyline, pineapple EDEN VALE	97	11.6	5.3	3.5	0.2
Cracker Barrel Cheddar KRAFT	415	25	0.1	34.5	0
Cream Cheese	439	3.1	Tr	47.4	0
Danish Blue	342	20.5	Tr	28.9	0
Davidstow Mature DAIRY CREST	410	25	0.1	34.4	0
Dolcelatte	396	17.3	0.8	36	0
Double Gloucester	404	24.4	0.1	34	0
Edam	341	26.7	Tr	26	0

All amounts per 100g/100ml unless otherwise stated	Cal kcal	Pro g	Carb g	Fat g	Fibre g
Emmenthal	370	29	0.4	28	0
Feta	250	15.6	1.5	20.2	0
Goats' Milk Soft Cheese	320	21.1	1	25.8	0
Gorgonzola	310	19	0	36	0
Gouda	377	25.3	Tr	30.6	0
Grana Padano	384	33	0	28	0
Gruyère	396	27	0.1	32	0
Jarlsberg	360	27	0.1	28	0
Lancashire	381	23.7	0.1	31.8	0
Laughing Cow FROMAGERIES BEL	269	10	6.5	22.5	n/a
Mascarpone	426	3.5	3	44.5	0
Mature Cheese, reduced fat HEINZ WEIGHT WATCHERS	306	27	0.1	22	0
Medium Fat Soft Cheese	199	9.8	3.5	16.3	0
Mendip Hills DAIRY CREST	410	25	0.1	34.4	0
Mild Cheese, reduced fat HEINZ WEIGHT WATCHERS	306	27	0.1	22	0
Mozzarella	257	18.6	Tr	20.3	0

Calorie Counter

All amounts per 100g/100ml unless otherwise stated	Cal kcal	Pro g	Carb g	Fat g	Fibre g
Parmesan, fresh	**415**	36.2	0.9	29.7	0
Philadelphia Soft Cheese KRAFT					
Full Fat	**250**	5.9	3.2	24	0.2
Light Medium Fat	**190**	7.6	3.4	16	0.3
Light with chives	**185**	7.5	3.4	15.5	0.3
Light with garlic & herbs	**180**	7.2	3.4	15.5	0.2
Light with tomato & basil	**179**	7.6	4.5	14	0.4
Quark	**61**	11	3.9	0.2	0
Red Leicester	**399**	23.8	0.1	33.7	0
Ricotta	**134**	9	2	10	0
Roquefort	**355**	23	Tr	29.2	0
Sage Derby	**415**	24.4	2.7	34	0
Shropshire Blue	**409**	22.3	0.1	35.5	0
Stilton					
blue	**410**	23.7	0.1	35	0
white	**359**	19.9	0.1	31	0
white, with apricots	**351**	16.9	10.4	26.9	1.8
Wensleydale	**375**	22.8	0.1	31.5	0
with cranberries	**366**	21.2	9.4	27.2	0
Wilson's Mighty Strong Cheddar DAIRY CREST	**410**	25	0.1	34.4	0

All amounts per 100g/100ml unless otherwise stated	Cal kcal	Pro g	Carb g	Fat g	Fibre g
CHEESE SPREADS AND PROCESSED CHEESE					
Cheese Spread					
plain	**267**	11.3	4.4	22.8	0
reduced fat	**175**	15	7.9	9.5	0
Cheese Slices KRAFT					
singles	**260**	13.5	7.6	14.5	0.5
singles light	**205**	20	6	11	0
Dairylea Cheese Food Slices KRAFT	**315**	13	8	24.5	0
light	**215**	19.5	7.1	11.5	0
thick light	**205**	17.3	8.6	10.5	0
Dairylea Cheese Portions KRAFT	**225**	9.9	7.3	17.5	0
Dairylea Cheese Strip Cheese KRAFT	**360**	24.5	1	27.5	0
Primula PRIMULA					
original	**240**	13	2	20	0
cheese & chive	**236**	12.9	1	20	0
cheese & shrimp	**240**	13.3	1.8	20	0
cheese & ham	**236**	13	1.5	20	0
cheese & garlic	**247**	15.7	4.3	18.6	0
light	**171**	16	6.6	9	0
Processed Cheese, plain	**297**	7.8	5	23	0

See also: **SAVOURY SPREADS AND PASTES**

DELI AND COLD MEAT

All amounts per 100g/100ml unless otherwise stated	Cal kcal	Pro g	Carb g	Fat g	Fibre g
Beef, roasted					
silverside	**138**	19.1	2.4	5.8	Tr
topside	**158**	25.4	0.4	6.1	0
Chicken, roasted					
breast	**153**	30.2	0	3.6	0
Chorizo	**387**	23	4	31	0
Corned Beef					
canned	**205**	25.9	1	10.9	ni
canned LIBBY	**224**	24.5	1	13.5	0
Garlic Sausage	**189**	15.3	5.8	11.6	0.5
coarse	**222**	21.7	0.9	14.6	0.4
Haggis, boiled	**310**	10.7	19.2	21.7	N
Ham & Pork, chopped, canned	**275**	14.4	1.4	23.6	0.3
Ham					
canned	**120**	18.4	0	5.1	ni
honey-roast	**135**	20.1	2.8	4.3	1
mustard	**140**	22.6	1.1	5	0.8
on the bone	**136**	20.9	0.8	15.5	0.7
Parisian HERTA	**105**	20.6	0.5	2.6	0
Parisian beechwood smoked HERTA	**150**	20.6	0.5	2.6	0
Parma	**240**	25.4	0.1	15.3	0
Wiltshire	**201**	19.9	1.5	12.8	1.1
Yorkshire	**191**	15.4	1.2	13.8	0

All amounts per 100g/100ml unless otherwise stated	Cal kcal	Pro g	Carb g	Fat g	Fibre g
Haslet	144	12.9	18.6	2	0.8
Kabanos	240	24.4	1	15.4	0.5
Liver Pâté	348	12.6	0.8	32.7	Tr
reduced fat	191	18	3	12	Tr
Liver Sausage	226	13.4	6	16.7	0.7
Luncheon Meat, canned	279	12.9	3.6	23.8	0.2
Pâté, Brussels	326	13	1	30	0
Peperami PEPERAMI					
Hot	554	19	2.5	52	1.2
Pork Salami Sausage	536	22	1.7	49	0.1
Polony	281	9.4	14.2	21.1	N
Pork					
luncheon meat	261	13.9	3.3	21.5	0
oven-baked	183	26.1	1.4	8.1	0.8
roast with stuffing	160	18.1	3.3	8.2	1.1
stuffed pork roll TYNE BRAND	147	4.5	9.6	7	n/a
Salami	438	20.9	0.5	39.2	0.1
Danish	604	15.6	0.5	59.9	0
German	395	19	1	35	0
Milano	428	23	3	36	0
Scotch Eggs	241	12	13.1	16	N
Tongue, lunch	175	19.5	0.3	10.4	0
Turkey					
breast, roasted	108	23.1	0.4	1.6	0.8
stuffed turkey roll TYNE BRAND	150	13	7.8	7.4	n/a

DESSERTS AND PUDDINGS

All amounts per 100g/100ml unless otherwise stated	Cal kcal	Pro g	Carb g	Fat g	Fibre g
PUDDINGS AND TRIFLES					
Bread Pudding, recipe	**289**	5.9	48	9.5	1.2
Chocolova McVITIE'S	**351**	3.4	42.3	18.7	Tr
Christmas Pudding	**329**	3	56.3	11.8	1.7
Cider & Sherry Pudding, Mrs Peek's JACOB'S	**326**	2.6	63.2	7	3.1
Meringue	**379**	5.3	95.4	Tr	0
Pavlova McVITIE'S					
fruits of the forest	**293**	2.7	43.6	12	Tr
raspberry	**297**	2.5	45	11.9	Tr
strawberry	**330**	2.3	32.7	21.1	0
Profiteroles McVITIE'S	**358**	6.2	18.5	29.2	0.4
Rum & Brandy Pudding, Mrs Peek's JACOB'S	**335**	2.9	34.9	7.1	4.5
Sago Pudding					
as sold WHITWORTHS	**355**	0.2	94	0.2	0
made with semi-skimmed milk	**93**	4	20.1	0.2	0.1
made with whole milk	**130**	4.1	19.6	4.3	0.1

All amounts per 100g/100ml unless otherwise stated	Cal kcal	Pro g	Carb g	Fat g	Fibre g
Semolina Pudding					
as sold WHITWORTHS	350	10.7	77.5	1.8	2.1
made with semi-skimmed milk	93	4	20.1	0.2	0.1
made with whole milk	130	4.1	19.6	4.3	0.1
Tapioca Pudding					
as sold WHITWORTHS	348	0.4	86.4	0.1	0.4
made with semi-skimmed milk	93	4	20.1	0.2	0.1
made with whole milk	130	4.1	19.6	4.3	0.1
Torte, raspberry McVITIE'S	271	3.5	24.5	17.8	0.4
Trifle	160	3.6	22.3	6.3	0.5
mango & passionfruit ST IVEL SHAPE	154	2.3	26.7	4.3	0.3
raspberry, luxury HEINZ WEIGHT WATCHERS	110	3.2	18.4	1.8	0.4
strawberry ST IVEL	172	2.4	21	8.7	0.2
strawberry ST IVEL SHAPE	146	2.3	24.8	4.3	0.3
strawberry YOUNG'S	142	1.4	26.6	3.7	0.2
Trifle Mixes, as sold BIRD'S					
fruit cocktail	420	2.5	77	10.5	1.5
raspberry	420	2.5	77	10.5	1.5
sherry flavour	420	2.5	77	10.5	1.5
strawberry	420	2.5	77	10.5	1.5
Trifle with Fresh Cream	166	2.4	19.5	9.2	0.5

Calorie Counter

All amounts per 100g/100ml unless otherwise stated	Cal kcal	Pro g	Carb g	Fat g	Fibre g
Trifle, Luxury Devonshire St Ivel					
fruit cocktail	166	2	23.3	7.2	0.2
mandarin & banana	190	2.4	22.5	10.1	0.1
raspberry	167	2.1	23.2	7.3	0.3
strawberry	166	2.1	23.2	7.2	0.2
Trifles, fruit Mr Kipling	392	3.4	52.3	17.8	n/a

SPONGE AND RICE PUDDINGS

	Cal kcal	Pro g	Carb g	Fat g	Fibre g
Creamed Macaroni Ambrosia	88	3.6	14.6	1.7	0.3
Creamed Rice Ambrosia	90	3.1	15.2	1.9	Tr
Creamed Rice Dessert Pot Ambrosia					
as sold	101	3.2	16.5	2.5	Tr
low fat	86	3.3	16.1	0.9	Tr
Creamed Rice Pudding Libby	89	3.1	15.4	1.6	0.2
Creamed Rice Ambrosia					
low fat	81	3.2	15.2	0.8	Tr
organic	107	3.4	15.1	3.7	Tr
Creamed Sago Ambrosia	79	2.5	13.6	1.6	0.2
Creamed Semolina Ambrosia	81	3.3	13.1	1.7	0.2
Creamed Tapioca Ambrosia	80	2.5	13.8	1.6	Tr

Desserts and Puddings

All amounts per 100g/100ml unless otherwise stated	Cal kcal	Pro g	Carb g	Fat g	Fibre g
Müllerice MÜLLER					
apple	83	3.5	15.3	0.9	n/a
apple, fat free	83	3.5	15.3	0.9	n/a
original	72	3.9	11.9	1	n/a
original, fat free	72	3.9	11.8	1	n/a
strawberry	77	3.5	13.6	0.9	n/a
strawberry, fat free	77	3.5	13.6	0.9	n/a
toffee	79	3.3	14.6	1	n/a
toffee, fat free	79	3.3	14.3	1	n/a
Rice Pudding					
recipe	130	4.1	19.6	4.3	0.1
canned	89	3.4	14	2.5	0.2
canned CREAMOLA	380	6.4	85	1	2.4
canned, low fat, no added sugar					
HEINZ WEIGHT WATCHERS	73	3.7	11.4	1.5	0
Rice Pudding with Sultanas & Nutmeg, traditional AMBROSIA	105	3.2	16.6	2.9	0.1
Sponge Pudding HEINZ	340	5.8	45.3	16.3	1.1
Banana with Toffee Sauce	291	2.7	48.8	9.4	0.7
Chocolate with Chocolate Sauce	285	2.7	48.2	9.1	1.4
Lemon	306	2.7	50.1	10.6	0.6
Mixed Fruit	302	4	44.5	12	1.3
Sticky Toffee	313	3.2	46.9	12.5	0.7
Strawberry Jam	282	2.7	51.2	7.4	0.6
Treacle	278	2.3	49.2	8	0.6
Spotted Dick MCVITIE'S	357	5.7	51.2	15	2.3

Calorie Counter

All amounts per 100g/100ml unless otherwise stated	Cal kcal	Pro g	Carb g	Fat g	Fibre g
CHILLED DESSERTS					
Aero Milk Chocolate Mousse NESTLÉ	**225**	5	25.9	11.5	0.2
Aero Twist NESTLÉ					
Cappucino	**180**	4.2	16.8	10.8	0.2
Chocolate	**170**	4.3	17.7	9.2	0.2
Black Cherry Ripple Mousse, each FIESTA	**87**	2	11.6	4	n/a
Cadbury's Crunchie Twinpot ST IVEL	**262**	5.3	31.7	12.7	0
Cadbury's Flake Twinpot ST IVEL	**266**	5.7	28.6	14.1	0
Cadbury's Light Chocolate Mousse ST IVEL	**123**	6.2	17.3	3.2	0
Cadbury's Light Chocolate Trifle ST IVEL	**180**	5.3	23.8	7.3	0.7
Cadbury's Milk Chocolate Mousse ST IVEL	**192**	6	25.8	7.2	0
Cadbury's Milk Chocolate Trifle ST IVEL	**276**	5	23.6	17.9	0.2
Caramel Soya Dessert, each PROVAMEL	**103**	3.8	17.1	2.1	0.4

All amounts per 100g/100ml unless otherwise stated	Cal kcal	Pro g	Carb g	Fat g	Fibre g
Chocolate Dessert, organic, each PROVAMEL	131	3.8	24.3	2.1	2.1
Chocolate Mousse	139	4	19.9	5.4	N
HEINZ WEIGHT WATCHERS	97	4.8	10.3	3.6	0.4
each FIESTA	83	1.9	10.2	3.8	n/a
Chocolate Soya Dessert, each PROVAMEL	113	3.8	17.8	2.9	1.8
Corner Dessert, sticky toffee pudding MÜLLER	159	3.6	24.7	5.1	n/a
Creme Brulee, raspberry & redcurrant MCVITIE'S	251	1.3	23.5	17	0.2
Creme Caramel	109	3	20.6	2.2	N
La Laitiere NESTLÉ	135	5	20	4	0
Crunch Corner MÜLLER					
rum & raisin	146	4.2	22	4.6	n/a
vanilla & chocolate balls	145	4.1	22.5	4.3	n/a
Fruit Juice Mousse ST IVEL SHAPE					
lemon	116	3.5	18.6	2.8	0
orange	116	3.5	18.5	2.8	0
strawberry	115	3.5	18.5	2.8	0
Fruit Mousse	137	4.5	18	5.7	N
Milky Bar Dessert NESTLÉ	460	3.6	75.6	15.7	0.2
Mini Smarties Dessert NESTLÉ	425	4.3	72.3	13	1.2

Calorie Counter

All amounts per 100g/100ml unless otherwise stated	Cal kcal	Pro g	Carb g	Fat g	Fibre g
Mint Choc Chip Mousse, each FIESTA	84	1.8	10.6	4.1	n/a
More than a Mousse NESTLÉ					
chocolate	190	4	17.7	11.2	1.1
vanilla	195	4	16.3	12.5	0.1
Munchies Dessert Split Pot NESTLÉ	247	4.3	29.7	12.4	0.3
Raspberry Ripple Mousse, each FIESTA	90	2	11.4	4	n/a
Rowntree Swirly Yoghurt Dessert NESTLÉ	100	2.5	19.2	1.2	0.8
Smarties Split Pot NESTLÉ	243	3.1	33.2	12.2	1.1
Smatana RAINES	130	4.7	5.6	10	n/a
Strawberry Mousse, each FIESTA	75	1.7	9	3.6	n/a
Tiramisu					
McVITIE'S	337	3.5	31.2	22.2	0.3
chocolate HEINZ WEIGHT WATCHERS	181	4.1	26.9	3.7	0.8
Toffee Chocolate Dessert HEINZ WEIGHT WATCHERS	190	5.9	32.9	3.6	0.4
Toffee Mousse, each FIESTA	78	1.8	9.6	3.8	n/a

All amounts per 100g/100ml unless otherwise stated	Cal kcal	Pro g	Carb g	Fat g	Fibre g
Vanilla Dessert, organic, each PROVAMEL	131	3.8	23.9	2.3	1.3
Vanilla Soya Dessert, each PROVAMEL	101	3.8	16.4	2.3	1.3

FROZEN DESSERTS

	Cal kcal	Pro g	Carb g	Fat g	Fibre g
Bounty, dark, ice cream MARS	330	4	28.8	22.1	n/a
Chocolate & Honeycomb Pieces Iced Dessert HEINZ WEIGHT WATCHERS	159	3.1	26.2	4.3	0.8
Chocolate Creme de Creme, each LYONS MAID	161	3.2	17.5	8.8	n/a
Chocolate Ice Cream					
FIESTA	187	3.5	20.6	10.6	n/a
LYONS MAID	91	2	11.4	4.2	n/a
Chocolate Nut Sundae	243	2.6	26.2	14.9	0.2
Chocolate Ripple Ice Cream LYONS MAID	98	2	14.2	3.7	n/a
Chocolate Swirl Iced Dessert HEINZ WEIGHT WATCHERS	133	2.6	19.6	4.6	0.5
Chunky Choc Ice WALLS	163	2.1	15.3	10.6	n/a

Calorie Counter

All amounts per 100g/100ml unless otherwise stated	Cal kcal	Pro g	Carb g	Fat g	Fibre g
Cornetto WALLS					
classico	**225**	3.5	25.4	12.4	n/a
mint	**225**	3.4	27.1	11.5	n/a
strawberry	**190**	2.5	27.6	7.7	n/a
whippy	**230**	3.2	31.1	10.5	n/a
Cornish Ice Cream LYONS MAID	**92**	19	11.3	4.4	n/a
Crème Caramel Ice Cream CARTE D'OR	**120**	1.6	19	4.5	n/a
Dark Classico, each LYONS MAID	**135**	1.5	13.5	8.5	n/a
Feast WALLS	**315**	3.3	23	23.1	n/a
Galaxy Bar MARS	**346**	4.1	32.2	22.3	n/a
Galaxy Caramel Swirl Ice Cream MARS	**338**	3.8	33	21.3	n/a
Galaxy Triple Chocolate Swirls Ice Cream MARS	**345**	3.9	32.7	22.1	n/a
Ice Cream: *see* **Individual flavours**					
Ice Cream Bar, chocolate coated	**311**	5	21.8	23.3	Tr
Ice Cream Desserts, frozen	**251**	3.5	21	17.6	Tr
King Cone, each LYONS MAID					
Mega Mint	**367**	6.2	46.4	18.7	n/a
Mint Chocolate Chip	**185**	3	23.6	8.6	n/a
Strawberry	**186**	2	28.9	6.8	n/a
Vanilla	**174**	2.8	23.6	7.6	n/a

All amounts per 100g/100ml unless otherwise stated	Cal kcal	Pro g	Carb g	Fat g	Fibre g
M & Ms Ice Cream Cone MARS	321	3.8	36.8	17.6	n/a
Magnum Caramel & Nuts WALLS	205	2.9	21.7	12	n/a
Magnum Classic WALLS	280	3.9	27.3	17.4	n/a
Magnum Cone WALLS	350	3.5	34	22	n/a
Magnum Double Caramel WALLS	340	3.7	34	21	n/a
Magnum Double Chocolate WALLS	371	4.5	33	24.5	n/a
Magnum White WALLS	300	3.8	26.6	19.6	n/a
Magnum Yogurt Fresh WALLS	296	3.1	30.5	18	n/a
Mars Bar Ice Cream MARS	346	4.4	37.3	19.6	n/a
Milk Classico, each LYONS MAID	141	1.7	13.5	9	n/a
Mint Crisp, each LYONS MAID	198	1.7	22	11.4	n/a
Montego NESTLÉ					
Lemon	105	1	20.6	2.1	n/a
Orange	110	0.6	21.6	2.3	n/a
Raspberry	103	0.6	21.8	1.6	n/a
Napoli LYONS MAID					
banana	95	1.7	10.5	5.1	n/a
blueberry	104	1.8	12.7	5.2	n/a
chocolate ripple	121	2.3	14.9	5.9	n/a
coffee	98	1.9	10.4	5.5	n/a
maple walnut	118	2	12.9	6.5	n/a
mint chocolate chip	124	2.1	13.7	6.8	n/a

Calorie Counter

All amounts per 100g/100ml unless otherwise stated	Cal kcal	Pro g	Carb g	Fat g	Fibre g
rum & raisin	104	1.8	12.4	5.1	n/a
strawberry	102	1.8	12.2	5.1	n/a
toffee	107	1.8	14.5	5.8	n/a
vanilla	100	1.9	10.6	5.6	n/a
Neapolitan Ice Cream					
FIESTA	173	3.6	20.1	9.3	n/a
LYONS MAID	87	1.8	11	4	n/a
Peach Melba Ice Cream					
LYONS MAID	94	1.7	13.2	3.8	n/a
Raspberry Ripple Ice Cream					
FIESTA	192	3.2	24.3	9.8	n/a
LYONS MAID	114	1.6	19	3.5	n/a
Raspberry Swirl Iced Dessert					
HEINZ WEIGHT WATCHERS	124	1.7	23.4	2.5	0.3
Snickers Ice Cream Bar MARS	376	7.6	34.5	23.1	n/a
Solero Exotic WALLS	115	1.5	19.6	3.1	n/a
Sorbet					
fruit	97	0.2	24.8	0.3	Tr
blackcurrant CARTE D'OR	85	0.5	20.2	0.2	n/a
blackcurrant DEL MONTE	106	0.4	27.1	Tr	n/a
lemon CARTE D'OR	74	0.2	18.2	0.1	n/a
lemon	131	0.9	34.2	Tr	0
lemon DEL MONTE	114	0.1	29.2	Tr	n/a
lemon FIESTA	114	0	28.1	0	n/a

All amounts per 100g/100ml unless otherwise stated	Cal kcal	Pro g	Carb g	Fat g	Fibre g
mango CARTE D'OR	77	0.3	19	0	n/a
mango DEL MONTE	115	0.2	29.6	Tr	n/a
orange DEL MONTE	125	0.2	32.1	Tr	n/a
pineapple DEL MONTE	120	0.3	30.6	Tr	n/a
Starburst Joosters MARS	131	1.2	31.4	0	n/a
Starburst MARS					
orange & lemon	119	0.2	29.3	0.1	n/a
strawberry	127	0.1	31.8	0.1	n/a
Stracciatella Ice Cream CARTE D'OR	130	2.2	19.5	4.8	n/a
Strawberry Creme de Creme, each LYONS MAID	174	2.3	26	7.2	n/a
Strawberry Ice Cream					
CARTE D'OR	105	1.6	15.3	4.3	n/a
FIESTA	176	3.8	18.5	10.2	n/a
LYONS MAID	84	1.7	10.5	3.8	n/a
Tiramisu Ice Cream CARTE D'OR	112	2.1	15.2	4.6	n/a
Toffee Crumble, each LYONS MAID	170	1.9	19.6	9.3	n/a
Toffee Flavour & Toffee Sauce Iced Dessert HEINZ WEIGHT WATCHERS	163	2.7	26.2	4.8	0.2
Toffee Flavour Fudge Swirl Iced Dessert HEINZ WEIGHT WATCHERS	143	2.5	22.6	4.4	0.4

Calorie Counter

All amounts per 100g/100ml unless otherwise stated	Cal kcal	Pro g	Carb g	Fat g	Fibre g
Tornado, each LYONS MAID	61	0	15.2	0	n/a
Tropical Juice Bar, each LYONS MAID	37	Tr	9.9	Tr	n/a
Twix Ice Cream MARS	400	5.4	43	22.9	n/a
Vanilla & Raspberry Compote Iced Dessert HEINZ WEIGHT WATCHERS	142	2.6	23.3	3.9	0.3
Vanilla & Strawberry Compote Iced Dessert HEINZ WEIGHT WATCHERS	142	2.5	23.4	3.9	0.2
Vanilla Creme de Creme, each LYONS MAID	166	3	21.3	8.3	n/a
Vanilla Cup, each LYONS MAID	181	3.3	25.5	8.1	n/a
Vanilla Ice Cream					
CARTE D'OR	110	1.6	14.8	4.9	n/a
FIESTA	155	3.6	19.2	7.6	n/a
LYONS MAID	87	1.7	11	4.5	n/a
WALLS	90	1.5	11.4	4.5	n/a
soft scoop WALLS	85	1.3	10.2	4.1	n/a
soft serve FIESTA	161	3.3	19.4	8.3	n/a
super value FIESTA	154	3.4	20.4	7.1	n/a
Vanilla Iced Dessert HEINZ WEIGHT WATCHERS	124	2.4	20.1	3.5	0.2

Desserts and Puddings

All amounts per 100g/100ml unless otherwise stated	Cal kcal	Pro g	Carb g	Fat g	Fibre g
Viennetta WALLS					
chocolate	130	2.1	12.4	8	n/a
original vanilla	130	1.7	11.7	8.7	n/a

See also: **KIDS' FOODS**

CHEESECAKES

Blackcurrant Cheesecake					
EDEN VALE	261	2.8	38.8	11.6	n/a
HEINZ WEIGHT WATCHERS	159	6	24	4.1	0.7
MCVITIE'S	296	4.5	31.9	17.1	0.7
SARA LEE	275	3.4	35.1	13.4	1.4
Blackcurrant Party Cheesecake					
MCVITIE'S	295	4.4	33.8	16.1	0.8
Cheesecake, frozen	242	5.7	33	10.6	0.9
Cherry Cream Cheesecake					
MCVITIE'S	336	4.9	30	22	1.4
Chocolate Truffle Cheesecake					
MCVITIE'S	340	5.9	35.4	19.7	0.6
Fruits of the Forest Cheesecake					
MCVITIE'S	302	4.5	31.9	17.7	0.6
Raspberry and Redcurrant Souffle					
ENTENMANN'S	267	3.4	36.1	12.2	1
Raspberry Cheesecake YOUNG'S	299	4.7	31.9	17.2	0.6

Calorie Counter

All amounts per 100g/100ml unless otherwise stated	Cal kcal	Pro g	Carb g	Fat g	Fibre g
Strawberry Cheesecake					
HEINZ WEIGHT WATCHERS	159	5.9	24	4.1	0.4
MCVITIE'S	390	4.9	31.9	22.7	0.4
SARA LEE	272	3.1	35.3	13.2	1
Strawberry & Cream Cheesecake					
YOUNG'S	296	4.6	31.9	16.9	0.2

See also: **FLOUR AND BAKING**

JELLY

Blackcurrant Jelly Pots, Rowntree, ready to eat NESTLÉ	80	Tr	18.9	0	0
Blackcurrant Flavour Jelly Crystals, sugar free BIRD'S	330	57.5	13	0.1	0
Jelly, made with water, all varieties	61	1.2	15.1	0	0
Jelly, Rowntree, tablet, all varieties NESTLÉ	300	5.6	67.3	0.4	n/a
Lemon Flavour Jelly Crystals, as sold DIETADE	7	1.3	0	0	0
Orange Flavour Jelly Crystals					
as sold, DIETADE	7	1.3	0	0	0
sugar free, as sold BIRD'S	335	62.5	6.4	1.9	0
Orange Jelly Pots, Rowntree, ready to eat NESTLÉ	80	Tr	18.9	0	0

Desserts and Puddings

All amounts per 100g/100ml unless otherwise stated	Cal kcal	Pro g	Carb g	Fat g	Fibre g
Raspberry Flavour Jelly Crystals, as sold DIETADE	8	1.4	0.2	0	0
Raspberry Flavour Jelly, sugar free BIRD'S	325	57	12.5	0.1	0.7
Strawberry Flavour Jelly Crystals, as sold DIETADE	7	1.3	0.1	0	0
Strawberry Flavour Jelly, sugar free BIRD'S	325	57.5	11.5	0.2	0.2
Strawberry Jelly Pots, Rowntree, ready to eat NESTLÉ	76	Tr	18.8	0	0

DESSERT POWDERS

	Cal kcal	Pro g	Carb g	Fat g	Fibre g
Instant Dessert Powder					
as sold	391	2.4	60.1	17.3	1
made up with whole milk	111	3.1	14.8	6.3	0.2
Angel Delight, as sold BIRD'S					
banana	490	2.5	72	21	0
butterscotch	475	2.4	73.5	19	0
butterscotch, no added sugar	480	4.5	61	24	0
chocolate	455	3.7	69.5	18	0.4
chocolate, no added sugar	450	6.3	56.5	22	0.6
raspberry	490	2.5	72	21	0
strawberry	485	2.5	71	21	0
strawberry, no added sugar	490	4.8	59	26.5	0

Calorie Counter

All amounts per 100g/100ml unless otherwise stated	Cal kcal	Pro g	Carb g	Fat g	Fibre g
Blancmange Powder, as sold					
BROWN & POLSON					
chocolate	**339**	2.7	78	1.7	0.8
strawberry	**342**	0.6	83	0.7	n/a
vanilla	**341**	0.6	83	0.7	n/a

CUSTARD DESSERTS

	Cal kcal	Pro g	Carb g	Fat g	Fibre g
Splat Custard Dessert Pot AMBROSIA					
banana flavour	**104**	2.7	16.6	3	0
milk chocolate flavour	**119**	3	20	3	0.7
strawberry flavour	**104**	2.7	16.6	3	0
vanilla flavour	**105**	2.7	16.7	3	0
toffee flavour	**105**	2.7	16.9	3	0
Devon Custard Dessert Pot AMBROSIA					
as sold	**103**	2.7	16.4	3	0.1
low fat	**72**	2.9	12.7	1.1	0.1

SWEET SAUCES AND TOPPINGS

	Cal kcal	Pro g	Carb g	Fat g	Fibre g
Angel Delight Topples BIRD'S					
chocolate	**465**	5	67	20	0.5
strawberry	**450**	2.8	74.5	14	0.7
Brandy Flavour Sauce Mix, as sold BIRD'S	**415**	6.1	76.5	9.5	0

Desserts and Puddings

All amounts per 100g/100ml unless otherwise stated	Cal kcal	Pro g	Carb g	Fat g	Fibre g
Brandy Sauce, ready to serve, as sold BIRD'S	97	2.7	16.5	1.5	0
Chocolate Custard Mix, as sold BIRD'S					
chocolate flavour	415	5.9	78.5	8.8	0.1
low fat	405	4.3	78.5	8.2	0
Custard					
canned	95	2.6	15.4	3	0.1
made up with skimmed milk	79	3.8	16.8	0.1	Tr
made up with whole milk	117	3.7	16.6	4.5	Tr
powder, as sold CREAMOLA	350	0.4	92	0.7	n/a
Custard Complete Mix ROWNTREE	412	4.2	77.8	10.2	n/a
Custard, Original BIRD'S					
powder, as sold	355	0.4	87	0.5	0
ready to serve	102	2.8	15.5	3	0
Devon Custard AMBROSIA	103	2.7	16.4	3	0.1
low fat	72	2.9	12.7	1.1	0.1
organic	108	2.7	16.6	3.4	0
Dream Topping, as sold BIRD'S	690	6.7	32.5	58.5	0.5
sugar free	695	7.3	30.5	60.5	0.5
Maple Syrup, organic MERIDIAN FOODS LTD	262	0	67.2	0.2	0
Rum Flavour Sauce Mix, as sold BIRD'S	415	6.1	76.5	9.5	0

Calorie Counter

All amounts per 100g/100ml unless otherwise stated	Cal kcal	Pro g	Carb g	Fat g	Fibre g
Rum Sauce, ready to serve, as sold BIRD'S	91	2.8	15.5	1.5	0
Saucy Syrup TATE & LYLE					
chocolate flavour	305	1	74	0.5	0
maple flavour	306	Tr	76.5	0	0
strawberry flavour	308	Tr	77.5	0	0
toffee flavour	306	Tr	76.5	0	0
Tip Top NESTLÉ	112	4.8	9	6.3	0
White Sauce, sweet, recipe					
made with semi-skimmed milk	152	4	18.5	7.4	0.2
made with whole milk	171	3.9	18.3	9.5	0.2

DIPS AND PRE-DRESSED SALADS

All amounts per 100g/100ml unless otherwise stated	Cal kcal	Pro g	Carb g	Fat g	Fibre g
Beetroot Salad	46	0.9	10.3	0.1	1.8
Coleslaw					
chunky	194	1	7.1	18	1.6
HEINZ	135	1.6	9.4	10.2	1.2
with cheese	165	3.3	6.4	14	1.1
with prawns	171	2	6.8	15.1	1.6
Coronation Chicken	264	4.9	18.1	19.1	1.1
Curry & Mango Dip PRIMULA	334	4.5	6.1	32.4	n/a
Dairylea Breadstick Dunkers, each KRAFT	M140	4.3	14	7.8	0.5
Dairylea Chipsticks Dunkers, each KRAFT					
jumbo munch	150	3.6	13.5	9.2	0.6
salt & vinegar	155	3.5	12	10.5	0.6
Dairylea Double Dunkers, each KRAFT					
Mexican	185	3.9	19	10	0.9
pizza	180	4.7	17	10	1.2
Dairylea Pizza Baguette Dunkers, each KRAFT	160	4.4	11.8	10.6	0.7

Calorie Counter

All amounts per 100g/100ml unless otherwise stated	Cal kcal	Pro g	Carb g	Fat g	Fibre g
Doritos Dippas Mexican Dips WALKERS					
guacamole	159	1.2	0.6	16	0.1
Mexican bean	89	2.7	12.1	3.3	2.4
soured cream & chive	322	2.5	3.1	33.3	0.1
Florida Salad	201	0.7	10.5	17.3	1.5
Garlic & Herb Dip, per pack PRIMULA	344	4.8	3.6	34.5	n/a
Guacamole	143	2.8	6.3	11.9	2.3
Hummus	187	7.6	11.6	12.6	2.4
Nacho Dippits PRIMULA	336	7.8	18.4	25.7	n/a
Onion & Chive Dip PRIMULA	341	4.6	2.1	34.9	n/a
Pasta Salad					
pasta & tomato	176	4.1	18.1	9.7	3.8
pasta, ham & pineapple	242	3.9	17	17.6	0.6
pasta, prawn & cucumber	264	3.6	17.5	20	0.7
Philadelphia Dip Plain & Ciabatta Baguette Crackers, each KRAFT	118	4	8.3	7.6	1
Philadelphia Dip Plain & Smokey Bacon Baguette Crackers, each KRAFT	115	3.8	7.3	7	1
Pizza Cheese Xtreme Dipz PRIMULA	318	12.2	29.8	16.7	n/a

Dips and Pre-dressed Salads

All amounts per 100g/100ml unless otherwise stated	Cal kcal	Pro g	Carb g	Fat g	Fibre g
Potato Salad HEINZ	141	1.4	14.8	8.5	0.8
(non-branded)	126	1.2	13.3	7.5	1.3
Rice Salad					
savoury rice	95	2.4	18.5	1.3	4.4
vegetable	143	2.1	22.5	4.9	0.4
Salsa Dippits PRIMULA	101	3.7	20.7	0.4	n/a
Salsa					
Cheese OLD EL PASO	143	2.5	9.3	10.7	n/a
Chunky OLD EL PASO	32	1.2	6.6	0.1	n/a
Cool, organic MERIDIAN FOODS	141	1.1	6.3	0.4	1.2
Hot, organic MERIDIAN FOODS	141	1.2	6.2	0.4	1.1
Picante, Thick 'n Chunky OLD EL PASO	28	1.4	4.6	0.5	n/a
Salsa, Taco OLD EL PASO					
hot	41	1	8.6	0.3	n/a
mild	43	1.2	9.4	0.1	n/a
Sour Cream Based Dips	360	2.9	4	37	N
Sour Cream & Chive Dip PRIMULA	345	5	1.8	35.3	n/a
Spicy Mexican Dip PRIMULA	324	4.7	4.8	31.7	n/a
Taramosalata	523	2.7	7.4	53.6	1.8
Tzatziki	66	3.8	1.9	4.9	0.3
Vegetable Salad HEINZ	133	1.5	12.6	8.5	1.3

DRIED FRUIT, NUTS AND SEEDS

All amounts per 100g/100ml unless otherwise stated	Cal kcal	Pro g	Carb g	Fat g	Fibre g
DRIED FRUIT					
Apple Rings, dried					
HOLLAND & BARRETT	238	2	60.1	0.5	9.7
Apricots, ready to eat	240	4	62	0.5	8
Banana, dried, ready to eat					
HOLLAND & BARRETT	221	3.1	53.7	0.8	9.5
Banana Chips, dried					
HOLLAND & BARRETT	511	1	59.9	31.4	1.1
WHITWORTHS	526	1	59.9	31.4	1.7
Currants, dried	267	2.3	67.8	0.4	1.9
HOLLAND & BARRETT	248	2.3	67.7	0.4	1.9
Dates, flesh and skin, dried	270	3.3	68	0.2	4
Figs, dried	227	3.6	52.9	1.6	7.5
Fruit Salad, dried					
HOLLAND & BARRETT	185	3.1	40.9	1	8
WHITWORTHS	145	2.6	39.9	0.5	4.2
Mixed Fruit, dried	227	3.6	52.9	1.6	2.2
Pineapple, diced & dried					
HOLLAND & BARRETT	276	2.5	67.9	1.3	8.1

Dried Fruit, Nuts and Seeds

All amounts per 100g/100ml unless otherwise stated	Cal kcal	Pro g	Carb g	Fat g	Fibre g
Prunes,					
canned in juice	79	0.7	19.7	0.2	2.4
canned in syrup	90	0.6	23	0.2	2.8
ready to eat HOLLAND & BARRETT	134	2	33.5	Tr	13.4
Raisins, seedless	272	2.1	69.3	0.4	2
HOLLAND & BARRETT	246	1.1	64.4	Tr	6.8
WHITWORTHS	289	2.1	69.3	0.4	2
Sultanas	275	2.7	69.4	0.4	2
HOLLAND & BARRETT	292	2.7	69.4	0.4	2

NUTS AND SEEDS

	Cal kcal	Pro g	Carb g	Fat g	Fibre g
Almonds					
weighed with shells	229	7.8	2.5	20.6	4.8
flaked/ground	612	21.1	6.9	55.8	12.9
Brazils					
weighed with shells	314	6.5	1.4	31.4	3.7
kernel only	682	14.1	3.1	68.2	8.1
HOLLAND & BARRETT	691	16.3	2.9	68.2	4.3
Cashews					
kernel only	585	19	21	47	8
pieces HOLLAND & BARRETT	624	24.2	17.3	50.9	3.2
Chestnuts, kernel only	170	2	36.6	2.7	4.1

Coconut: *see* FRUIT AND VEGETABLES

Calorie Counter

All amounts per 100g/100ml unless otherwise stated	Cal kcal	Pro g	Carb g	Fat g	Fibre g
Hazelnuts					
weighed with shell	247	5.4	2.3	24.1	2.5
kernel only	650	14.1	6	63.5	6.5
Hickory Nuts: *see* **Pecan Nuts**					
Mixed Nuts	607	22.9	7.9	54.1	6
Monkey Nuts: *see* **Peanuts**					
Peanuts					
plain, weighed with shells	389	17.7	8.6	31.8	4.3
plain, kernel only	564	25.6	12.5	46.1	6.2
paleskin HOLLAND & BARRETT	564	25.5	12.5	46.1	6.2
Peanuts, salted: *see* **CRISPS AND NIBBLES**					
Pecans, kernel only	689	9.2	5.8	70.1	4.7
Pine Nuts, kernel only	688	14	4	68.6	1.9
Pistachios, weighed with shells	331	9.9	4.6	30.5	3.3
Poppy Seeds	556	20.6	19	44	0
Pumpkin Seeds HOLLAND & BARRETT	571	29	47	n/a	n/a
Sunflower Seeds HOLLAND & BARRETT	596	23.4	18.6	47.5	6
Walnuts					
weighed with shell	295	6.3	1.4	29.4	1.5
halves HOLLAND & BARRETT	688	14.7	3.3	68.5	3.5
halves WHITWORTHS	525	10.6	5	51.5	5.2

DRINKS (ALCOHOLIC)

All amounts per 100g/100ml unless otherwise stated	Cal kcal	Pro g	Carb g	Fat g	Fibre g
Advocaat	**272**	4.7	28.4	6.3	0
Bols	**257**	3.4	27	5.6	0
Bailey's Irish Cream	**320**	n/a	n/a	n/a	n/a
Beer, bitter					
canned	**32**	0.3	2.3	Tr	0
draught	**32**	0.3	2.3	Tr	0
keg	**31**	0.3	2.3	Tr	0
Beer, mild, draught	**25**	0.2	1.6	Tr	0
Brandy	**222**	Tr	Tr	0	0
Breezer, each BACARDI					
cranberry	**158.5**	n/a	n/a	n/a	n/a
lemon	**179.1**	n/a	n/a	n/a	n/a
lime	**179.4**	n/a	n/a	n/a	n/a
orange	**177.3**	n/a	n/a	n/a	n/a
peach	**171.4**	n/a	n/a	n/a	n/a
pineapple	**176.7**	n/a	n/a	n/a	n/a
ruby grapefruit	**180.4**	n/a	n/a	n/a	n/a
watermelon	**149**	n/a	n/a	n/a	n/a
Breezer, Twist BACARDI					
keylime	**187**	n/a	n/a	n/a	n/a
mango	**192**	n/a	n/a	n/a	n/a
watermelon	**184**	n/a	n/a	n/a	n/a

Calorie Counter

All amounts per 100g/100ml unless otherwise stated	Cal kcal	Pro g	Carb g	Fat g	Fibre g
Breezer, Mini, each BACARDI					
orange	131	n/a	n/a	n/a	n/a
cranberry	120	n/a	n/a	n/a	n/a
Brown Ale					
bottled	28	0.3	3	Tr	0
Newcastle, per bottle					
SCOTTISH & NEWCASTLE	165	n/a	n/a	n/a	n/a
Cherry Brandy	255	Tr	32.6	0	0
Cider					
dry	36	Tr	2.6	0	0
sweet	42	Tr	4.3	0	0
vintage	101	Tr	7.3	0	0
Cider, bottle/can H P BULMER					
Scrumpy Jack	45	n/a	2.64	n/a	n/a
Strongbow	36	n/a	1.47	n/a	n/a
Woodpecker	30	n/a	2.38	n/a	n/a
Cognac, Courvoisier	350	n/a	n/a	n/a	n/a
Cointreau	340	n/a	n/a	n/a	n/a
Curacao	311	Tr	28.3	0	0
Gin	222	Tr	Tr	0	0
Grand Marnier	320	n/a	n/a	n/a	n/a

All amounts per 100g/100ml unless otherwise stated	Cal kcal	Pro g	Carb g	Fat g	Fibre g
Lager					
bottled	29	0.2	1.5	Tr	0
per bottle HEINEKEN	85	n/a	n/a	n/a	n/a
per can TENNENT'S	140	n/a	n/a	n/a	n/a
Pale Ale, bottled	32	0.3	2	Tr	0
Port	157	0.1	12	0	0
Cockburn	151	n/a	n/a	n/a	n/a
Rum	222	Tr	Tr	0	0
Carta Blanca BACARDI	210	n/a	n/a	n/a	n/a
Sherry					
dry	116	0.2	1.4	0	0
medium	118	0.1	3.6	0	0
sweet	136	0.3	6.9	0	0
Sherry HARVEY					
Bristol Cream	154	n/a	n/a	n/a	n/a
Club Classic	115	n/a	n/a	n/a	n/a
Stout					
bottled	37	0.3	4.2	Tr	0
extra	39	0.3	2.1	Tr	0
Strong Ale	72	0.7	6.1	Tr	0
Tia Lusso	251	n/a	n/a	n/a	n/a
Tia Maria	262	n/a	n/a	n/a	n/a

Calorie Counter

All amounts per 100g/100ml unless otherwise stated	Cal kcal	Pro g	Carb g	Fat g	Fibre g
Vermouth					
dry	**118**	0.1	5.5	0	0
sweet	**151**	Tr	15.9	0	0
Martini Bianco BACARDI	**145**	n/a	n/a	n/a	n/a
Martini Extra Dry BACARDI	**95**	n/a	n/a	n/a	n/a
Martini Rosso BACARDI	**140**	n/a	n/a	n/a	n/a
Vintage Cider: *see* **Cider**					
Vodka	**222**	Tr	Tr	0	0
Whisky	**222**	Tr	Tr	0	0
Laphroaig, single malt	**222**	n/a	n/a	n/a	n/a
Teacher's, blended	**222**	n/a	n/a	n/a	n/a
Wine					
red	**68**	0.2	0.3	0	0
rosé	**71**	0.1	2.5	0	0
white, dry	**66**	0.1	0.6	0	0
white, medium	**75**	0.1	3.4	0	0
white, sparkling	**76**	0.2	5.9	0	0
white, sweet	**94**	0.2	5.9	0	0

DRINKS (NON-ALCOHOLIC)

All amounts per 100g/100ml unless otherwise stated	Cal kcal	Pro g	Carb g	Fat g	Fibre g
JUICES AND CORDIALS					
Apple Juice, unsweetened	38	0.1	9.9	0.1	Tr
Apple 'C' LIBBY	47	Tr	11.7	Tr	0
Apple Crush JUSODA	31	n/a	9.5	Tr	Tr
Apple Fruit Juice DEL MONTE	47	0.3	10.8	Tr	n/a
Apple Fruit Juice Concentrate, organic MERIDIAN FOODS LTD	308	0.8	76.1	Tr	0
Apple Juice COPELLA	44	0.4	10.3	0.1	n/a
Apple Juice Drink					
BRITVIC 55	47	Tr	11	Tr	n/a
original, ROBINSONS	98.4	Tr	22.9	Tr	n/a
Apple Juice, English CAWSTON VALE	42	0.1	10.8	Tr	n/a
Apple & Blackcurrant Drink					
QUOSH	72	Tr	16.6	Tr	n/a
original, ROBINSONS	43.7	Tr	9.7	Tr	n/a
Apple & Blackcurrant Fruit Burst DEL MONTE	45	0.1	11	Tr	n/a
Apple & Cranberry Fruit Break Drink, no added sugar ROBINSONS	7	Tr	1.3	Tr	n/a

Calorie Counter

All amounts per 100g/100ml unless otherwise stated	Cal kcal	Pro g	Carb g	Fat g	Fibre g
Apple & Elderflower Juice COPELLA	43	0.4	10.2	0.1	n/a
Apple & Lemon Fruit Concentrate, organic MERIDIAN FOODS LTD	304	1	71.7	0.1	0.1
Apple & Mango Juice COPELLA	43	0.4	10.1	0.1	n/a
Apple & Mango Juice Drink, J2O BRITVIC	49	0.2	11.3	Tr	n/a
Apple & Orange Fruit Concentrate, organic MERIDIAN FOODS LTD	262	0.9	63	Tr	Tr
Apple & Raspberry Juice COPELLA	41	0.5	9.4	0.1	n/a
Apple & Sour Cherry Juice CAWSTON VALE	44	0.1	10.8	Tr	n/a
Apple & Strawberry Juice COPELLA	39	n/a	10.1	0	Tr
Barley Water ROBINSONS					
Lemon, original	88	0.3	19.6	Tr	Tr
no added sugar	11	0.2	0.5	Tr	Tr
Orange, original	89	0.3	21	Tr	Tr
Blackcurrant & Apple Juice COPELLA	50	n/a	12.5	0	Tr
Blackcurrant 'C' LIBBY	54	Tr	13.5	Tr	0

178

Drinks (non-Alcoholic)

All amounts per 100g/100ml unless otherwise stated	Cal kcal	Pro g	Carb g	Fat g	Fibre g
Blackcurrant Cordial, undiluted					
BRITVIC	**57.3**	Tr	13.1	0	n/a
Blackcurrant C-Vit SMITH KLINE					
BEECHAM	**19**	Tr	4.5	0	n/a
Blackcurrant Juice Drink RIBENA	**59**	Tr	15.6	n/a	n/a
undiluted	**285**	Tr	76	n/a	n/a
Breakfast Juice DEL MONTE	**43**	0.6	9.6	Tr	n/a
Caribbean Fruit Burst DEL MONTE	**39**	0.1	9.5	Tr	n/a
Carrot Juice	**24**	0.5	5.7	0.1	N
Cherry Juice Special R, as sold					
ROBINSONS	**10.3**	0.2	1.3	Tr	n/a
Citrus Fruits Fruit Break Drink					
ROBINSONS	**5.5**	0.1	0.6	Tr	n/a
Cranberry & Apple Juice COPELLA	**45**	0.2	9.2	0.1	n/a
Cranberry Juice Drink BRITVIC	**43.8**	n/a	10.1	n/a	n/a
Five Alive COCA-COLA					
Blackcurrant	**62**	Tr	15.3	0	n/a
Citrus	**50**	Tr	12	0	n/a
Orange Breakfast	**46**	0	10.8	0	n/a
Tropical	**41**	Tr	10	0	0
Very Berry	**54**	0	13.2	0	n/a

Calorie Counter

All amounts per 100g/100ml unless otherwise stated	Cal kcal	Pro g	Carb g	Fat g	Fibre g
Five Fruit 'C' LIBBY	40	0.1	10	Tr	Tr
Five Fruits Fruit Burst DEL MONTE	53	0.2	12.4	Tr	n/a
Fruit & Barley Citrus Drink ROBINSONS	13.4	0.2	1.2	Tr	n/a
Fruit & Barley Orange Soft Drink ROBINSONS	16.2	0.3	2.6	Tr	n/a
Grape Juice					
unsweetened	46	0.3	11.7	0.1	0
unsweetened, red, sparkling SCHLOER	49	Tr	13.1	n/a	n/a
unsweetened, white SCHLOER	48	Tr	12.9	n/a	n/a
unsweetened, white, sparkling SCHLOER	49	Tr	13.1	n/a	n/a
unsweetened	33	0.4	8.3	0.1	Tr
BRITVIC	40	0.5	8.1	0.1	n/a
unsweetened DEL MONTE	41	0.5	8.8	Tr	n/a
Grapefruit 'C' LIBBY	36	0.2	8.8	Tr	0.3
Hi-Juice 66 SCHWEPPES	52	2.17	12.2	0	n/a
Lemon & Lime Drink JUSODA	28	n/a	6.9	Tr	Tr
Lemon Drink CITRUS SPRING	41	0.1	9.6	Tr	n/a
Lemon Drink Special R ROBINSONS	11	0.2	0.4	Tr	n/a
Lemon Juice Drink, organic ROBINSONS	263.5	0.1	60.5	Tr	n/a

Drinks (non-Alcoholic)

All amounts per 100g/100ml unless otherwise stated	Cal kcal	Pro g	Carb g	Fat g	Fibre g
Lemon Low Calorie Squash DIETADE	2	0.1	0.4	Tr	n/a
Lemonade, All Juice CAWSTON VALE	44	Tr	11.7	Tr	n/a
Lime Cordial, undiluted ROSES	105	0.1	24.4	0	n/a
Lime Drink CITRUS SPRING	45.8	0.1	10.5	Tr	n/a
Lime Juice Cordial					
undiluted	112	Tr	27	0	0
undiluted BRITVIC	46.8	0.1	9.1	Tr	n/a
Orange & Mango Fruit Juice DEL MONTE	46	0.6	10.4	Tr	n/a
Orange & Mango Special R ROBINSONS	8.6	0.2	0.8	Tr	n/a
Orange & Peach C-Vit Ready to Drink SMITH KLINE BEECHAM	37	Tr	9	0	n/a
Orange & Pineapple Drink					
original, ROBINSONS	53	0.1	12.1	Tr	n/a
as sold QUOSH	55	0.1	12.4	Tr	n/a
Orange & Pineapple Fruit Juice DEL MONTE	48	0.5	11	Tr	n/a
Orange & Pineapple Special R, as sold ROBINSONS	8.8	0.2	0.9	Tr	n/a

Calorie Counter

All amounts per 100g/100ml unless otherwise stated	Cal kcal	Pro g	Carb g	Fat g	Fibre g
Orange 'C' LIBBY	37	0.1	9.1	Tr	0.1
no added sugar	12	0.2	1.9	Tr	Tr
Orange Apple Passionfruit Juice DEL MONTE	45	0.5	10.1	Tr	n/a
Orange Drink					
undiluted	107	Tr	28.5	0	0
CITRUS SPRING	41.7	0.1	9.9	Tr	n/a
JUSODA	31	n/a	7.6	Tr	Tr
QUOSH	40	0.1	8.8	Tr	n/a
Orange Fruit Burst DEL MONTE	49	0.1	12	Tr	n/a
Orange Fruit Juice DEL MONTE	44	0.6	9.9	Tr	n/a
Orange Juice					
unsweetened	36	0.5	8.8	0.1	0.1
BRITVIC	45.8	0.3	9.9	Tr	n/a
CAWSTON VALE	43	0.6	10.5	Tr	n/a
Orange Juice Drink, organic ROBINSONS	258.7	0.2	60.8	Tr	n/a
Orange Low Calorie Squash DIETADE	10	0.1	2.4	Tr	n/a
Orange Peach Apricot Juice DEL MONTE	44	0.6	9.9	Tr	n/a
Orange Special R ROBINSONS	7.9	0.2	0.7	Tr	n/a
Orange Squash, undiluted ST CLEMENTS	120	0.7	31.8	0.1	n/a

All amounts per 100g/100ml unless otherwise stated	Cal kcal	Pro g	Carb g	Fat g	Fibre g
Orchard Fruits Juice COPELLA	45	0.2	9.2	0.1	n/a
Peach Fruit Break Drink ROBINSONS	6.2	0.2	1	Tr	n/a
Pineapple 'C' LIBBY	44	0.1	10.9	Tr	Tr
Pineapple Fruit Juice DEL MONTE	52	0.4	12	Tr	n/a
Pineapple Juice					
BRITVIC	51.2	0.2	11.1	Tr	n/a
unsweetened	41	0.3	10.5	0.1	Tr
Ribena: *see* **Blackcurrant Juice Drink**					
St Ivel Real Pure Apple Juice DAIRY CREST	49	0.1	11.6	Tr	0
St Ivel Real Pure Orange Juice DAIRY CREST	45	0.7	10	Tr	Tr
Summer Fruits Special R ROBINSONS	10	0.1	1.2	Tr	n/a
Tomato Juice	14	0.8	3	Tr	0.6
DEL MONTE	19	0.8	3.5	Tr	n/a
NAPOLINA	16	0.7	3.4	Tr	n/a
Cocktail BRITVIC	18.8	0.9	3.2	0.1	n/a
Tropical Fruit Burst DEL MONTE	45	0.2	10.9	Tr	n/a
Tropical Squash, undiluted ST CLEMENTS	186	0.3	44.4	0.2	n/a

Calorie Counter

All amounts per 100g/100ml unless otherwise stated	Cal kcal	Pro g	Carb g	Fat g	Fibre g
Whole Lemon Drink ROBINSONS	**59.2**	0.2	12.3	Tr	n/a
Whole Orange Drink ROBINSONS	**54.2**	0.1	12.3	Tr	n/a

See also: **CHILDREN'S FOODS**

FIZZY DRINKS

	Cal kcal	Pro g	Carb g	Fat g	Fibre g
7 Up PEPSI					
original	**46**	0	n/a	0	n/a
diet	**1.1**	0	n/a	0	n/a
Apple Drink, Sparkling					
ST CLEMENTS	**47**	n/a	11.6	Tr	Tr
Apple Soft Drink TANGO	**29**	Tr	6.8	Tr	n/a
low calorie	**4.5**	Tr	0.8	Tr	n/a
Bitter Lemon					
BRITVIC	**36.1**	0.1	8.3	Tr	n/a
SCHWEPPES	**33.9**	Tr	8.2	0	n/a
Canada Dry Ginger Ale					
SCHWEPPES	**37.5**	Tr	9.1	0	n/a
Cherry Coke COCA-COLA	**45**	0	11.2	0	n/a
Cherryade CORONA	**1.2**	Tr	n/a	Tr	n/a
Coca-Cola COCA-COLA					
original	**43**	0	10.6	0	n/a
diet	**0.5**	0	0	0	n/a

Drinks (non-Alcoholic)

All amounts per 100g/100ml unless otherwise stated	Cal kcal	Pro g	Carb g	Fat g	Fibre g
Cream Soda					
BARR	29	Tr	7.2	Tr	Tr
IDRIS	21.8	0	5.3	0	n/a
Dandelion & Burdock					
IDRIS	22.5	0	5.4	Tr	n/a
TOP DECK	4.5	Tr	0.9	0	n/a
Ginger Ale, American					
BRITVIC	38.2	0	9.2	0	n/a
SCHWEPPES	22	0	5.3	0	n/a
Ginger Ale, Dry SCHWEPPES	16	0	3.8	0	n/a
Ginger Beer IDRIS	36.3	0	8.5	0	n/a
Irn Bru BARR	41	Tr	10.1	Tr	0
diet	0.7	Tr	Tr	Tr	0
Lemon Drink, sparkling ST CLEMENTS	47	Tr	11.3	Tr	Tr
Lemon Soft Drink TANGO	40.4	Tr	9.3	Tr	n/a
low calorie	3	Tr	0.1	Tr	n/a
Lemonade, bottled	21	Tr	5.6	0	0
BARR	30	n/a	7.4	Tr	Tr
CORONA	10.5	Tr	2.3	0	n/a
R WHITES	22.8	0	5.4	Tr	n/a
low calorie BARR	0.9	n/a	Tr	Tr	Tr
low calorie CORONA	1	Tr	0	n/a	n/a
low calorie, R WHITES	1.4	Tr	Tr	Tr	n/a

Calorie Counter

All amounts per 100g/100ml unless otherwise stated	Cal kcal	Pro g	Carb g	Fat g	Fibre g
Lemonade, Premium R WHITES	26	Tr	6.1	Tr	n/a
Limeade, bottled CORONA	1.3	Tr	n/a	0	n/a
Lucozade SMITH KLINE BEECHAM	73	Tr	17.9	0	0
Lucozade Orange Crush SMITH KLINE BEECHAM	70	Tr	17.2	0	0
low calorie	5	Tr	0.7	0	0
Orange Drink					
TANGO	28.7	Tr	6.7	Tr	n/a
low calorie TANGO	5.5	Tr	0.7	Tr	n/a
sparkling ST CLEMENTS	47	n/a	11.1	Tr	Tr
Orangeade CORONA	1.5	Tr	Tr	0	n/a
Pepsi PEPSI	47	0	n/a	0	n/a
Pepsi Max PEPSI	0.6	n/a	n/a	n/a	n/a
Pepsi, Diet PEPSI	0.3	n/a	n/a	0	n/a
Ribena Spark SMITH KLINE BEECHAM	54	Tr	13.3	0	n/a
low calorie	2	Tr	0.1	0	n/a
Tizer BARR	3.9	Tr	9.6	Tr	0
Tonic Water SCHWEPPES	21.8	0	5.1	0	n/a
Tropical Soft Drink TANGO	33.4	Tr	7.7	Tr	n/a
low calorie	4.1	Tr	0.5	Tr	n/a
Water, flavoured, all flavours	1	Tr	0.2	Tr	Tr

All amounts per 100g/100ml unless otherwise stated	Cal kcal	Pro g	Carb g	Fat g	Fibre g
COFFEE AND TEA					
Alta Rica NESCAFÉ	98	13.8	10	0.3	21
Cappuccino NESCAFÉ					
instant	398	11.4	66.5	9.5	n/a
unsweetened	428	14.8	54.7	16.6	n/a
Coffee					
infusion, 5 minutes	2	0.2	0.3	Tr	0
instant, powdered	100	14.6	11	Tr	0
Coffeemate CARNATION					
per 6.5g tsp	35	0.1	3.9	1.9	0
virtually fat free	25	0.1	5	0.8	0
Espresso, instant NESCAFÉ	104	15.2	10	0.4	11.5
Fine Tasses NESCAFÉ	98	14.1	10	0.2	10.4
Gold Blend NESCAFÉ	102	14.4	10	0.5	7.3
decaffinated	102	14.4	10	0.2	11.6
Ice Tea LIPTON'S					
lemon	30	0	7.2	0	n/a
peach	31	0	7.4	0	n/a
Lyle's Coffee Syrup TATE & LYLE					
almond	245	Tr	61	Tr	0
caramel	329	Tr	83	Tr	0
chocolate	275	Tr	69	Tr	0
cinnamon	279	Tr	69	Tr	0

Calorie Counter

All amounts per 100g/100ml unless otherwise stated	Cal kcal	Pro g	Carb g	Fat g	Fibre g
hazelnut	**329**	Tr	83	Tr	0
irish cream	**329**	Tr	83	Tr	0
vanilla	**329**	Tr	83	Tr	0
Nescafé Original NESCAFÉ	**103**	15.4	10	0.2	13.4
Tea, infusion, black	**Tr**	0.1	Tr	Tr	0
Tea BROOKE BOND					
PG Tips	**Tr**	0	0	0	0
Scottish Blend	**Tr**	0	0	0	0

HOT/MILK DRINKS

Aero Chocolate Drinks, all flavours, each NESTLÉ	**175**	8.3	22.3	5.8	0.4
Banana Nesquik NESTLÉ	**395**	0	97.3	0.5	0
made up with whole milk	**168**	6.8	18.9	7.8	0
ready to drink	**68**	3.2	10.2	1.6	0
with semi-skimmed	**155**	6.8	24.9	3.4	0
Beef Instant Drink BOVRIL	**181**	39.7	3.9	0.6	0
Bournvita Powder	**341**	7.7	79	1.5	N
made with semi-skimmed milk	**58**	3.5	7.6	1.6	Tr
made with whole milk	**76**	3.4	7.6	3.8	Tr
Chicken Instant Drink BOVRIL	**129**	9.7	19.4	1.4	2.1
Chocolate Nesquik NESTLÉ	**370**	0	97.3	0.5	0
made with whole milk	**168**	6.8	18.9	7.8	0

All amounts per 100g/100ml unless otherwise stated	Cal kcal	Pro g	Carb g	Fat g	Fibre g
ready to drink, each	**187**	8.5	29	4.3	0.4
with semi-skimmed milk	**155**	6.8	24.9	3.4	0
Cocoa Powder	**312**	18.5	11.5	21.7	12.1
made with semi-skimmed milk	**57**	3.5	7	1.9	0.2
made with whole milk	**76**	3.4	6.8	4.2	0.2
organic GREEN & BLACK	**322**	23	10.5	21	0
Rowntree NESTLÉ	**310**	17.5	11.5	21.5	4.9
Drinking Chocolate, powder	**366**	5.5	77.4	6	N
made with semi-skimmed milk	**71**	3.5	10.8	1.9	Tr
made with whole milk	**90**	3.4	10.6	4.1	Tr
Galaxy Chocolate Drink MARS	**89**	3.9	14.4	1.9	n/a
Horlicks					
made up with semi-skimmed milk	**181**	7.7	28.3	4.5	1
made up with whole milk	**222**	7.4	27.9	9.2	1
Horlicks Light Chocolate Malt Drink SMITHKLINE BEECHAM	**390**	9	71.6	7.5	5.6
Horlicks Light Hot Chocolate Drink SMITHKLINE BEECHAM	**399**	8.8	72.6	8.1	3.7
Horlicks Light Instant Powder SMITHKLINE BEECHAM	**381**	13.7	71.5	4.5	2.7
made up with water	**122**	4.4	22.3	1.4	0.9
Hot Chocolate, organic GREEN & BLACK	**376**	7.6	76.8	9.2	0

Calorie Counter

All amounts per 100g/100ml unless otherwise stated	Cal kcal	Pro g	Carb g	Fat g	Fibre g
Maltissimo Chocolate Drink, low fat SMITHKLINE BEECHAM					
Milk	**394**	14.6	62.4	9.6	6.8
Mocha Flavoured	**65**	2.2	10.6	1.5	1.5
Tiramisu Flavoured	**65**	2.3	10.6	1.5	1.5
Ovaltine					
powder	**358**	9	79.4	2.7	N
made up with semi-skimmed milk	**79**	3.9	13	1.7	Tr
made up with whole milk	**97**	3.8	12.9	3.8	Tr
Strawberry Nesquik NESTLÉ	**390**	0	96.7	0.5	0
made up with whole milk	**168**	6.8	18.9	7.8	0
ready to drink, each	**170**	8	25.5	4	0
with semi-skimmed milk	**155**	6.8	24.9	3.4	0

EGGS

All amounts per 100g/100ml unless otherwise stated	Cal kcal	Pro g	Carb g	Fat g	Fibre g
Eggs, chicken					
raw, whole	**151**	12.5	Tr	11.2	0
raw, white only	**36**	9	Tr	Tr	0
raw, yolk only	**339**	16.1	Tr	30.5	0
boiled	**147**	12.5	Tr	10.8	0
fried, in vegetable oil	**179**	13.6	Tr	13.9	0
poached	**147**	12.5	Tr	10.8	0
scrambled with milk, recipe	**257**	10.9	0.7	23.4	0
Eggs, duck, raw, whole	**163**	14.3	Tr	11.8	0
Omelette, recipe					
plain	**195**	10.9	Tr	16.8	0
cheese	**271**	15.9	Tr	23	0

FISH AND SEAFOOD

All amounts per 100g/100ml unless otherwise stated	Cal kcal	Pro g	Carb g	Fat g	Fibre g
FISH AND SEAFOOD					
Anchovies, canned in oil, drained	**280**	25.2	0	19.9	0
Cockles, boiled	**48**	17.2	Tr	2	0
Cod					
baked fillets	**96**	21.4	0	1.2	0
dried, salted, boiled	**138**	32.5	0	0.9	0
in batter, fried	**247**	16.1	11.7	15.4	0.5
in crumbs, frozen, fried	**235**	12.4	15.2	14.3	0
in parsley sauce, frozen, boiled	**84**	12	2.8	2.8	0
poached fillets	**94**	20.9	0	1.1	0
steaks, grilled	**95**	20.8	0	1.3	0
Cod Roe, hard, fried	**202**	20.9	3	11.9	0.1
Coley Fillets, steamed	**99**	23.3	0	0.6	0
Crab					
boiled	**127**	20.1	0	5.2	0
canned	**81**	18.1	0	0.9	0
dressed YOUNG'S	**105**	16.9	0	14.2	0
Eels, jellied	98	8.4	Tr	7.1	0
Fish Fillets, Fish Shop ROSS	**257**	11.8	20.1	14.6	0.6

All amounts per 100g/100ml unless otherwise stated	Cal kcal	Pro g	Carb g	Fat g	Fibre g
Haddock					
in crumbs, frozen, fried	**196**	14.7	12.6	10	0
smoked, steamed, flesh only	**101**	23.3	0	0.9	0
steamed, flesh only	**98**	22.8	0	0.8	0
Halibut, steamed, flesh only	**131**	23.8	0	4	0
Herring					
fried, flesh only	**234**	23.1	1.5	15.1	N
grilled, flesh only	**199**	20.4	0	13	0
Kippers, grilled, flesh only	**205**	25.5	0	11.4	0
Lemon Sole					
steamed	**91**	20.6	0	0.9	0
goujons, baked	**187**	16	14.7	14.6	N
goujons, fried	**374**	15.5	14.3	28.7	N
Lobster, boiled	**119**	22.1	0	3.4	0
Mackerel, fried, flesh only	**188**	21.5	0	11.3	0
Mussels, boiled	**87**	17.2	Tr	2	0
Pilchards, canned in tomato sauce	**126**	18.8	0.7	5.4	Tr
Plaice					
in batter, fried	**257**	15.2	12	16.8	0
in crumbs, fried	**228**	18	8.6	13.7	0
goujons, baked	**304**	8.8	27.7	18.3	N
goujons, fried	**426**	8.5	27	32.3	0
steamed	**93**	18.9	0	1.9	0

Calorie Counter

All amounts per 100g/100ml unless otherwise stated	Cal kcal	Pro g	Carb g	Fat g	Fibre g
Prawns					
boiled	**107**	22.6	0	1.8	0
boiled, weighed in shells	**41**	8.6	0	0.7	0
boiled LYONS SEAFOODS	**61**	13.5	0	0.6	n/a
king, freshwater LYONS SEAFOODS	**70**	16.8	0	0.3	n/a
king, gourmet LYONS SEAFOODS	**51**	12	0	0.5	n/a
North Atlantic, peeled YOUNG'S	**61**	15.1	0	0.1	0
tiger king, cooked					
LYONS SEAFOODS	**61**	13.5	0	0.6	n/a
tiger, headless & unpeeled					
LYONS SEAFOODS	**84**	19.6	0	0.7	n/a
tropical LYONS SEAFOODS	**51**	12	0	0.5	n/a
tropical, cooked & peeled					
LYONS SEAFOODS	**53**	12	0	0.6	n/a
tropical, in brine					
LYONS SEAFOODS	**71**	14.3	2	0.7	n/a
Roe					
cod, hard, fried	**202**	20.9	3	11.9	0.1
herring, soft, fried	**244**	21.1	4.7	15.8	N
Saithe: *see* **Coley**					
Salmon					
pink, canned, in brine, drained	**155**	203	0	8.2	0
grilled steak	**215**	24.2	0	13.1	0
smoked	**142**	25.4	0	4.5	0
steamed, flesh only	**197**	20.1	0	13	0
Pacific, slices YOUNG'S	**182**	18.4	0	12	0

All amounts per 100g/100ml unless otherwise stated	Cal kcal	Pro g	Carb g	Fat g	Fibre g
Scottish, side YOUNG'S	**182**	18.4	0	12	0
Scottish, slices YOUNG'S	**182**	18.4	0	12	0

Salt Cod: *see* **Cod**

Sardines

| canned in oil, drained | **217** | 23.7 | 0 | 13.6 | 0 |
| canned in tomato sauce | **177** | 17.8 | 0.5 | 11.6 | Tr |

Scampi Tails, premium
LYONS SEAFOODS

| | **230** | 8.4 | 26 | 10.9 | n/a |

Seafood Selection

| LYONS SEAFOODS | **81** | 14.9 | 1.3 | 2.3 | n/a |
| YOUNG'S | **66** | 11.5 | 0 | 2.2 | 0 |

Shrimps

| canned, drained | **94** | 20.8 | 0 | 1.2 | 0 |
| frozen, without shells | **73** | 16.5 | 0 | 0.8 | 0 |

Skate, fried in butter

| | **199** | 17.9 | 4.9 | 12.1 | 0.2 |

Sole: *see* **Lemon Sole**

Swordfish, grilled

| | **139** | 17 | 1.4 | 9.9 | 0 |

Trout

brown, steamed, flesh only	**135**	23.5	0	4.5	0
rainbow, grilled	**135**	21.5	0	5.4	0
rainbow YOUNG'S	**89**	13.8	0	3.8	0

Calorie Counter

All amounts per 100g/100ml unless otherwise stated	Cal kcal	Pro g	Carb g	Fat g	Fibre g
Tuna, chunks/steaks, drained					
canned in brine	99	23.5	0	0.6	0
canned in oil	189	27.1	0	9	0
Whelks, boiled, weighed with shells	14	2.8	Tr	0.3	0
Whitebait, fried	525	19.5	5.3	47.5	0.2
Whiting					
steamed, flesh only	92	20.9	0	0.9	0
in crumbs, fried	191	18.1	7	10.3	0.3
Winkles, boiled, weighed with shells	14	2.9	Tr	0.3	0

BREADED, BATTERED OR IN SAUCES

Calamari, Golden YOUNG'S	299	13.7	15.8	20.4	0.7
Cod Fillet Fish Fingers					
BIRDS EYE	177	12.7	14.1	7.7	1
ROSS	182	11.5	17.4	8.7	0.7
Chip Shop, jumbo ROSS	232	10.2	14.2	15.2	0.7
Cod Fillets ROSS					
breaded	180	11.1	17.9	7.4	0.8
in natural crumb	180	11.1	17.9	7.4	0.8

All amounts per 100g/100ml unless otherwise stated	Cal kcal	Pro g	Carb g	Fat g	Fibre g
Cod Steak					
in batter, fried in oil	199	19.6	0	10.3	0.3
Chip Shop, jumbo Ross	180	10.4	11.5	10.5	0.5
in Butter Sauce Birds Eye	97	10	3.9	4.6	0.1
in Butter Sauce Ross	84	10.5	3	3.4	0.1
in Cheese Sauce Birds Eye	96	10.9	5.2	3.5	0.1
in Crispy Crunch Crumb, each Birds Eye	225	14	13	13	0.9
in Mushroom Sauce Birds Eye	99	9.8	5	4.4	0.1
in Natural Crumb Ross	180	11.1	17.9	7.4	0.8
in Parsley Sauce Birds Eye	85	10.4	5	2.6	0.1
in Parsley Sauce Ross	89	10.4	2.9	4	0.1
lemon & herb, each Birds Eye	195	11	16	9.8	0.8
Oven Crispy, each Birds Eye	240	13	13	15	1.3
Fish Cakes					
Chip Shop Ross	232	10.6	19.7	12.7	0.8
Chip Shop, battered Ross	232	10.6	19.7	12.7	0.8
each Birds Eye	172	11.4	15.2	7.3	0.9
fried	188	9.1	15.1	10.5	N
Fish Dip-Ins, Crispy Birds Eye	229	10.7	15.6	13.7	0.7
Fish Fingers					
Ross	186	11.5	16.3	8.6	0.7
fried in oil	233	13.5	17.2	12.7	0.6
grilled	214	15.1	19.3	9	0.7
Oven Crispy Birds Eye	218	10.4	15.8	12.6	0.4
grilled Birds Eye	178	12.1	16.4	7.1	0.5

Calorie Counter

All amounts per 100g/100ml unless otherwise stated	Cal kcal	Pro g	Carb g	Fat g	Fibre g
Fish Portions in Crispy Crumb ROSS	206	10.9	19.2	9.8	0.8
Fish Steaks in Butter Sauce ROSS	93	9.4	2.9	4.9	0.1
Fish Steaks in Parsley Sauce ROSS	85	9.4	2.9	4.9	0.1
Fish Steaks, Chip Shop, ROSS	186	11	13.9	9.9	0.6
Haddock, in crumbs, fried in oil	174	21.4	3.6	8.3	0.2
Haddock Cutlets, smoked ROSS	77	17.8	0	0.6	0
Haddock Fillet Fish Fingers BIRDS EYE	167	12.4	13.2	7.2	0.9
Haddock Fillets breaded ROSS	183	11.6	19.6	6.8	0.8
smoked, with butter BIRDS EYE	85	16	0	2.3	0
Haddock Steaks in Butter Sauce ROSS	90	10.2	2.9	4.2	0.1
Haddock Steaks in Crispy Crunch Crumb, each BIRDS EYE	225	14	13	13	0.9
Haddock Steaks in Natural Crumb ROSS	189	11.2	13.4	10.3	0.6
Haddock Steaks, Oven Crispy, each BIRDS EYE	255	13	17	15	0.6
Hake Fillets, Golden ROSS	256	9	17.4	17	0.7

All amounts per 100g/100ml unless otherwise stated	Cal kcal	Pro g	Carb g	Fat g	Fibre g
King Prawns, sweet & sour ROSS	195	6.6	15.1	12.2	0.4
Kipper Fillets with Butter BIRDS EYE	205	15	0	16	0
Lemon Sole Goujons, Golden YOUNG'S	246	10.9	26.4	11.2	1.1
Plaice					
in batter, fried in oil	279	15.8	14.4	18	N
in crumbs, fried, fillets	228	18	8.6	13.7	N
Prawn Cocktail LYONS SEAFOODS	429	5.7	4.5	42.9	n/a
Prawn Nuggets, Golden YOUNG'S	175	11.5	11.1	9.6	0.5
Prawns					
golden garlic YOUNG'S	223	10	19.6	12	0.8
Hot 'n' Spicy LYONS SEAFOODS	275	6.5	32.1	14.3	n/a
King, Golden YOUNG'S	241	8.7	15.6	16.3	0.7
Prawns, Popcorn LYONS SEAFOODS	280	9.1	18.9	19.4	n/a
Scampi in Breadcrumbs					
frozen, fried	316	12.2	28.9	17.6	N
Golden YOUNG'S	172	9.4	22.1	5.5	0.9
Scampi, Chip Shop ROSS	228	8.3	22.8	11.9	1
Seafood Cocktail LYONS SEAFOODS	72	14	2	1.8	n/a
Seafood Sticks YOUNG'S	97	10.7	14.1	0.1	0
Shrimps, potted YOUNG'S	358	16.5	0	32.4	0

Calorie Counter

All amounts per 100g/100ml unless otherwise stated	Cal kcal	Pro g	Carb g	Fat g	Fibre g
Whitebait, Golden YOUNG'S	**338**	13.3	17.1	24.4	0.7
Whiting, in crumbs, fried	**191**	18.1	7	10.3	0.3

MEALS

Cod & Chips, Chip Shop, jumbo ROSS	**169**	6.1	19.1	7.9	0.8
Cod & Prawn Pie ROSS	**164**	8.7	11.9	9.3	0.5
Cod Crumble ROSS	**179**	8.9	12.7	10.5	0.5
Cod Pie, Captain's, each BIRDS EYE	**455**	21	36	25	n/a
Fish & Potato Bake ROSS	**83**	5.8	8.1	3.3	0.1
Fish & Tomato Gratin ROSS	**120**	7.3	9.3	6.2	0.4
Fish Mornay ROSS	**137**	6.6	11.8	7.3	0.5
Fish Pie, recipe	**102**	8	12.3	3	0.7
Haddock & Prawn Crumble ROSS	**181**	8.7	12.6	11.2	0.5
Haddock Bake ROSS	**142**	7.7	11.9	7.3	0.5
Haddock, fillet, with julienne vegetables ROSS	**125**	13	3.2	6.8	0.1
Kedgeree, recipe	**176**	16	8	9.1	0
Ocean Pie ROSS	**121**	7	9.8	6.2	0.4

Fish and Seafood

All amounts per 100g/100ml unless otherwise stated	Cal kcal	Pro g	Carb g	Fat g	Fibre g
Ocean Pie with Cod HEINZ WEIGHT WATCHERS	85	5.4	10	2.6	0.8
Prawn Kievs LYONS SEAFOODS	224	9.1	16	13.8	n/a
Prawns, Indian Tandoori, stir fry ROSS	67	3.8	11.6	1.6	2.1
Salmon & Brocolli Pie, each BIRDS EYE	450	23	40	22	n/a
Salmon Mornay with Broccoli HEINZ WEIGHT WATCHERS	91	9	9.1	2.1	0.7
Seafood Crumble ROSS	197	8.7	11.3	13.2	0.5
Seafood Lasagne ROSS	117	7.2	10.7	5.3	1
Tuna Creamy Pasta Bake NAPOLINA	88	3.1	10.6	3.7	0.4
Tuna Crumble ROSS	191	7.5	14.4	11.9	0.6
Tuna Twists Italiana HEINZ WEIGHT WATCHERS	62	4.3	8.1	1.4	0.6

FLOUR AND BAKING

All amounts per 100g/100ml unless otherwise stated	Cal kcal	Pro g	Carb g	Fat g	Fibre g
FLOUR					
Cornflour	354	0.6	92	0.7	0.1
BROWN & POLSON	343	0.6	83.6	0.7	0.1
Flour					
rye, whole	335	8.2	75.9	20	11.7
wheat, brown	323	12.6	68.5	1.8	6.4
wheat, white, breadmaking	341	11.5	75.3	1.4	3.1
wheat, white, plain	341	9.4	77.7	1.3	3.1
wheat, white, self-raising	330	8.9	75.6	1.2	3.1
wheat, wholemeal	310	12.7	63.9	2.2	9
Ground Rice WHITWORTHS	361	6.5	86.8	1	0.5
PASTRY					
Pastry					
filo, uncooked	311	9	62	3	2
flaky, cooked	560	5.6	45.9	40.6	1.4
puff, uncooked	419	5	30	31	1.6
shortcrust, cooked	521	6.6	54.2	32.3	2.2
shortcrust, mix WHITWORTHS	467	7.4	60.8	23.2	2.3
wholemeal, cooked	499	8.9	44.6	32.9	6.3
BAKING AGENTS					
Baking Powder	163	5.2	37.8	Tr	0

All amounts per 100g/100ml unless otherwise stated	Cal kcal	Pro g	Carb g	Fat g	Fibre g
Yeast, bakers					
compressed	53	11.4	1.1	0.4	N
dried	169	35.6	3.5	1.5	N

MIXES

	Cal kcal	Pro g	Carb g	Fat g	Fibre g
Carmelle Mix GREEN'S	117	3	17	4	n/a
Batter Mix, Quick WHITWORTHS	338	9.3	77.2	1.2	3.7
Crumble Mix WHITWORTHS	422	5.5	67.6	16.3	1.5
Egg Custard Mix, no bake GREEN'S	109	3.5	13.5	4.5	n/a
Lemon Cheesecake Mix GREEN'S	298	4	34.5	16	n/a
Lemon Meringue Crunch Mix GREEN'S	249	2.5	39	9	n/a
Lemon Pie Filling Mix, Royal GREEN'S	390	0.5	94.5	1.4	n/a
Madeira Loaf Mix GREEN'S	339	4.9	56	12.4	n/a
Mississippi Mud Pie GREEN'S	323	4	37.5	17.5	n/a
Pancake Mix WHITWORTHS	322	13.4	65.9	2.5	2.3
Strawberry Cheesecake GREEN'S	258	3	31.5	12	n/a
Toffee Cheesecake GREEN'S	342	3.2	37.5	19.3	n/a
Victoria Sponge Mix GREEN'S	367	6	52	15	n/a

Calorie Counter

All amounts per 100g/100ml unless otherwise stated	Cal kcal	Pro g	Carb g	Fat g	Fibre g
SUNDRIES					
Cherries					
cocktail BURGESS	**247**	0.3	61.4	0	10
glacé	**251**	0.4	66.4	Tr	0.9
Cherry Pie Filling	**82**	0.4	21.5	Tr	0.4
Ginger, glacé WHITWORTHS	**303**	0.1	74.2	0.7	Tr
Lemon Juice, fresh	**7**	0.3	1.6	Tr	0.1
Marzipan					
homemade	**461**	10.4	50.2	25.8	3.3
retail	**404**	5.3	67.6	14.4	1.9
Mincemeat	**274**	0.6	62.1	4.3	1.3
Mixed Peel	**231**	0.3	59.1	0.9	4.8
Royal Icing TATE & LYLE	**390**	1.4	97.5	0	0

FRUIT AND VEGETABLES

All amounts per 100g/100ml unless otherwise stated	Cal kcal	Pro g	Carb g	Fat g	Fibre g

FRUIT

Apples, cooking

flesh only	35	0.3	8.9	0.1	1.6
stewed with sugar	74	0.3	19.1	0.1	1.2
stewed without sugar	33	0.3	8.1	0.1	1.5

Apples, eating, flesh only	45	0.4	11.2	0.1	1.6

Apricots

flesh and skin	31	0.9	7.2	0.1	1.7
canned in juice	34	0.5	8.4	0.1	0.9
canned in syrup	63	0.4	16.1	0.1	0.9
canned halves in syrup					
DEL MONTE	78	0.4	18.5	0.2	n/a
LIBBY	74	0.4	18	Tr	0.4
dried, ready to eat	240	4	62	0.5	8

Avocado Pears: *see* **Vegetables**

Bananas

peeled	95	1.2	23.2	0.3	1.1
dried, ready to eat HOLLAND & BARRETT	221	3.1	53.7	0.8	9.5

Blackberries

	25	0.9	5.1	0.2	3.1
stewed with sugar	56	0.7	13.8	0.2	2.4
stewed without sugar	21	0.8	4.4	0.2	5.6

Calorie Counter

All amounts per 100g/100ml unless otherwise stated	Cal kcal	Pro g	Carb g	Fat g	Fibre g
Blackcurrants	28	0.9	6.6	Tr	3.6
canned in juice	31	0.8	7.6	Tr	4.2
JOHN WEST	34	0.6	7.9	n/a	2.2
canned in syrup	72	0.7	18.4	Tr	3.6
stewed with sugar	58	0.7	15	Tr	2.8
Boysenberries, in syrup LIBBY	68	n/a	n/a	Tr	n/a
Breadfruit, canned, drained	66	0.6	16.4	0.2	2.5
Cherries					
flesh and skin	48	0.9	11.5	0.1	0.9
canned in syrup	71	0.5	18.5	Tr	0.6
Cherries, black					
canned in juice PEK MORELLO	87	0.8	22.1	n/a	2
canned in syrup LIBBY	73	n/a	n/a	Tr	n/a
Cherries, cocktail: *see* BAKING					
Cherries, glacé: *see* BAKING					
Clementines					
flesh only	37	0.9	8.7	0.1	1.2
canned in natural juice LIBBY	41	n/a	n/a	Tr	n/a
Coconut					
creamed	669	6	7	68.8	N
desiccated	604	5.6	6.4	62	13.7
Cranberries	15	0.4	3.5	Tr	4.2

All amounts per 100g/100ml unless otherwise stated	Cal kcal	Pro g	Carb g	Fat g	Fibre g
Damsons					
flesh and skin	38	0.5	9.6	Tr	1.8
stewed with sugar	74	0.4	19.3	Tr	1.5
Dates					
flesh and skin	124	1.5	31.3	0.1	1.8
block WHITWORTHS	288	3.3	68	0.2	n/a
chopped HOLLAND & BARRETT	241	2.8	57.1	0.2	3.4
stoned WHITWORTHS	287	3.2	68	0.2	3.9
Figs	122	0.4	7.2	Tr	6.9
canned in syrup LIBBY	88	n/a	n/a	Tr	n/a
canned in syrup PREMIER GOLD	59	0.5	14	n/a	n/a
dried, ready to eat	209	3.3	48.6	1.5	6.9
Fruit cocktail					
canned in juice	57	0.4	14.8	Tr	1
DEL MONTE	49	0.4	11.2	0.1	n/a
LIBBY	52	0.2	12.7	Tr	0.3
canned in syrup	77	0.4	20.1	Tr	1
DEL MONTE	75	0.4	18	0.1	n/a
LIBBY	74	0.2	18.2	Tr	0.4
Fruits of the forest, canned in syrup LIBBY	82	0.4	20.2	Tr	0.5
Gooseberries	54	0.7	12.9	0.3	2.4
stewed with sugar	73	0.4	18.5	0.2	2

Calorie Counter

All amounts per 100g/100ml unless otherwise stated	Cal kcal	Pro g	Carb g	Fat g	Fibre g
Grapefruit, flesh only	30	0.8	6.8	0.1	1.3
canned in juice DEL MONTE	48	0.6	10.5	0.1	n/a
canned segments in syrup					
LIBBY	78	0.5	18.9	Tr	0.3
Grapes, black/white, seedless	60	0.4	15.4	0.1	0.7
Greengages					
flesh and skin	34	0.5	8.6	Tr	1.6
stewed with sugar	107	1.3	26.9	0.1	1.5
Guavas	26	0.8	5	0.5	3.7
canned in syrup	60	0.4	15.7	Tr	n/a
JOHN WEST	64	0.4	15.7	n/a	3.1
Honeydew melon: *see* **Melon**					
Jackfruit	88	1.3	21.4	0.3	N
canned, drained	104	0.5	26.3	0.3	N
Kiwi fruit					
peeled	49	1.1	10.6	0.5	1.9
canned in syrup LIBBY	69	n/a	n/a	Tr	n/a
Lemons, whole	19	1	3.2	0.3	N
Lychees	58	0.9	14.3	0.1	0.7
canned in syrup	68	0.4	17.7	Tr	0.5
LIBBY	74	n/a	n/a	Tr	n/a
JOHN WEST	72	0.4	17.7		0.2

Fruit and Vegetables

All amounts per 100g/100ml unless otherwise stated	Cal kcal	Pro g	Carb g	Fat g	Fibre g
Mandarin oranges					
canned in juice	32	0.7	7.7	Tr	0.3
LIBBY	41	n/a	n/a	Tr	n/a
canned in syrup	52	0.5	14.4	Tr	0.2
LIBBY	57	n/a	n/a	Tr	n/a
Mangos					
flesh only	57	0.7	14.1	0.2	2.6
canned in syrup	57	0.7	14.1	0.2	2.6
LIBBY	70	n/a	n/a	Tr	n/a
Melon, flesh only,					
cantaloupe-type	19	0.6	4.2	0.1	1
galia	24	0.5	5.6	0.1	0.4
honeydew	28	0.6	6.6	0.1	0.6
watermelon	31	0.5	7.1	0.3	0.1
Nectarines, flesh and skin	40	1.4	9	0.1	1.2
Oranges, flesh only	37	1.1	8.5	0.1	1.7
Papaya: *see* **Paw-paw**					
Passionfruit, flesh and pips only	36	2.6	5.8	0.4	3.3
Paw-paw					
flesh only	36	0.5	8.8	0.1	2.2
canned in juice	65	0.2	17	Tr	0.7

Calorie Counter

All amounts per 100g/100ml unless otherwise stated	Cal kcal	Pro g	Carb g	Fat g	Fibre g
Peaches	**33**	1	7.6	0.1	1.5
canned in natural juice	39	0.6	9.7	Tr	0.8
DEL MONTE	49	0.5	11.2	0.1	n/a
LIBBY	52	0.4	12.4	0.1	0.3
canned in syrup	55	0.5	14	Tr	0.9
DEL MONTE	77	0.4	18.5	0.1	n/a
LIBBY	82	0.4	20	Tr	0.3
Pears	**40**	0.3	10	0.1	2.2
canned in natural juice	33	0.3	8.5	Tr	1.4
DEL MONTE	45	0.3	10.5	0.1	n/a
LIBBY	54	0.1	13.3	Tr	0.5
canned in syrup	50	0.2	13.2	Tr	1.1
DEL MONTE	70	0.2	17	0.1	n/a
LIBBY	77	0.1	19.2	Tr	0.6
Pineapple					
flesh only	**41**	0.4	10.1	0.2	1.2
canned in natural juice	47	0.3	12.2	Tr	0.5
DEL MONTE	57	0.4	13	0.1	n/a
LIBBY	50	n/a	n/a	Tr	n/a
canned in syrup	64	0.5	16.5	Tr	0.7
canned rings in syrup LIBBY	80	0.4	19.6	Tr	0.4
diced & dried HOLLAND & BARRETT	276	2.5	67.9	1.3	8.1
Plums	**36**	0.6	8.8	0.1	1.6
canned in syrup	59	0.3	15.5	Tr	0.8
JOHN WEST	73	0.3	18	n/a	0.8

All amounts per 100g/100ml unless otherwise stated	Cal kcal	Pro g	Carb g	Fat g	Fibre g
Prunes					
canned in juice	79	0.7	19.7	0.2	2.4
canned in syrup	90	0.6	23	0.2	2.8

Prunes, dried: *see* **DRIED FRUIT AND NUTS**

Raisins: *see* **DRIED FRUIT AND NUTS**

Raspberries	25	1.4	4.6	0.3	2.5
canned in juice JOHN WEST	32	0.9	6.7	0.2	1.5
canned in syrup	31	0.5	7.6	Tr	0.8
JOHN WEST	82	0.8	19.3	0.2	1.5
stewed with sugar	48	0.9	11.5	0.1	1.2
Rhubarb	7	0.9	0.8	0.1	1.4
canned in syrup	31	0.5	7.6	Tr	0.8
stewed with sugar	48	0.9	11.5	0.1	1.2
stewed without sugar	7	0.9	0.7	0.1	1.3
Satsumas, flesh only	36	0.9	8.5	0.1	1.3
Strawberries	27	0.8	6	0.1	1.1
canned in syrup	65	0.5	16.9	Tr	0.7
canned in juice	50	0.4	12	Tr	0.7
DEL MONTE	74	0.5	16.9	0.1	n/a
Tangerines, flesh only	35	0.9	8	0.1	1.3
Watermelon, flesh only	31	0.5	7.1	0.3	0.1

See also: **DRIED FRUIT AND NUTS**

Calorie Counter

All amounts per 100g/100ml unless otherwise stated	Cal kcal	Pro g	Carb g	Fat g	Fibre g
VEGETABLES					
Artichoke, globe, base of leaves and heart, boiled	**18**	2.8	2.7	0.2	N
Artichoke, Jerusalem, flesh only, boiled	**41**	1.6	10.6	0.1	N
Asparagus					
soft tips only, boiled	**26**	3.4	1.4	0.8	1.4
canned, drained	**24**	3.4	1.5	0.5	2.9
Aubergine, sliced, fried in corn oil	**302**	1.2	2.8	31.9	2.3
Avocado Pear	**190**	1.9	1.9	19.5	3.4
Bamboo Shoots					
canned	**11**	1.5	0.7	0.2	1.7
canned SHARWOOD	**6**	0.8	0.3	0.2	1.6
Beans, Broad					
boiled	**48**	5.1	5.6	0.8	5.4
canned	**77**	5.9	13	0.5	5.2
frozen, boiled	**81**	7.9	11.7	0.6	6.5
young, frozen BIRDS EYE	**56**	5.9	7.4	0.3	4.8
Beans, Green/French					
trimmed	**24**	1.9	3.2	0.5	2.2
trimmed, boiled	**22**	1.8	2.9	0.5	2.4
canned	**22**	1.5	4.1	0.1	2.6
frozen, boiled	**25**	1.7	4.7	0.1	4.1
frozen, sliced, boiled ROSS	**31**	1.8	7.6	0.2	2.2

All amounts per 100g/100ml unless otherwise stated	Cal kcal	Pro g	Carb g	Fat g	Fibre g
Beans, Runner, trimmed, boiled	18	1.2	2.3	0.5	3.1

For dried and canned beans see: **BEANS, PULSES AND CEREALS**

	Cal kcal	Pro g	Carb g	Fat g	Fibre g
Beansprouts, mung	31	2.9	4	0.5	1.5
stirfried in blended oil	72	1.9	2.5	6.1	0.9
Beetroot					
trimmed, peeled	36	1.7	7.6	0.1	1.9
trimmed, peeled, boiled	46	2.3	9.5	0.1	1.9
pickled, whole and sliced	28	1.2	5.6	0.2	1.7
pickled, all varieties BAXTERS	30	1.5	6	Tr	1.2
Beets, sliced, organic BAXTERS	47	1.5	9.9	0.1	1.2
Broccoli					
florets, boiled	24	3.1	1.1	0.8	2.3
Premium Choice, frozen ROSS	24	2.9	4.1	0.7	2.6
Brussels Sprouts					
trimmed, boiled	35	2.9	3.5	1.3	3.1
Premium Choice, frozen ROSS	35	4.1	6.6	0.5	3.2
Cabbage, (January King, Savoy, Summer)					
trimmed	26	1.7	4.1	0.4	2.4
shredded & boiled	18	0.8	2.5	0.6	2.1
white, trimmed	27	1.4	5	0.2	2.1
shredded, frozen ROSS	19	1.1	5.5	0.2	2.3
Spring greens	33	3	3.1	1	3.4
Spring greens, boiled	20	1.9	1.6	0.7	2.6

Calorie Counter

All amounts per 100g/100ml unless otherwise stated	Cal kcal	Pro g	Carb g	Fat g	Fibre g
Carrots					
old	35	0.6	7.9	0.3	2.4
old, boiled	24	0.6	4.9	0.4	2.5
young	30	0.7	6	0.5	2.4
young, boiled	22	0.6	4.4	0.4	2.3
canned	20	0.5	4.2	0.3	1.9
baby, frozen, boiled BIRDS EYE	22	0.8	4.6	Tr	2
frozen, boiled	22	0.4	4.7	0.3	2.3
grated	37	0.6	8	0.3	2.4
Cassava					
baked	155	0.7	40.1	0.2	1.7
boiled	130	0.5	33.5	0.2	1.4
fresh	142	0.6	36.8	0.2	1.6
Cauliflower	34	3.6	3	0.9	1.8
boiled	28	2.9	2.1	0.9	1.6
frozen, boiled	20	2	2	0.5	1.2
Celeriac					
flesh only	18	1.2	2.3	0.4	3.7
flesh only, boiled	15	0.9	1.9	0.5	3.2
Celery					
stem only	7	0.5	0.9	0.2	1.1
stem only, boiled	8	0.5	0.8	0.3	1.2
Chicory	11	0.5	2.8	0.6	0.9

Fruit and Vegetables

All amounts per 100g/100ml unless otherwise stated	Cal kcal	Pro g	Carb g	Fat g	Fibre g
Corn-on-the-cob					
boiled	111	4.2	19.6	2.3	2.2
mini corncobs, canned	23	2.9	2	0.4	1.5
mini corncobs, fresh/frozen, boiled	24	2.5	2.7	0.4	2
See also: **Sweetcorn**					
Courgettes (zucchini)					
trimmed	18	1.8	1.8	0.4	0.9
trimmed, boiled	19	2	2	0.4	1.2
trimmed, sliced, fried in corn oil	63	2.6	2.6	4.8	1.2
Cucumber, trimmed	10	0.7	1.5	0.1	0.6
Eggplant: *see* **Aubergine**					
Fennel, Florence	12	0.9	1.8	0.2	2.4
boiled	11	0.9	1.5	0.2	2.3
Garlic	98	7.9	16.3	0.6	4.1
purée	423	2.7	13	40	6
Gherkins, pickled	14	0.9	2.6	0.1	1.2
Ginger Root	38	1.4	7.2	0.6	N
Greens, spring: *see* **Cabbage**					
Gumbo: *see* **Okra**					
Kale, Curly	33	3.4	1.4	1.6	3.1
shredded & boiled	24	2.4	1	1.1	2.8

Calorie Counter

All amounts per 100g/100ml unless otherwise stated	Cal kcal	Pro g	Carb g	Fat g	Fibre g
Kohlrabi	**23**	1.6	3.7	0.2	2.2
boiled	**18**	1.2	3.1	0.2	1.9
Lady's Fingers: *see* **Okra**					
Leeks					
trimmed	**22**	1.6	2.9	0.5	2.2
trimmed, chopped, boiled	**21**	1.2	2.6	0.7	1.7
Lettuce	**14**	0.8	1.7	0.5	0.9
iceberg	**13**	0.7	1.9	0.3	0.6
mixed leaf	**17**	1.3	2.7	0.1	2.8
mediterranean	**15.**	0.9	2.7	0.3	1
Mange-tout	**32**	3.6	4.2	0.2	2.3
boiled	**26**	3.2	3.3	0.1	2.2
stir-fried	**71**	3.8	3.5	4.8	2.4
Marrow					
flesh only	**12**	0.5	2.2	0.2	0.5
flesh only, boiled	**9**	0.4	1.6	0.2	0.6
Mooli: *see* **Radish, white**					
Mushrooms, common	**13**	1.8	0.4	0.5	1.1
boiled	**11**	1.8	0.4	0.3	1.1
canned	**12**	2.1	Tr	0.4	1.3
fried in oil	**157**	2.4	0.3	16.2	1.5
sliced, dried WHITWORTHS	**223**	16.5	40	1	22.9
Mushrooms, oyster	**8**	1.6	Tr	0.2	N

All amounts per 100g/100ml unless otherwise stated	Cal kcal	Pro g	Carb g	Fat g	Fibre g
Mushrooms, shiitake					
cooked	55	1.6	12.3	0.2	N
dried	296	9.6	63.9	1	N
Mushrooms, straw					
canned, drained	15	2.1	1.2	0.2	N
Neeps (England): see **Swede**					
Neeps (Scotland): see **Turnip**					
Okra (gumbo, lady's fingers)	31	2.8	3	1	4
boiled	28	2.5	2.7	0.9	3.6
canned, drained	21	1.4	2.5	0.7	2.6
stir-fried	269	4.3	4.4	26	6.3
Olives, pitted, in brine	103	0.9	Tr	11	2.9
Onions					
flesh only	36	1.2	7.9	0.2	1.4
boiled	17	0.6	3.7	0.1	0.7
cocktail/silverskin, drained	15	0.6	3.1	0.1	N
dried	313	10.2	68.6	1.7	12.1
fried in oil	164	2.3	14.1	11.2	3.1
pickled, drained	24	0.9	4.9	0.2	1.2
Parsnips, trimmed, peeled, boiled	66	1.6	12.9	1.2	4.7
Peas					
no pod	83	6.9	11.3	1.5	4.7
boiled	79	6.7	10	1.6	4.5
canned	80	5.3	13.5	0.9	5.1

Calorie Counter

All amounts per 100g/100ml unless otherwise stated	Cal kcal	Pro g	Carb g	Fat g	Fibre g
dried, boiled	109	6.9	19.9	0.8	5.5
frozen, boiled	69	6	9.7	0.9	5.1
Peas, Garden					
frozen BIRDS EYE	62	4.9	9	0.7	4.5
frozen ROSS	72	6	14.5	0.8	4.3
Peas, Mushy					
canned	81	5.8	13.8	0.7	1.8
Original Style, canned					
BATCHELORS	81	5.4	14	0.2	2.8
Mint Sauce Flavoured, canned					
BATCHELORS	74	5.7	12.1	4	2.6
Chip Shop Mushy, frozen ROSS	117	7.5	23	0.2	1.8
Peas, Processed, canned					
(unbranded)	99	6.9	17.5	0.7	4.8
Bigga Marrowfat BATCHELORS	66	5.6	10.1	0.3	4
Farrow's Giant Marrowfat					
BATCHELORS	77	5.9	12.3	0.5	4.9
Mushy, Chip Shop Style					
BATCHELORS	84	5.2	14.6	0.3	3.5
Small Processed BATCHELORS	87	5.4	15.5	0.4	4.8

See also: **Petit Pois**

See also: **BEANS, PULSES AND CEREALS**

Peppers					
green, stalk & seeds removed	15	0.8	2.6	0.3	1.6
green, boiled	18	1	2.6	0.5	1.8

All amounts per 100g/100ml unless otherwise stated	Cal kcal	Pro g	Carb g	Fat g	Fibre g
red, stalk & seeds removed	32	1	6.4	0.4	1.6
red, boiled	34	1.1	7	0.4	1.7
yellow, stalk & seeds removed	26	1.2	5.3	0.2	1.7
mixed, sliced, frozen	28	1.1	4.9	0.4	1.8
chilli	20	2.9	0.7	0.6	N
jalapeños, sliced OLD EL PASO	22	1.3	3.4	0.3	n/a
Petits Pois	100	6.9	17.5	0.8	4.1
canned	45	5.2	4.9	0.6	4.3
frozen, boiled	49	5	5.5	0.9	4.5
frozen ROSS	51	4.2	10.4	1.2	4.6
Potatoes, new					
boiled, peeled	75	1.5	17.8	0.3	1.1
boiled in skins	66	1.4	15.4	0.3	1.5
canned	63	1.5	15.1	0.1	0.8
Potatoes, old					
baked, flesh & skin	136	3.9	31.7	0.2	2.7
baked, flesh only	77	2.2	18	0.1	1.4
boiled, peeled	72	1.8	17	0.1	1.2
mashed with butter & milk	104	1.8	15.5	4.3	1.1
roast in oil/lard	149	2.9	25.9	4.5	1.8
Potato Powder, Instant					
made up with semi-skimmed milk	70	2.4	14.8	1.2	1
made up with skimmed milk	66	2.4	14.8	0.1	1
made up with water	57	1.5	13.5	0.1	1
made up with whole milk	76	2.4	14.8	1.2	1

Calorie Counter

All amounts per 100g/100ml unless otherwise stated	Cal kcal	Pro g	Carb g	Fat g	Fibre g
See also: **CHIPS, FRIES AND SHAPED POTATO PRODUCTS**					
Pumpkin					
flesh only	13	0.7	2.2	0.2	1
flesh only, boiled	13	0.6	2.1	0.3	1.1
Raddiccio	14	1.4	1.7	0.2	1.8
Radish, red	12	0.7	1.9	0.2	0.9
Radish, white/mooli	15	0.8	2.9	0.1	N
Ratatouille, canned	48	1	6.5	2	1
Salad: *see also* **Lettuce**					
Salsify					
flesh only	27	1.3	10.2	0.3	3.2
flesh only, boiled	23	1.1	8.6	0.4	3.5
Shallots	20	1.5	3.3	0.2	1.4
Spinach	25	2.8	1.6	0.8	2.1
boiled	19	2.2	0.8	0.8	2.1
frozen, boiled	21	3.1	0.5	0.8	2.1
Spring Onions, bulbs & tops	23	2	3	0.5	1.5
Sprouts: *see* **Brussels Sprouts**					
Squash: *see* **Marrow**					

Fruit and Vegetables

All amounts per 100g/100ml unless otherwise stated	Cal kcal	Pro g	Carb g	Fat g	Fibre g
Swede, flesh only, boiled	11	0.3	2.3	0.1	0.7
Sweet Potato, boiled	84	1.1	20.5	0.3	2.3
Sweetcorn, kernels					
canned, drained, re-heated	122	2.9	26.6	1.2	1.4
Niblets, canned GREEN GIANT	100	2.7	20.8	0.7	1.2
Niblets, no salt, no sugar					
GREEN GIANT	77	2.6	16.7	0	2.6
Niblets, Extra Crisp					
GREEN GIANT	70	2.7	13.3	0.7	2.7
Niblets with Peppers					
GREEN GIANT	82	2.6	17.9	0	1.3
Tomatoes	17	0.7	3.1	0.3	1
canned, whole	16	1	3	0.1	0.7
cherry	18	0.8	3	0.4	1
fried in oil	91	0.7	5	7.7	1.3
grilled	49	2	8.9	0.9	2.9
sun-dried	209	4.3	11	16.4	6.5
purée	86	6	15	0.2	Tr
passata	25	1.4	4.5	0.1	0.2
Tomatoes, chopped, canned					
NAPOLINA	15	1.2	2.5	Tr	n/a
for bolognese	24	1.4	5	Tr	n/a
with herbs	15	1.2	2.5	Tr	n/a
with onions & herbs	16	1.2	3	Tr	n/a

Calorie Counter

All amounts per 100g/100ml unless otherwise stated	Cal kcal	Pro g	Carb g	Fat g	Fibre g
Turnip					
flesh only	**23**	0.9	4.7	0.3	2.4
flesh only, boiled	**12**	0.6	2	0.2	1.9
Water Chestnuts					
canned	**31**	0.9	7.4	Tr	N
canned AMOY	**42**	0.9	10.1	0	n/a
Yam					
flesh only	**114**	1.5	28.2	0.3	1.3
flesh only, boiled	**133**	1.7	33	0.3	1.4

Zucchini: *see* **Courgettes**

JAMS, MARMALADES AND SWEET SPREADS

All amounts per 100g/100ml unless otherwise stated	Cal kcal	Pro g	Carb g	Fat g	Fibre g
JAM, MARMALADE AND HONEY					
Apricot Conserve BAXTERS	252	Tr	63	Tr	0.8
Apricot Fruit Spread					
HEINZ WEIGHT WATCHERS	110	0.3	27.2	0	0.5
organic MERIDIAN FOODS LTD	148	0.4	36	Tr	3
Apricot Jam					
reduced sugar BAXTERS	210	Tr	53	Tr	0.8
sucrose free DIETADE	162	0.3	64.4	Tr	n/a
Blackcurrant Fruit Spread					
HEINZ WEIGHT WATCHERS	106	0.2	26.3	0	0.9
organic MERIDIAN FOODS LTD	148	0.4	36	Tr	3
Blackcurrant Jam					
reduced sugar BAXTERS	210	Tr	53	Tr	1.3
sucrose free DIETADE	170	0.3	67	Tr	n/a
Blueberry & Blackberry Jam, organic BAXTERS	252	Tr	63	Tr	1.4
Grapefruit Fruit Spread MERIDIAN FOODS LTD	138	0.4	37.5	0.1	2.2

Calorie Counter

All amounts per 100g/100ml unless otherwise stated	Cal kcal	Pro g	Carb g	Fat g	Fibre g
Honey					
clear GALES	245	0.32	60.8	0	n/a
comb	288	0.4	76.4	0	0
comb HOLLAND & BARRETT	307	0.4	76.5	0.1	0
set	307	0.4	76.4	0	0
Lemon Curd	283	0.6	62.7	5.1	0.2
GALES	290	0.7	61	4.6	n/a
Marmalade	261	0.1	69.5	0	0.6
Orange sucrose free DIETADE	165	0.2	66.4	Tr	n/a
Orange, Lemon & Grapefruit, organic BAXTERS	252	Tr	63	Tr	0.1
Scotch Orange BAXTERS	210	Tr	53	Tr	0.1
Vintage Orange BAXTERS	252	Tr	63	Tr	0.8
Morello Cherry Fruit Spread, organic MERIDIAN FOODS LTD	148	0.4	36	Tr	3
Pineapple & Ginger Fruit Spread MERIDIAN FOODS LTD	137	0.2	37.5	Tr	1.6
Raspberry Conserve BAXTERS	252	Tr	63	Tr	1.2
Raspberry Fruit Spread					
HEINZ WEIGHT WATCHERS	111	0.4	27.1	0.1	0.9
organic MERIDIAN FOODS LTD	149	0.5	36	Tr	2.6
Raspberry Jam					
organic BAXTERS	252	Tr	63	Tr	1.2
reduced sugar BAXTERS	210	Tr	53	Tr	1.2
sucrose free DIETADE	161	0.5	63.9	0.1	n/a

Jams, Marmalades and Sweet Spreads

All amounts per 100g/100ml unless otherwise stated	Cal kcal	Pro g	Carb g	Fat g	Fibre g
Rhubarb & Ginger Jam, reduced sugar BAXTERS	210	Tr	53	Tr	0.6
Seville Orange Fruit Spread					
HEINZ WEIGHT WATCHERS	111	0.2	27.5	0	0.3
organic MERIDIAN FOODS LTD	148	0.4	36	Tr	2.2
Strawberry Conserve BAXTERS	252	Tr	63	Tr	0.5
Strawberry Fruit Spread					
HEINZ WEIGHT WATCHERS	115	0.2	28.4	0	0.4
organic MERIDIAN FOODS LTD	147	0.3	36	Tr	2.5
Strawberry Jam					
reduced sugar BAXTERS	210	Tr	53	Tr	0.5
sucrose free DIETADE	159	0.3	63.8	Tr	n/a
Wild Blackberry Jelly, reduced sugar BAXTERS	210	Tr	53	Tr	1.2
Wild Blueberry Fruit Spread, organic MERIDIAN FOODS LTD	148	0.2	36	Tr	3.8

NUT BUTTERS

	Cal	Pro	Carb	Fat	Fibre
Almond Butter MERIDIAN FOODS LTD	626	25.3	6.5	55.5	n/a
Cashew Butter MERIDIAN FOODS LTD	612	20.4	18.7	51.1	n/a
Chocolate Nut Spread	549	6	60.5	33	0.8

Calorie Counter

All amounts per 100g/100ml unless otherwise stated	Cal kcal	Pro g	Carb g	Fat g	Fibre g
Hazel Butter MERIDIAN FOODS LTD	672	15	5.3	65.3	n/a
Nutella FERRERO	533	6.5	75	31	n/a
Peanut Butter					
American Stripy Chocolate SUNPAT	617	13.2	34.7	46.8	3.4
creamy crunch SUNPAT	605	22.9	19.8	48.6	5.3
creamy smooth SUNPAT	620	24	17.5	50.2	6.1
crunchy HOLLAND & BARRETT	591	25.5	10.3	49.8	7.4
organic MERIDIAN FOODS LTD	606	31.2	12.1	48.7	6.5
organic, no salt MERIDIAN FOODS LTD	612	31.2	12.2	48.7	6.5
original crunchy SUNPAT	600	27	14.5	48.2	6.8
original smooth SUNPAT	585	27.9	14.4	46.3	7.1
smooth	623	22.6	13.1	53.7	5.4
Tahini Paste	607	18.5	0.9	58.9	8

MEAT AND POULTRY

All amounts per 100g/100ml unless otherwise stated	Cal kcal	Pro g	Carb g	Fat g	Fibre g
BACON AND GAMMON					
Bacon, rashers, back					
dry fried	**295**	24.2	0	22	0
fat trimmed, grilled	**214**	25.7	0	12.3	0
grilled	**287**	23.2	0	21.6	0
microwaved	**307**	24.2	0	23.3	0
uncooked	**215**	16.5	0	16.5	0
uncooked, smoked WALL'S	**188**	16.2	0.5	13.5	n/a
uncooked, unsmoked WALL'S	**188**	16.2	0.5	13.5	n/a
Bacon, rashers, middle, grilled	**307**	24.8	0	23.1	0
Bacon, rashers, streaky					
fried	**335**	23.8	0	26.6	0
grilled	**337**	23.8	0	26.9	0
Gammon, joint, boiled	**204**	23.3	0	12.3	0
Gammon, rashers, grilled	**199**	27.5	0	9.9	0
SAUSAGES					
Beef sausages, grilled	**278**	13.3	13.1	19.5	0.7
Cumberland sausages, uncooked WALL'S	**318**	11.6	9.8	25.6	0.8
Frankfurters HERTA	**335**	12	2	31	Tr

Calorie Counter

All amounts per 100g/100ml unless otherwise stated	Cal kcal	Pro g	Carb g	Fat g	Fibre g
Lincolnshire sausages, uncooked WALL'S	307	12.4	8.7	24.3	1.4
Pork sausages					
fried	308	13.9	9.9	23.9	0.7
lean recipe, uncooked WALL'S	132	15.4	8.5	4.1	2.1
skinless, uncooked WALL'S	313	11.4	11.6	24.6	0.1
Pork & apple sausages, lean recipe, uncooked WALL'S	139	14.5	9.4	4.5	2.3
Pork & beef sausages, thick, uncooked WALL'S	300	9.3	18.5	21	1
Premium sausages, grilled	292	16.8	6.3	22.4	N
Saveloy	296	13.8	10.8	22.3	0.8

BEEF

	Cal kcal	Pro g	Carb g	Fat g	Fibre g
Beef, fore-rib, roasted	300	29.1	0	20.4	0
Beef, mince, stewed	209	21.8	0	13.5	0
Beef, rump steak					
lean, grilled	177	31	0	5.9	0
lean, fried	183	30.9	0	6.6	0
lean & fat, fried	228	28.4	0	12.7	0
Beef, silverside, lean only, boiled	184	30.4	0	6.9	0
Beef, stewing steak, lean & fat, stewed	223	30.9	0	11	0

All amounts per 100g/100ml unless otherwise stated	Cal kcal	Pro g	Carb g	Fat g	Fibre g
Beef, topside					
lean only, roasted well-done	**202**	36.2	0	6.3	0
lean & fat, roasted	**244**	32.8	0	12.5	0
Grillsteaks, grilled	**305**	22.1	0.5	23.9	Tr
Oxtail, stewed	**243**	30.5	0	13.4	0
Tongue, fat & skin removed, stewed	**289**	18.2	0	24	0

Beef, sausages: *see* SAUSAGES

LAMB

Lamb, breast					
lean only, roasted	**273**	26.7	0	18.5	0
lean & fat, roasted	**359**	22.4	0	29.9	0
Lamb, loin chops					
lean only, grilled	**213**	29.2	0	10.7	0
lean & fat, grilled	**305**	26.5	0	22.1	0
Lamb, cutlets					
lean only, grilled	**238**	28.5	0	13.8	0
lean & fat, grilled	**367**	24.5	0	29.9	0
Lamb, leg					
whole, lean only, roasted	**203**	29.7	0	9.4	0
whole, lean & fat, roasted	**240**	28.1	0	14.2	0
Lamb, mince, stewed	**208**	24.4	0	12.3	0

Calorie Counter

All amounts per 100g/100ml unless otherwise stated	Cal kcal	Pro g	Carb g	Fat g	Fibre g
Lamb, stewing, lean only, stewed	**240**	26.6	0	14.8	0
Lamb, shoulder					
lean only, roasted	**218**	27.2	0	12.1	0
lean & fat, roasted	**298**	24.7	0	22.1	0

PORK

	Cal kcal	Pro g	Carb g	Fat g	Fibre g
Pork, belly rashers, lean & fat, grilled	**320**	27.4	0	23.4	0
Pork, loin chops, lean only, grilled	**184**	31.6	0	6.4	0
Pork, leg					
lean only, roasted	**182**	33	0	5.5	0
lean & fat, roasted	**215**	30.9	0	10.2	0
Pork, steaks	**162**	18	0	10	0

Pork, sausages: *see* SAUSAGES

VEAL

	Cal kcal	Pro g	Carb g	Fat g	Fibre g
Veal, escalope fried	**196**	33.7	4.4	6.8	0

CHICKEN

	Cal kcal	Pro g	Carb g	Fat g	Fibre g
Chicken, breast					
in crumbs, fried	**242**	18	14.8	12.7	0.7
meat only, casseroled	**160**	28.4	0	5.2	0

All amounts per 100g/100ml unless otherwise stated	Cal kcal	Pro g	Carb g	Fat g	Fibre g
meat only, grilled	**148**	32	0	2.2	0
meat only, stir fried	**161**	29.7	0	4.6	0
Chicken, drumsticks, meat & skin, roasted	**185**	25.8	0	9.1	0
Chicken, leg quarter, meat & skin, roasted	**236**	20.9	0	16.9	0
Chicken, light & dark meat, roasted	**177**	27.3	0	7.5	0
Chicken, wing quarter, meat & skin, roasted	**226**	24.8	0	14.1	0
Chicken, light meat, roasted	**153**	30.2	0	3.6	0

TURKEY

Turkey, breast fillet, meat only, grilled	**155**	35	0	1.7	0
Turkey, dark meat, roasted	**177**	29.4	0	6.6	0
Turkey, light meat, roasted	**153**	33.7	0	2	0
Turkey, meat only, roasted	**166**	31.2	0	4.6	0

GAME

Duck

meat only, roasted	**195**	25.3	0	10.4	0
meat, fat & skin, roasted	**423**	20	0	38.1	0

Calorie Counter

All amounts per 100g/100ml unless otherwise stated	Cal kcal	Pro g	Carb g	Fat g	Fibre g
Duck, crispy, Chinese style	331	27.9	0.3	24.2	0
Goose, meat, fat & skin, roasted	301	27.5	0	21.2	0
Pheasant, meat only, roasted	220	27.9	0	12	0
Rabbit, meat only, stewed	114	21.2	0	3.2	0
Venison, haunch, meat only, roasted	165	35.6	0	2.5	0

OFFAL

Black Pudding, dry fried	297	10.3	16.6	21.5	0.2
Heart, lamb, roasted	226	25.3	0	13.9	0
Kidney, lamb, fried	188	23.7	0	10.3	0
Kidney, ox, stewed	138	24.5	0	4.4	0
Kidney, pig, stewed	153	24.4	0	6.1	0
Liver, calf, fried	176	22.3	Tr	9.6	0
Liver, chicken, fried	169	22.1	Tr	8.9	0
Liver, lamb, fried	237	30.1	Tr	12.9	0
Liver, ox, stewed	198	24.8	3.6	9.5	Tr
Liver, pig, stewed	189	25.6	3.6	8.1	Tr
Tripe, dressed, raw	33	7.1	0	0.5	0
White Pudding	450	7	36.3	31.8	N

OILS AND FATS

All amounts per 100g/100ml unless otherwise stated	Cal kcal	Pro g	Carb g	Fat g	Fibre g
OILS					
Crisp 'n' Dry SPRY	**828**	0	0	92	0
Coconut Oil	**899**	Tr	0	99.9	0
Corn Oil MAZOLA	**900**	Tr	0	100	0
Olive Oil	**899**	Tr	0	99.9	0
CARAPELLI	**822**	0	0	91.3	0
FILIPPO BERRIO	**822**	0	0	91.3	0
Extra Virgin NAPOLINA	**828**	0	0	92	0
OLIVIO	**900**	0	0	100	0
Palm Oil	**899**	Tr	0	99.9	0
Peanut Oil	**899**	Tr	0	99.9	0
Rapeseed Oil	**899**	Tr	0	99.9	0
Safflower Oil	**899**	Tr	0	99.9	0
Sesame Oil	**881**	0.2	0	99.7	0
Soya Oil	**899**	Tr	0	99.9	0
Stir Fry Oil SHARWOOD	**897**	0	0	99.7	0
Sunflower Oil FLORA	**828**	0	0	92	0
Sunflower Oil Seed	**899**	Tr	0	99.9	0
Vegetable Oil	**899**	Tr	0	99.9	0
Wheatgerm Oil	**899**	Tr	0	99.9	0

Calorie Counter

All amounts per 100g/100ml unless otherwise stated	Cal kcal	Pro g	Carb g	Fat g	Fibre g
FATS					
Cooking Fat					
COOKEEN	900	0	0	100	0
White Fat VAN DEN BERGH	900	0	0	100	n/a
Crisp 'n' Dry, solid SPRY	900	0	0	100	0
White Flora FLORA	900	0	0	100	0
Dripping, beef	891	Tr	Tr	99	0
Ghee					
butter	898	Tr	Tr	99.8	0
palm	897	Tr	Tr	99.7	0
vegetable	898	Tr	Tr	99.8	0
vegetable SHARWOOD	897	Tr	Tr	99.7	0
Lard	891	Tr	Tr	99	0
Suet, shredded	826	Tr	12.1	86.7	0.5

PASTA

All amounts per 100g/100ml unless otherwise stated	Cal kcal	Pro g	Carb g	Fat g	Fibre g
Cooked Lasagne sheets BUITONI					
standard	89	3.1	18.1	0.4	n/a
verdi	93	3.2	18.3	0.4	n/a
Cooked Pasta, all shapes BUITONI					
standard	89	3.1	18.1	0.4	n/a
verdi	93	3.2	18.3	0.4	n/a
Dry Lasagne sheets BUITONI					
standard	362	12.2	74.4	1.7	n/a
verdi	367	12.8	75.2	1.7	n/a
Dry Pasta, all shapes					
standard BUITONI	362	12.2	74.4	1.7	n/a
verdi BUITONI	367	12.8	75.2	1.7	n/a
organic MERIDIAN FOODS	357	13	72.5	1.7	2.4
wholewheat, organic MERIDIAN FOODS	332	12	65.7	2.3	8.9
Fresh Egg Pasta					
conchiglie, penne, fusilli	170	7	31	2	1.4
Lasagne sheets	150	6	29	1.1	4.6
Spaghetti	135	6	23	2.1	1.6
Tagliatelle	134	5	25	1.6	1.5
Macaroni, boiled	86	3	18.5	0.5	0.9
Spaghetti					
cooked	104	3.6	22.2	0.7	1.2
wholemeal, cooked	113	4.7	23.2	0.9	3.5

Calorie Counter

All amounts per 100g/100ml unless otherwise stated	Cal kcal	Pro g	Carb g	Fat g	Fibre g
Stuffed Fresh Pasta					
cheese & porcini ravioli	164	7.8	21.6	5.2	2.8
chicken & mushroom tortellini	136	6.6	21.7	2.5	1
four cheese tortellini	133	5.6	20.1	3.3	0.9
garlic, basil & ricotta tortellini	133	6	22.5	2.1	1.8
ham & cheese tortellini	131	6.1	19.7	3.1	0.5
mushroom & ricotta tortellini	133	6	22.5	2.1	1.8
spinach & ricotta tortellini verdi	149	6	21	4.5	2.4

CLASSIC PASTA SAUCES

See also: **COOKING SAUCES AND MARINADES (ITALIAN)**

Amatriciana, fresh, low fat	50	2.3	6.3	1.9	1.2
Arrabbiata, fresh, low fat	42	1.5	6.3	1.3	1.1
Beef Bolognese Sauce, fresh	77	4.7	3.4	5	0.4
Bolognese Sauce, recipe	161	11.8	2.5	11.6	0.6
Carbonara					
fresh	197	5.2	5.7	17.3	0.6
fresh, low fat	97	4.8	5.5	6	0.6
Pesto					
creamy fresh	45	2.2	6	1.3	1.4
jar	427	4.7	3.5	43.8	1.4
red, jar	358	4.1	3.1	36.6	0.4
Tomato & basil, fresh	51	1.8	8.8	0.9	1.3
Tomato Pasta Sauce, jar	57	2.2	7.7	1.9	1.4

All amounts per 100g/100ml unless otherwise stated	Cal kcal	Pro g	Carb g	Fat g	Fibre g
TINNED PASTA					
Ravioli in Tomato Sauce HEINZ	73	2.6	13	1.1	0.6
Spaghetti Bolognese HEINZ	86	3.4	12.8	2.3	0.7
Spaghetti Hoops HEINZ	56	1.9	11.7	0.2	0.6
Spaghetti Hoops 'n' Hotdogs in a Smoky Bacon Sauce HEINZ	76	2.8	11	2.4	0.4
Spaghetti in Tomato Sauce					
CROSSE & BLACKWELL	88	3.3	15	1.7	n/a
HEINZ	61	1.7	13	0.2	0.5
no added sugar HEINZ WEIGHT WATCHERS	50	1.8	10.1	0.2	0.6
Spaghetti with Sausages in Tomato Sauce HEINZ	82	3.7	11	2.6	0.5
Spicy Pepperoni Pasta HEINZ	83	2.9	9.1	3.9	0.5
Spicy Salsa Twists HEINZ	75	2.7	10.9	2.3	0.8

See also: **CHILDREN'S FOOD**

PIZZA

All amounts per 100g/100ml unless otherwise stated	Cal kcal	Pro g	Carb g	Fat g	Fibre g
Cheese & Onion Deep Topped Pizza, slices MCVITIE'S	223	8.4	30.3	8.2	1.3
Cheese & Onion Pizza, 5″ MCCAIN	177	8.8	27.6	3.5	n/a
Cheese & Tomato Pizza					
recipe	235	9	24.8	11.8	1.5
deep pan base	249	12.4	35.1	7.5	2.2
French bread base	230	10.6	31.4	7.8	N
thin base	277	14.4	33.9	10.3	1.9
SAN MARCO	244	11.8	24.7	11.3	1
5″ MCCAIN	235	11.6	22.4	10.1	n/a
Cheese, Tomato & Vegetable Deep Crust Pizza, slice MCCAIN	193	9.4	26.7	5.4	n/a
Cheese, Tomato & Vegetable Pizza, slice MCCAIN	159	7.4	27.8	2.8	n/a
French Bread Pizza FINDUS	235	9.3	32.4	7.8	1.8
Ham & Mushroom Pizza SAN MARCO	227	11.4	29.5	7.5	1.1
Ham & Mushroom Pizza, 5″ MCCAIN	184	8.7	27.7	4.3	n/a
Mushroom & Garlic Pizza SAN MARCO	241	11.3	28.5	10.4	1.2

All amounts per 100g/100ml unless otherwise stated	Cal kcal	Pro g	Carb g	Fat g	Fibre g
Pepperoni & Sausage Pizza SAN MARCO	226	10.9	24.8	9.9	1.3
Pepperoni Deep Crust Pizza, slice McCAIN	229	10.1	26.8	9	n/a
Pepperoni Feast Deep Pizza McCAIN	218	10.5	27	8.3	n/a
Pizza Bases NAPOLINA					
deep pan	298	8.5	56	4.4	n/a
mini	298	8.5	56	4.4	n/a
standard	298	8.5	56	4.4	n/a
stone baked	274	8.5	55	2.2	n/a
Pizza Slice, pepperoni McCAIN	229	10.1	26.8	9	n/a
Pizza Topping NAPOLINA					
spicy tomato	66	1.6	9	2.6	1
tomato, cheese, onion & herbs	80	3	8.1	4	0.9
tomato, herbs & spices	67	1.5	9.4	2.6	0.8
Super Deluxe SGFY Pizza McCAIN	167	10.7	25.9	3.6	n/a

See also: **FAST FOOD**

QUICHES, PIES AND SAVOURY PASTRIES

All amounts per 100g/100ml unless otherwise stated	Cal kcal	Pro g	Carb g	Fat g	Fibre g
Beef & Kidney Pie, canned					
TYNE BRAND	154	8.7	13.3	8.1	n/a
Beef & Mushroom Pie, canned					
TYNE BRAND	162	10.1	11.8	8.3	n/a
Beef & Potato Pie, canned					
TYNE BRAND	191	7.1	22.2	8.2	n/a
Beef & Vegetable Pie, canned					
TYNE BRAND	185	6.5	22.5	7.7	n/a
Cheese & Onion Pie, individual	324	6.7	27	21	1.2
Chicken & Mushroom Pie					
canned, FRAY BENTOS	161	7.3	11.5	9.5	n/a
individual	294	7.7	25.6	17.9	1.1
Chicken & Vegetable Pie					
frozen ROSS	251	7.3	26.5	13.4	1.1
canned TYNE BRAND	162	4.7	14.3	9.6	n/a
Cornish Pastie	267	6.7	25	16.3	0.9
giant ROSS	228	6.5	24.5	12	1
Game Pie	381	12.2	34.7	22.5	1.3
Minced Beef & Onion Deep Pie, frozen ROSS	249	6	24.6	14.5	1

Quiches, Pies and Savoury Pastries

All amounts per 100g/100ml unless otherwise stated	Cal kcal	Pro g	Carb g	Fat g	Fibre g
Minced Beef & Onion Pastie, giant, frozen ROSS	259	6	28	14.2	1.2
Minced Beef & Onion Pie	295	8.3	25.7	17.7	1.1
canned FRAY BENTOS	175	4.8	13.9	11.1	n/a
frozen ROSS	295	6.6	24.6	19.4	1
canned TYNE BRAND	161	8.7	13.3	8.1	n/a
Pork Pie, individual	363	10.8	23.7	25.7	0.9
Pork & Egg Pie	343	15.4	16.2	24.1	2.5
Quiche Lorraine, recipe	358	13.7	19.6	25.5	0.7
Quiche					
cheese & egg, recipe	315	12.4	17.1	22.3	0.6
three cheese & spring onion	281	9.8	18.6	18.6	0.7
Sausage Rolls					
flaky pastry	383	9.9	25.4	27.6	1
short pastry ROSS	289	11.1	19.4	19.3	0.8
vegetarian LINDA MCCARTNEY FOODS	260	10.9	23.1	14.5	1.6
Shepherd's Pie, frozen, per pack BIRDS EYE	101	4.1	11	4.5	0.8
Steak Pie, individual	298	9	25	18	1.1
Steak & Ale Pie, canned FRAY BENTOS	164	7.6	13	9.1	n/a

Calorie Counter

All amounts per 100g/100ml unless otherwise stated	Cal kcal	Pro g	Carb g	Fat g	Fibre g
Steak & Kidney Deep Pie, frozen, family Ross	**270**	7.2	23.9	16.7	1
Steak & Kidney Pie					
canned Fray Bentos	**163**	8.2	12.9	8.8	n/a
individual	**323**	9.1	25.6	21.2	0.9
frozen, individual Ross	**232**	8.5	22.4	12.4	0.9
pastry top only	**286**	15.2	15.9	18.4	0.6
Steak & Mushroom Pie, canned Fray Bentos	**157**	7.5	12.9	8.3	n/a
Vegetable Pie, frozen Ross	**246**	5.1	27.5	13.9	2.5
Yorkshire Pudding	**210**	6.7	24.6	10.1	0.9

READY MEALS
(FROZEN, TINNED OR FRESH)

All amounts per 100g/100ml unless otherwise stated	Cal kcal	Pro g	Carb g	Fat g	Fibre g
TRADITIONAL					
Beef & Kidney TYNE BRAND	97	10.5	2	5.2	n/a
Beef Casserole TYNE BRAND	93	6.2	6.5	4.7	n/a
Beef Stew					
recipe	107	12	4.7	4.6	0.7
TYNE BRAND	83	4.8	7.2	3.8	n/a
Beef Stew, Spicy TYNE BRAND	106	7.5	8.1	5.1	n/a
Beef Stew & Dumpling, each BIRDS EYE	355	23	39	12	n/a
Braised Beef TYNE BRAND	102	10.9	3.2	5.1	n/a
Bubble & Squeak ROSS	111	1.7	13.8	6	1.3
Cheese & Potato Bake TYNE BRAND	93	3.4	10.6	4.1	n/a
Cheesey Pasta, made up KRAFT	235	6.1	26.5	11.5	1.1
Chicken Casserole TYNE BRAND	100	4.2	7.1	6.3	n/a
Chicken Hotpot HEINZ WEIGHT WATCHERS	89	5	11.4	2.6	0.9
Chicken Kiev, frozen	289	13	12	21	1.5
low fat	207	13	14	11	0.7

Calorie Counter

All amounts per 100g/100ml unless otherwise stated	Cal kcal	Pro g	Carb g	Fat g	Fibre g
Chicken in Peppercorn Sauce HEINZ WEIGHT WATCHERS	84	4.8	11.9	1.8	0.7
Chicken Ravioli in a Spicy Indian Sauce HEINZ	81	2.8	13.7	1.6	0.5
Chicken Stew TYNE BRAND	74	2.8	5.9	4.4	n/a
Chicken Stew & Dumplings, each BIRDS EYE	370	20	32	18	n/a
Chicken Supreme with Rice HEINZ WEIGHT WATCHERS	85	5.5	11.7	1.7	0.5
each BIRDS EYE	485	23	75	10.5	n/a
Chunky Chicken Casserole & Dumplings, canned SHIPPAMS	126	8.5	9	6.2	n/a
Chunky Chicken Supreme, canned SHIPPAMS	140	12.5	3.5	8.4	n/a
Chunky Hot Chicken Curry, canned SHIPPAMS	112	8.7	7.3	5.3	n/a
Chunky Sweet & Sour Chicken, canned SHIPPAMS	108	8.6	12.2	2.8	n/a
Creamy Mustard Chicken with Rice, each BIRDS EYE	530	23	64	20	n/a
Faggots	268	11.1	15.3	18.5	N

Ready Meals (Frozen, Tinned or Fresh)

All amounts per 100g/100ml unless otherwise stated	Cal kcal	Pro g	Carb g	Fat g	Fibre g
Faggots in West Country Sauce, **Mr Brain's** HIBERNIA BRANDS	131	7.2	11.7	6.2	0.3
Glazed Chicken FINDUS LEAN CUISINE	90	6	12.5	1.5	0.8
Glazed Chicken Dinner, 97% fat free, each BIRDS EYE	340	30	32	10	n/a
Irish Stew					
recipe	107	7.7	8.6	4.9	1
TYNE BRAND	89	4.3	9.4	3.8	n/a
Lancashire Hotpot					
recipe	119	7.4	7.4	6.9	0.9
TYNE BRAND	77	4.5	7.2	3.3	n/a
Macaroni Cheese					
recipe	162	6.7	12.2	9.9	0.5
FINDUS RED BOX	160	7	13.9	8.5	0.7
HEINZ	95	3.4	9.8	4.7	0.3
Macaroni with Chicken & Bacon FINDUS	145	5.5	14.2	7.4	0.7
Macaroni with Ham & Leek FINDUS	140	4.5	15.5	6.6	0.8
Mince & Vegetables, Farmhouse TYNE BRAND	74	5.9	6.7	2.6	n/a
Minced Beef & Onion TYNE BRAND	115	9.5	7	5.5	n/a
Pork Sausage Casserole, as sold FINDUS RED BOX	80	2.5	7.7	4.5	1.3

Calorie Counter

All amounts per 100g/100ml unless otherwise stated	Cal kcal	Pro g	Carb g	Fat g	Fibre g
Roast Beef Dinner, each BIRDS EYE	370	29	39	11	n/a
Roast Chicken Dinner, each BIRDS EYE	500	37	39	22	n/a
Roast Lamb Dinner, each BIRDS EYE	350	23	40	11	n/a
Roast Pork Dinner, each BIRDS EYE	340	27	39	8.2	n/a
Roast Turkey Dinner, each BIRDS EYE	330	24	34	11	n/a
Savoury Mince TYNE BRAND	86	9.8	13.4	7.3	0.6
Shepherd's Pie BIRDS EYE	220	11	25	8.5	n/a
Stewed Steak with Gravy	176	14.8	1	1.25	Tr
Vegetable Bake ROSS	80	2.4	13	2.9	1.9
Vegetable Hotpot HEINZ WEIGHT WATCHERS	68	2.6	9.9	1.9	1.5

CHINESE

	Cal kcal	Pro g	Carb g	Fat g	Fibre g
Beef in Black Bean Sauce Readymeal UNCLE BEN'S	85	6.3	8.1	3	n/a
Chicken Sweet & Sour Readymeal UNCLE BEN'S	103	6.1	17.5	0.9	n/a

Ready Meals (Frozen, Tinned or Fresh)

All amounts per 100g/100ml unless otherwise stated	Cal kcal	Pro g	Carb g	Fat g	Fibre g
Chinese Chicken & Prawn Foo Yeung Stir Fry ROSS	77	5.5	12.3	1.4	1.8
Chinese Chicken Stir Fry ROSS	57	5.7	9.6	0.8	2.8
Chinese Prawns Stir Fry ROSS	60	3.3	12.4	0.4	1.5
Chinese Sizzling Prawns Stir Fry ROSS	39	3.3	8.2	0.3	2.5
Chinese Spring Rolls ROSS	114	4	22.5	1.6	1.7
Chinese Sweet & Sour Pork Stir Fry ROSS	63	4.1	12	0.8	2.1
Chow Mein, as sold VESTA	318	14.8	54	4.7	7.7
Lemon & Ginger Sauce & Vegetables Stir Fry UNCLE BEN'S	61	0.6	13	0.6	n/a
Lemon Chicken FINDUS LEAN CUISINE	120	5.5	19.7	1.7	0.8
Sweet & Sour Sauce & Vegetable Stir Fry UNCLE BEN'S	94	0.4	23.2	Tr	n/a
Sweet Chilli Chicken, each BIRDS EYE	440	28	34	21	n/a

247

Calorie Counter

All amounts per 100g/100ml unless otherwise stated	Cal kcal	Pro g	Carb g	Fat g	Fibre g
ITALIAN					
Bacon & Mushroom Filled Pasta FINDUS	90	3	12.5	2.5	1.1
Bolognese Shells Italiana HEINZ WEIGHT WATCHERS	71	5.2	9.6	1.3	0.8
Bolognese, mince TYNE BRAND	116	10.2	4.7	6.3	n/a
Cannelloni Bolognese DOLMIO	149	6.1	11.8	8.3	n/a
Cannelloni Cheese & Spinach Ready Meal DOLMIO	125	4.3	8.7	8.1	n/a
Chicken & Broccoli Pasta Bake HEINZ WEIGHT WATCHERS	92	6.4	11	2.5	0.7
Chicken Risotto, each BIRDS EYE	860	43	70	45	n/a
Deep Pasta Bake, chicken & tomato FINDUS	95	4.5	13	3	1.3
Lasagne					
recipe	119	9.8	14.6	10.8	0.8
beef HEINZ WEIGHT WATCHERS	98	5.9	13.5	2.3	0.7
Bolognese Ready Meal DOLMIO	132	7	11.7	6.3	n/a
cheese, onion & tomato, each BIRDS EYE	375	16	46	14	n/a
chicken & bacon FINDUS RED BOX	145	6.4	11.2	8.3	0.4
each BIRDS EYE	440	24	46	18	n/a
frozen, cooked	102	5	12.8	3.8	N

Ready Meals (Frozen, Tinned or Fresh)

All amounts per 100g/100ml unless otherwise stated	Cal kcal	Pro g	Carb g	Fat g	Fibre g
frozen, cooked FINDUS PASTA CHOICE	120	6.3	10.7	5.7	0.7
frozen, cooked FINDUS RED BOX	115	6.4	10.4	5.3	0.7
spicy FINDUS RED BOX	85	4.9	11.2	2.3	0.7
vegetable ROSS	110	5.3	12.6	4.7	0.9
vegetable HEINZ WEIGHT WATCHERS	78	3.2	12.9	1.5	1
Vegetable Ready Meal DOLMIO	101	3	11.6	4.7	n/a
Mushroom & Cheese Filled Pasta, as sold FINDUS	100	3	13.7	3.9	0.5
Pasta Bolognese, 97% fat free, each BIRDS EYE	375	18	54	9.6	n/a
Pasta Bows & Spicy Pepperoni, as sold FINDUS	115	3.8	12.1	5.6	0.7
Ravioli Bianche, as sold DOLMIO	200	9.6	29.7	4.7	n/a
Ravioli, Italiana, vegetable with tomato sauce, HEINZ WEIGHT WATCHERS	69	1.7	10.9	2.1	0.5
Ricotta and Spinach Filled Pasta, as sold FINDUS	115	3.4	14.5	4.7	0.5
Risotto	224	3	34.4	9.3	0.4
beef, as sold VESTA	346	15.3	57.8	5.9	5.6
Spaghetti Bolognese, each BIRDS EYE	405	17	48	16	n/a

Calorie Counter

All amounts per 100g/100ml unless otherwise stated	Cal kcal	Pro g	Carb g	Fat g	Fibre g
Spaghetti Napoli FINDUS RED BOX	75	2.8	13.3	1.4	1.4
Tagliatelle					
Bianche, as sold DOLMIO	291	10.9	56.7	2.3	n/a
Carbonara HEINZ WEIGHT WATCHERS	88	5.3	12.2	2	0.4
Garlic & Herbs, as sold DOLMIO	294	11.7	51.9	4.4	n/a
chicken Tuscany & pesto, as sold FINDUS LEAN CUISINE	120	6.8	15.1	3.4	0.9
Tortellini					
Italiana HEINZ WEIGHT WATCHERS	62	2	9.4	1.8	0.6
spicy Italiana HEINZ WEIGHT WATCHERS	60	2.8	9.9	1	0.9
5 cheese, as sold DOLMIO	334	14.7	44.6	10.7	n/a
Italian ham, as sold DOLMIO	297	15.3	41.1	7.9	n/a
mushroom & garlic, as sold DOLMIO	275	10.3	45.2	5.8	n/a
vegetables, cheese, garlic & herbs, as sold DOLMIO	329	13.4	46.2	10.1	n/a

INDIAN

	Cal kcal	Pro g	Carb g	Fat g	Fibre g
Beef Curry					
FINDUS RED BOX	140	5.4	18.3	4.9	1
TYNE BRAND	98	5.5	9.2	4.3	n/a
as sold VESTA	359	13.4	60.7	7	5.6

Ready Meals (Frozen, Tinned or Fresh)

All amounts per 100g/100ml unless otherwise stated	Cal kcal	Pro g	Carb g	Fat g	Fibre g
Beef Curry with Rice, each					
BIRDS EYE	525	26	80	11	n/a
Chicken Biryani, tandoori, each					
BIRDS EYE	550	37	64	16	n/a
Chicken Curry					
FINDUS RED BOX	125	6	18.1	3.1	0.8
TYNE BRAND	149	4.5	11	9.7	n/a
Chicken Curry, Creamy COLMAN'S	371	11	49	14	n/a
Chicken Curry with Rice					
each BIRDS EYE	475	22	78	8.4	n/a
HEINZ WEIGHT WATCHERS	98	5	15.6	1.7	0.5
Chicken Dhansak & Indian Potatoes FINDUS LEAN CUISINE	85	5.5	9.9	2.5	1.2
Chicken Jalfrezi with Rice, each					
BIRDS EYE	470	23	70	11	n/a
Chicken Korma					
Readymeal UNCLE BEN'S	123	9.1	6.3	6.8	n/a
with Rice HEINZ WEIGHT WATCHERS	97	5.8	13.5	2.1	0.2
with Rice, 97% fat free, each BIRDS EYE	465	24	75	7.4	n/a
Chicken Tikka Balti					
HEINZ WEIGHT WATCHERS	71	4.2	10	1.6	0.7

Calorie Counter

All amounts per 100g/100ml unless otherwise stated	Cal kcal	Pro g	Carb g	Fat g	Fibre g
Chicken Tikka Masala Dinner, 97% fat free, each BIRDS EYE	405	32	50	8.5	n/a
Chicken Tikka with Pilau Rice, each BIRDS EYE	515	22	75	14	n/a
Curried Beef & Vegetables TYNE BRAND	87	3.7	11	3.4	n/a
Curried Mince & Vegetables TYNE BRAND	100	5.7	9.6	4.3	n/a
Indian Chicken Stir Fry Meal ROSS	74	5.8	15.2	0.6	3.7
Lamb Curry TYNE BRAND	99	6.1	7.2	5.1	n/a
Prawn Curry					
ROSS	117	5	21.5	1.4	0.4
as sold FINDUS RED BOX	115	4.4	18.3	2.4	0.8
Prawn Curry with Rice, each BIRDS EYE	440	13	78	8.4	n/a
Samosas					
meat	593	5.1	17.9	56.1	1.2
vegetable	472	3.1	22.3	41.8	1.8
Southern Indian Spiced Chicken, each BIRDS EYE	840	44	62	46	n/a
Vegetable Curry TYNE BRAND	57	2	9.6	1.4	n/a

Ready Meals (Frozen, Tinned or Fresh)

All amounts per 100g/100ml unless otherwise stated	Cal kcal	Pro g	Carb g	Fat g	Fibre g
MEXICAN					
Burrito Dinner Kit OLD EL PASO	294	8	55	4.8	n/a
Chicken Mexicana with Rice HEINZ WEIGHT WATCHERS	97	5.8	13.5	2.1	0.2
Chili Con Carne Kit OLD EL PASO	219	6.7	46.4	0.7	n/a
Chilli Con Carne					
OLD EL PASO	118	9.3	8.3	5.3	n/a
TYNE BRAND	106	9.4	6.6	4.7	n/a
Chilli Con Carne with Rice, each BIRDS EYE	325	12	53	7	n/a
Chilli with Beans and Vegetables TYNE BRAND	111	5.9	12.5	4.2	n/a
Enchilada Dinner Kit OLD EL PASO	194	5	30	6	n/a
Fajita Dinner Kit OLD EL PASO	246	7	41	6	n/a
Mexican Chilli with Deep Fried Potato Wedges HEINZ WEIGHT WATCHERS	84	5.1	10.3	2.5	1.7
Spicy Mexican Chicken BIRDS EYE	247	14.6	16.5	13.6	0.6
Taco Dinner Kit OLD EL PASO	286	48	46.6	13.4	n/a

Calorie Counter

All amounts per 100g/100ml unless otherwise stated	Cal kcal	Pro g	Carb g	Fat g	Fibre g
WORLD					
Caribbean Chicken Stir Fry ROSS	88	5.9	13.8	1.7	1.5
Chicken à l'Orange FINDUS LEAN CUISINE	120	6	19.8	1.8	0.5
Japanese Beef Oriental Stir Fry ROSS	62	5.4	9.4	1	1.5
Moussaka	184	9.1	7	13.6	0.9
lamb HEINZ WEIGHT WATCHERS	79	3.6	10.9	2.3	0.8
Paella					
as sold VESTA	349	10.9	69.6	2.9	3
each BIRDS EYE	750	39	81	30	n/a
fast cook ROSS	93	5.6	15.6	1.4	0.9
Thai Chicken Rice, each BIRDS EYE	665	35	66	29	n/a
Thai Green Chicken Curry, each BIRDS EYE	500	21	68	20	n/a
Thai Red Chicken Curry with Rice, 97% fat free, each BIRDS EYE	425	21	70	7	n/a
Vegetable Stroganoff HEINZ WEIGHT WATCHERS	85	2.2	15	1.9	0.6

RICE AND NOODLES

All amounts per 100g/100ml unless otherwise stated	Cal kcal	Pro g	Carb g	Fat g	Fibre g
PLAIN RICE COOKED					
White Rice					
boiled	**138**	2.6	30.9	1.3	0.1
Easy Cook, boiled	**138**	2.6	30.9	1.3	0.1
Brown Rice, boiled	**141**	2.6	32.1	1.1	0.8
PRE-COOKED RICE					
Chinese Special Rice, frozen ROSS	**99**	4.1	21.1	0.3	1
Chinese Style Rice, Stir Fry UNCLE BEN'S	**143**	2.7	26.3	3	n/a
Egg Fried Rice, recipe	**208**	4.2	25.7	10.6	0.4
Fried White Rice, recipe	**144**	2.5	25.9	4.1	0.5
Golden Vegetable Rice, frozen BIRDS EYE	**112**	3.5	23.7	0.4	1.4
Indian Special Rice, frozen ROSS	**118**	2.8	26.1	0.8	1.3
Long Grain Rice UNCLE BEN'S					
3 minute	**127**	2.7	27.3	0.8	n/a
frozen	**140**	3	30.3	0.7	n/a
Original Vegetable Rice, frozen BIRDS EYE	**105**	4	20.8	0.6	1.1
Pilau Rice, frozen UNCLE BEN'S	**148**	3.4	30.5	1.4	n/a

Calorie Counter

All amounts per 100g/100ml unless otherwise stated	Cal kcal	Pro g	Carb g	Fat g	Fibre g
Savoury Rice, cooked	**142**	2.9	26.3	3.5	1.4
Simply Basmati Rice SHARWOOD	**152**	2.7	27.6	3.4	0.5
Simply Egg Fried SHARWOOD	**154**	3.1	25.2	4.5	0.5
Wholegrain Rice UNCLE BEN'S					
3 minute	**164**	3.9	33.4	1.6	n/a
frozen	**147**	3.7	30.9	1.8	n/a

DRY RICE

Arborio Risotto Rice	**350**	7.4	77.5	1.1	1.1
Arrosito Seasoned Rice OLD EL PASO	**357**	9	78	1	n/a
Basmati Rice					
UNCLE BEN'S	**343**	9	75.5	0.6	n/a
WHITWORTHS	**339**	7.4	79.8	0.5	0.5
Beef Savoury Rice BATCHELORS	**358**	9.4	74.9	2.3	3.2
Chinese Rices of the World BATCHELORS	**354**	9.9	73.1	2.4	2.8
Chicken Savoury Rice BATCHELORS	**357**	9.9	74.5	2.2	2.9
Coriander & Herbs Delicately Flavoured Rice BATCHELORS	**369**	7.9	79.6	3.5	5

All amounts per 100g/100ml unless otherwise stated	Cal kcal	Pro g	Carb g	Fat g	Fibre g
Curry Savoury Rice BATCHELORS	355	8.4	76	1.9	1.8
Garlic & Butter Delicately Flavoured Rice BATCHELORS	350	8	79.8	2.8	5
Golden Savoury Rice BATCHELORS	364	10.1	74.7	2.8	2.4
Long Grain Rice					
UNCLE BEN'S	342	7.8	75.4	1	n/a
WHITWORTHS	361	6.5	86.8	1	0.5
Long Grain & Wild Rice UNCLE BEN'S	347	11.2	92.8	1.2	n/a
Mushroom Savoury Rice BATCHELORS	360	10.9	74.3	2.1	2.5
Pilau Delicately Flavoured Rice BATCHELORS	369	7.9	79.6	3.5	5
Pilau Rice SHARWOOD	354	9	76.8	1.2	1.8
Pudding Rice	355	6.3	80.5	0.9	0.5
Risotto Rice WHITWORTHS	324	7	77.8	0.6	0.2
Short Grain Rice WHITWORTHS	361	6.5	86.8	1	2.4
Sweet & Sour Rices of the World BATCHELORS	359	9.4	75.6	2.1	3.1

Calorie Counter

All amounts per 100g/100ml unless otherwise stated	Cal kcal	Pro g	Carb g	Fat g	Fibre g
Tandoori Rices of the World BATCHELORS	358	10.3	73.5	2.5	3
Tomato & Herb Delicately Flavoured Rice BATCHELORS	387	7.8	79.4	4.2	5
Wholegrain Rice UNCLE BEN'S	340	8.9	70.8	2.4	n/a

NOODLES, COOKED

Egg Noodles, boiled	62	2.2	13	0.5	0.6

DRY NOODLES

BBQ Chicken Sauce & Sweet Oriental Noodles Mix COLMAN'S	358	3.2	85	0.5	2.3
Oriental Beef Sauce & Sweet Red Pepper Noodle Mix COLMAN'S	317	4.2	73.2	0.7	5.1
Stir Fry Noodles SHARWOOD	358	7.3	79.6	1.2	3.7
Thai Rice Noodles SHARWOOD	361	6.5	86.8	1	2.4
Thread Noodles AMOY	169	6	24.5	5.2	n/a
Anchovy Paste SHIPPAMS	148	19.2	4.1	6.1	n/a
Bacon & Tomato Filler PRIMULA	220	7.7	2.3	20	1.3
Beany Cheez Xtreme Sqeez PRIMULA	291	14	8.7	22.2	N

SAVOURY SPREADS AND PASTES

All amounts per 100g/100ml unless otherwise stated	Cal kcal	Pro g	Carb g	Fat g	Fibre g
Beef Spread SHIPPAMS	177	15.5	2.2	11.8	n/a
Bloater Paste SHIPPAMS	174	17.7	3.1	10.1	n/a
Cheese Spread	267	11.3	4.4	22.8	0
KERRYGOLD	213	n/a	8.5	15	0
reduced fat	175	15	7.9	9.5	0
with Herbs, ultra plus, very low fat PRIMULA	137	16	7	5	n/a

See also: **DAIRY PRODUCTS (Cheese spreads and processed cheese)**

Chicken & Mayonnaise-style Dressing Sandwich Filler HEINZ	191	6.3	7.7	15	0.3
Chicken Spread SHIPPAMS	164	15.5	1.8	10.5	n/a
Chilli Bean Filler PRIMULA	203	6.4	12	15	2.7
Crab Spread SHIPPAMS	138	14.1	6	6.4	n/a
Curried Chicken Sandwich Filler HEINZ	192	6.2	9.6	14.2	0.7
Fish Paste	169	15.3	3.7	10.4	0.2
Ham Sandwich Filler HEINZ	198	5.4	11	14.7	0.5
Hot Dog Spread PRIMULA	222	13.5	6	16	n/a
Marmite Yeast Extract MARMITE	234	43	14.8	0.4	2.6

Calorie Counter

All amounts per 100g/100ml unless otherwise stated	Cal kcal	Pro g	Carb g	Fat g	Fibre g
Meat Paste	**173**	15.2	3	11.2	0.1
Pizza Cheese Xtreme Sqeez PRIMULA	**298**	13.9	8.2	23.3	n/a
Prawn & Salad Vegetables Sandwich Filler HEINZ	**129**	4.4	9.5	8.1	0.6
Salmon Spread SHIPPAMS	**172**	14.8	4.9	10.4	n/a
Sandwich Spread HEINZ	**221**	1.3	25.3	12.7	0.8
cucumber	**185**	1.3	18.9	11.5	0.5
Savoury Spread PRIMULA	**261**	17	1	21	n/a
Spicy Chicken Filler PRIMULA	**242**	9	6	20.3	1
Tangy Tomato Spread PRIMULA	**259**	15.2	2.2	21	n/a
Toast Topper HEINZ					
chicken & mushroom	**56**	5.1	5.7	1.4	0.2
ham & cheese	**96**	7.4	7.3	4.1	0.1
mushroom & bacon	**94**	6.9	6.6	4.4	0.3
Tuna & Sweetcorn Filler PRIMULA	**186**	10.7	4.1	14.1	1.2
Tuna Sandwich Filler HEINZ	**192**	6.3	11.7	13.4	0.3
Vegemite KRAFT	**173**	23.5	19.7	0	0

SNACK MEALS

All amounts per 100g/100ml unless otherwise stated	Cal kcal	Pro g	Carb g	Fat g	Fibre g
Bacon Supernoodles BATCHELORS	457	9.8	60.9	19.7	3.2
Balti Pot Curry POT NOODLE COMPANY	89	3.1	17.8	0.5	0.5
Barbecue Beef Supernoodles BATCHELORS	451	9.4	60.6	19.7	3.2
Barbecue Pot Noodle POT NOODLE COMPANY	433	10.4	61.5	16.2	3
Beef & Tomato Pot Noodle POT NOODLE COMPANY	424	10.7	60.3	15.5	3.7
Bolognese Pot Pasta POT NOODLE COMPANY	349	17.7	59.8	4.4	n/a
Bolonese Micropasta, as prepared KNORR	98	3.8	19.4	0.6	1
Bombay Potato Tastebreaks Potato Snack, as prepared KNORR	75	3.3	12.4	1.3	0.9
Burger Fun Pot Noodle POT NOODLE COMPANY	420	12.3	59.4	14.9	3.3
Carbonara Tastebreaks Pasta Snacks, as prepared KNORR	116	3.2	15.5	4.6	0.8
Chargrilled Chicken Salad Sandwich HEINZ WEIGHT WATCHERS	153	9.4	17.7	4.9	2.1

Calorie Counter

All amounts per 100g/100ml unless otherwise stated	Cal kcal	Pro g	Carb g	Fat g	Fibre g
Cheese & Ham Tastebreaks Potato Snack, as prepared KNORR	90	3.8	12.4	2.8	0.7
Cheese & Pepperoni New Snack Stop CROSSE & BLACKWELL	100	2.9	13.3	4.1	0.4
Chicken & Broccoli Pasta Snackpot, as sold FINDUS LEAN CUISINE	100	7	14.8	1.3	0.9
Chicken & Mushroom Fun Pot POT NOODLE COMPANY	430	13.7	59.5	15.3	3.7
Chicken & Mushroom Pot Noodle POT NOODLE COMPANY	437	12.1	60.9	16.1	3.1
Chicken & Prawn Creole Snackpot, as sold FINDUS LEAN CUISINE	100	5.2	14.9	1.9	0.8
Chicken & Sweetcorn New Snack Stop CROSSE & BLACKWELL	100	2.7	13.8	3.9	0.5
Chicken & Sweetcorn Pot Rice POT NOODLE COMPANY	357	13.1	65.8	4.6	4
Chicken Curry Pot Rice POT NOODLE COMPANY	342	11	67.2	2.3	3.3
Chicken Micropasta, as prepared KNORR	101	3.7	19.7	0.8	1

All amounts per 100g/100ml unless otherwise stated	Cal kcal	Pro g	Carb g	Fat g	Fibre g
Chicken Supernoodles BATCHELORS	449	8.7	60.3	19.2	2.5
Chicken Tikka Sandwich HEINZ WEIGHT WATCHERS	177	13.1	21.4	4.4	1.5
Chow Mein Pot Noodle POT NOODLE COMPANY	433	11.6	60.5	16	2.7
Chow Mein Supernoodles BATCHELORS	458	9.2	60.5	19.8	2.9
Creamy Korma Tastebreaks Indian Snack, as prepared KNORR	104	2.3	17.1	2.9	0.7
Creamy Mushroom Tastebreaks Pasta Snack, as prepared KNORR	119	3	16.5	4.5	0.9
Creamy Vegetable Tastebreaks Pasta Snacks, as prepared KNORR	120	3.1	16.8	4.4	0.9
Dairylea Lunchables KRAFT					
chicken, per pack	325	18.5	19.5	18	0.8
double cheese, per pack	405	21.5	19.5	26	0.8
ham, per pack	320	17	20	18	0.8
hotdog	270	12.5	16.5	17	0.5
turkey, per pack	315	17.5	20	17.5	0.8
Egg Salad Sandwich with Salad Cream HEINZ WEIGHT WATCHERS	155	6.9	21	4.8	0.9

Calorie Counter

All amounts per 100g/100ml unless otherwise stated	Cal kcal	Pro g	Carb g	Fat g	Fibre g
Ham & Cheese Pasta New Snack Stop CROSSE & BLACKWELL	115	4	15.5	4	0.1
Hot Chicken Curry Pot Noodle POT NOODLE COMPANY	440	10.1	63.6	16.1	2.7
Korma Pot Curry POT NOODLE COMPANY	91	2.9	17.4	1	0.4
Micro Noodles, as prepared KNORR					
barbecue beef flavour	176	3.4	22.1	8.2	0.6
chicken flavour	178	3.6	21.6	8.4	1
chow mein flavour	176	3.5	21.9	8.2	0.7
mild curry flavour	179	3.3	22.2	8.5	0.8
Mild Curry Supernoodles BATCHELORS	457	9.5	60.6	19.7	3
Mushroom Supernoodles BATCHELORS	454	9.3	60.5	19.7	3
Nice 'n' Cheesy Pot Pasta POT NOODLE COMPANY	379	10.3	67.5	7.5	0.3
Nice 'n' Spicy Pot Noodle POT NOODLE COMPANY	437	9.7	61.5	16.9	2.7
Prawn Cocktail Sandwich HEINZ WEIGHT WATCHERS	145	8.9	16.6	4.8	2.5
Roast Onion & Potato New Snack Stop CROSSE & BLACKWELL	100	1.7	14.4	3.7	0.6

All amounts per 100g/100ml unless otherwise stated	Cal kcal	Pro g	Carb g	Fat g	Fibre g
Roast Parsnip & Potato New Snack Stop CROSSE & BLACKWELL	95	1.7	13.6	3.6	1.1
Saucy BBQ Pasta New Snack Stop CROSSE & BLACKWELL	95	2.6	17.5	0.8	0.2
Sausage & Tomato Pot Noodle POT NOODLE COMPANY	437	10	63.1	16	2.7
Singapore Noodles Snackpot, as sold FINDUS LEAN CUISINE	90	2.7	15.3	1.8	1.1
Soft Cheese & Roasted Peppers Sandwich, low fat HEINZ WEIGHT WATCHERS	181	9.7	27	3.9	1.5
Spanish Paella Snackpot, as sold FINDUS LEAN CUISINE	115	4.8	17	3.2	0.8
Spicy Balti Curry Supernoodles BATCHELORS	457	8.3	59.4	20.7	3.1
Spicy Curry Pot Noodle POT NOODLE COMPANY	426	9.8	61.5	15.6	3
Spicy Tex-Mex Supernoodles BATCHELORS	453	8.1	59.1	20.5	2.8
Spicy Thai Curry Supernoodles BATCHELORS	459	8.5	59.8	20.6	2.8
Spicy Tomato Pasta New Snack Stop CROSSE & BLACKWELL	87	2.4	15.9	1.5	0.2

Calorie Counter

All amounts per 100g/100ml unless otherwise stated	Cal kcal	Pro g	Carb g	Fat g	Fibre g
Spicy Tomato Pot Pasta POT NOODLE COMPANY	331	7.6	70.3	2.1	1
Spicy Vindaloo Supernoodles BATCHELORS	443	7	64.9	17.3	1.9
Sweet & Sour Pot Noodle POT NOODLE COMPANY	437	9.4	63.2	16.2	2.7
Sweet & Sour Supernoodles BATCHELORS	455	8.8	60.8	19.7	3.1
Take Out Curry Pasta New Snack Stop CROSSE & BLACKWELL	100	2.7	16.9	2.1	0.5
Tikka Masala Pot Curry POT NOODLE COMPANY	82	3.1	17.5	0.8	0.3
Tikka Masala Tastebreaks Indian Snack, as prepared KNORR	100	2.4	17.3	2.3	1
Tomato & Ham Pasta New Snack Stop CROSSE & BLACKWELL	100	3.1	16.8	2.1	0.2
Tomato & Herb New Snack Stop CROSSE & BLACKWELL	85	2.6	16.1	1.1	0.5
Tomato & Mozzarella Tastebreaks Pasta Snacks, as prepared KNORR	110	3.6	16.3	3.3	1.4
Tuna Salad Sandwich HEINZ WEIGHT WATCHERS	137	10.5	13.9	4.4	2.4

SOUP

All amounts per 100g/100ml unless otherwise stated	Cal kcal	Pro g	Carb g	Fat g	Fibre g
American Potato & Leek Soup of the World, as sold KNORR	**359**	8.1	58.3	10.4	5.7
Austrian Cream of Herb Soup of the World, as sold KNORR	**464**	9.1	42.7	28.5	2.2
Autumn Vegetable Soup					
BAXTERS	**40**	1.8	8	0.2	1.5
blended HEINZ	**57**	1.2	6.4	3	0.7
Beef Broth HEINZ BIG SOUPS	**41**	2	6.8	0.6	0.7
Beef Consomme BAXTERS	**13**	2.4	0.7	Tr	0
Beef & Tomato Cup-A-Soup, per sachet BATCHELORS	**71**	1.3	15.5	0.4	1
Beef & Vegetable Soup HEINZ BIG SOUPS	**45**	2.4	7.3	0.7	0.9
Breton Chicken & Vegetable Soups of the World, as sold KNORR	**300**	13.6	52.1	4.1	5.8
Broccoli Soup BAXTERS	**45**	1.3	5.9	1.8	0.4
Broccoli & Cauliflower, per sachet BATCHELORS					
Cup-A-Soup Thick & Creamy	**120**	1.9	17.2	4.8	0.6
Slim-A-Soup	**59**	1.1	10.3	1.5	0.4
Broccoli & Potato Soup, organic BAXTERS	**31**	1.3	5.8	0.3	0.7

Calorie Counter

All amounts per 100g/100ml unless otherwise stated	Cal kcal	Pro g	Carb g	Fat g	Fibre g
Cajun Spicy Vegetable Slim-A-Soup, per sachet BATCHELORS	59	1.6	10.3	1.3	1.1
Carrot & Butter Bean Soup BAXTERS	55	1.6	7.9	1.9	1.7
Carrot & Coriander Soup					
BAXTERS	38	0.8	5.5	1.4	0.8
blended HEINZ	52	0.7	6.2	2.7	0.6
as sold KNORR	394	6.9	50.1	18.2	6.6
Carrot & Lentil Soup HEINZ WEIGHT WATCHERS	31	1.4	6	0.1	0.8
Carrot with Parsnip and Nutmeg Soup, organic BAXTERS	27	0.7	5.7	0.2	1
Carrot, Onion & Chick Pea Soup BAXTERS	34	1.7	7.1	0.1	1.5
Carrot, Potato & Coriander Soup HEINZ WEIGHT WATCHERS	24	0.5	5.4	0.1	0.6
Cheese & Broccoli Cup-A-Soup Extra, per sachet BATCHELORS	160	5.2	23.5	5	1.9
Chicken Broth BAXTERS	34	1.2	5.3	0.9	0.6

All amounts per 100g/100ml unless otherwise stated	Cal kcal	Pro g	Carb g	Fat g	Fibre g
Chicken Soup					
Cup-A-Soup, per sachet					
BATCHELORS	98	1.5	12.4	4.7	0.6
HEINZ WEIGHT WATCHERS	30	1.2	4.1	1	0
99% fat-free CAMPBELL'S	34	1.6	5	0.9	n/a
Chicken & Ham Soup HEINZ					
BIG SOUPS	46	2.3	6.9	1	0.7
Chicken & Leek Cup-A-Soup,					
per sachet BATCHELORS	77	1.2	14.1	1.8	0.7
Chicken & Mushroom, per sachet					
BATCHELORS					
Cup-A-Soup Extra	132	3.7	20.2	4	1.3
Slim-A-Soup	59	1.1	8.5	2.2	0.9
Chicken & Sweetcorn Soup					
BAXTERS	39	1.6	6.2	0.9	0.6
Slim-A-Soup, per sachet					
BATCHELORS	59	1.2	9.2	1.9	0.3
Chicken & Tarragon Cup-A-Soup					
Thick & Creamy, per sachet					
BATCHELORS	118	2.3	16	6.4	0.7
Chicken & Vegetable Soup					
BAXTERS	31	1.3	5.6	0.5	1.6
HEINZ BIG SOUPS	47	2.4	7.3	1	0.9

Calorie Counter

All amounts per 100g/100ml unless otherwise stated	Cal kcal	Pro g	Carb g	Fat g	Fibre g
Chicken & White Wine Soup					
CAMPBELL'S	49	1	4	3.3	n/a
Chicken Noodle Soup					
Cup-A-Soup, per sachet					
BATCHELORS	91	3.6	15.1	1.9	0.8
HEINZ	27	1.1	4.9	0.3	0.2
HEINZ WEIGHT WATCHERS	16	0.7	3.1	0.1	0.2
as sold, super KNORR	325	14.3	56	4.9	1.8
Chicken, Noodle & Vegetable Slim-A-Soup, per sachet					
BATCHELORS	59	1.6	10.2	1.4	0.7
Chicken Pasta & Vegetable Soup					
HEINZ BIG SOUP	34	1.8	5.9	0.4	0.8
Chinese Chicken & Noodle Tastebreaks Soup KNORR	44	1.6	8.10	0.6	0.4
Chinese Chicken Cup-A-Soup Extra, per sachet BATCHELORS	101	3.5	19.1	1.2	2
Chinese Chicken Noodle Soups of the World, as sold KNORR	307	15.1	51.8	4.4	2.9
Chinese Tomato & Noodle Soups of the World, as sold KNORR	329	9.3	60.1	5.7	4.6
Cock-a-Leekie Soup BAXTERS	29	0.9	4	1	0.3
Consommé CAMPBELL'S	7	1.3	0.5	Tr	n/a

All amounts per 100g/100ml unless otherwise stated	Cal kcal	Pro g	Carb g	Fat g	Fibre g
Cream of Asparagus Soup					
BAXTERS	66	1.1	5.8	4.3	0.2
CAMPBELL'S	45	0.5	4.6	2.8	n/a
Cup-A-Soup, per sachet					
BATCHELORS	133	2.1	19.9	5	1.1
HEINZ	46	1.1	4.5	2.6	0.2
as sold KNORR	426	8.3	54.0	19.6	1.3
Cream of Celery Soup					
CAMPBELL'S	47	0.6	3.2	3.4	n/a
HEINZ	44	0.8	4.1	2.7	0.2
Cream of Chicken Soup					
CAMPBELL'S	48	1.1	3.5	3.6	n/a
HEINZ	52	1.3	4.4	3.2	0.1
as sold KNORR	484	16.5	33.7	31.5	0.3
Cream of Chicken & Mushroom Soup					
CAMPBELL'S	56	0.9	3.5	4.4	n/a
HEINZ	50	1.3	4.6	2.9	0.1
Cream of Chicken & Vegetable Cup-A-Soup, per sachet					
BATCHELORS	113	2.1	18	5.9	0.6
Cream of Mushroom Soup					
CAMPBELL'S	69	1.7	5.3	4.5	n/a
Cup-A-Soup, per sachet					
BATCHELORS	129	1.2	15.4	6.6	0.7
as sold KNORR	496	8.5	39	34	1.3

Calorie Counter

All amounts per 100g/100ml unless otherwise stated	Cal kcal	Pro g	Carb g	Fat g	Fibre g
Cream of Sweetcorn Soup CAMPBELL'S	51	0.6	6.2	2.7	n/a
Cream of Tomato Soup					
BAXTERS	71	1.5	10.6	2.5	0.7
CAMPBELL'S	66	0.8	8.5	3.2	n/a
HEINZ	64	0.9	7.1	3.6	0.4
as sold KNORR	435	4.3	51.3	23.6	3.3
Cream of Tomato & Red Pepper Soup CAMPBELL'S	62	0.5	7.7	3.3	n/a
Cream of Vegetable Cup-A-Soup, per sachet BATCHELORS	144	1.9	19.8	6.3	1.2
Creamy Chicken & Sweetcorn Tastebreaks Soup KNORR	87	1.7	7.6	5.5	0.3
Creamy Chicken with Vegetables Fresh Soup BAXTERS	97	1.9	5.5	7.5	0.4
Creamy Potato, Bacon & Onion Cup-A-Soup, per sachet BATCHELORS	114	2.8	20.7	2.2	1.3
Creamy Potato, Leek & Ham Cup-A-Soup, per sachet BATCHELORS	109	2.5	3.1	2.6	1.7
Creamy Potato & Leek Cup-A-Soup, per sachet BATCHELORS	133	2.3	20.9	4.4	3.2

All amounts per 100g/100ml unless otherwise stated	Cal kcal	Pro g	Carb g	Fat g	Fibre g
Creamy Potato & Leek Tastebreaks Soup KNORR	71	1.1	9.3	3.3	0.5
Crofters' Chicken & Leek Soup, as sold KNORR	459	10.3	39.3	29	1.5
Crofters' Thick Vegetable Soup, as sold KNORR	364	10.8	52.9	12.2	3.3
Cullen Skink Soup BAXTERS	89	6.1	7.7	3.7	0.3
English Broccoli & Stilton Soups of the World, as sold KNORR	509	11.7	30.3	37.9	1.6
Florida Spring Vegetable Soup, as sold KNORR	29	7.8	52.2	5.6	5.2
French Mushroom Tastebreaks Soup KNORR	60	0.9	6.3	3.4	0.2
French Onion Soup					
BAXTERS	22	0.7	4.2	0.2	0.4
as sold KNORR	296	6	62.5	2.5	6.6
Garden Pea & Mint Fresh Soup, as sold BAXTERS	62	2.3	6.1	3.2	1.5
Garden Soup, Country BAXTERS	35	0.9	6.5	0.6	0.7

Calorie Counter

All amounts per 100g/100ml unless otherwise stated	Cal kcal	Pro g	Carb g	Fat g	Fibre g
Golden Vegetable Soup					
Cup-A-Soup, per sachet					
BATCHELORS	70	1	15.3	0.5	0.9
Slim-A-Soup, per sachet					
BATCHELORS	58	1.1	9.7	1.7	1.5
as sold KNORR	394	10.4	45.4	19	3.3
Highlander's Broth BAXTERS	43	1.6	6.1	1.4	0.5
Hot & Sour Cup-A-Soup Extra, per sachet BATCHELORS	91	2.5	18.7	0.7	1.2
Italian Bean & Pasta Soup BAXTERS	38	1.9	7	0.2	1.3
Italian Minestrone Soup of the World, as sold KNORR	311	11.5	57.1	4.1	7.8
Italian Tomato & Basil Tastebreaks Soup KNORR	67	1.6	11.5	1.6	1.1
Italian Tomato with Basil Soup CAMPBELL'S	68	1	5.3	4.8	n/a
Italian Tomato with Penne Pasta Soup BAXTERS	36	1.2	7.3	0.2	1
Leek & Bacon Soup, blended HEINZ	54	1.9	5	2.9	0.5
Leek & Potato Slim-A-Soup, per sachet BATCHELORS	57	0.9	10.2	1.4	0.5

All amounts per 100g/100ml unless otherwise stated	Cal kcal	Pro g	Carb g	Fat g	Fibre g
Lentil Soup					
CAMPBELL'S	27	1.3	4.3	0.6	n/a
HEINZ	39	2.3	7.1	0.2	1
Lentil & Bacon Soup BAXTERS	60	2.7	7.9	1.9	0.8
Lentil & Vegetable Soup BAXTERS	36	1.9	6.8	0.1	1.5
Lobster Bisque BAXTERS	51	3.4	4.7	2.1	0.2
Malaysian Chicken & Sweetcorn Soups of the World, as sold KNORR	370	10.6	56.3	11.4	1.8
Mediterranean Tomato Soup					
BAXTERS	33	1	6.9	0.2	0.7
CAMPBELL'S	27	0.4	5.9	0.2	n/a
Slim-A-Soup, per sachet					
BATCHELORS	58	1.1	9.6	1.7	0.7
Mediterranean Tomato & Courgette Soup, blended HEINZ	40	1	5.1	1.8	0.6
Mediterranean Tomato & Vegetable Soup HEINZ WEIGHT WATCHERS	18	0.6	3.3	0.3	0.4
Minestrone Soup					
BAXTERS	34	1.3	6	0.6	0.8
Chunky Fresh BAXTERS	42	1.7	7	0.8	1.2
Cup-A-Soup, per sachet					
BATCHELORS	100	1.9	17.9	2.3	1.1
Cup-A-Soup Extra, per sachet					
BATCHELORS	123	3.9	24.3	1.1	2.3

Calorie Counter

All amounts per 100g/100ml unless otherwise stated	Cal kcal	Pro g	Carb g	Fat g	Fibre g
Hearty CAMPBELL'S	26	0.6	5.6	0.1	n/a
HEINZ	30	1.3	4.8	0.6	0.6
HEINZ BIG SOUP	44	1.7	8.1	0.5	1
HEINZ WEIGHT WATCHERS	20	0.8	3.3	0.4	0.4
as sold KNORR	292	9.2	53.9	4.4	6.5
Slim-A-Soup, per sachet					
BATCHELORS	54	1.3	9.3	1.3	0.7
with Wholemeal Pasta BAXTERS	32	0.9	6.7	0.2	1
Miso	**203**	13.3	23.5	6.2	N
Mulligatawny Beef Curry Soup HEINZ	**60**	1.8	7.2	2.7	0.5
Mushroom Soup					
HEINZ WEIGHT WATCHERS	32	1.3	5	0.7	0.1
99% fat-free CAMPBELL'S	24	0.6	3.5	0.9	n/a
Mushroom & Cheese with Bacon & Croutons Cup-A-Soup					
BATCHELORS	131	1.7	17.1	6.2	0.3
Oxtail Soup					
CAMPBELL'S	40	1.4	5.3	1.5	n/a
canned HEINZ	41	1.9	6.7	0.8	0.3
Cup-A-Soup, per sachet					
BATCHELORS	76	1.5	13.7	1.7	1
Parsnip & Carrot Soup HEINZ WEIGHT WATCHERS	**25**	0.5	5.3	0.2	0.9

All amounts per 100g/100ml unless otherwise stated	Cal kcal	Pro g	Carb g	Fat g	Fibre g
Parsnip & Potato Soup, blended HEINZ	57	1.1	6.4	3	0.9
Pea & Ham Soup BAXTERS	58	2.9	8.1	1.6	1.2
Potato & Leek Soup BAXTERS	40	1	6.3	1.2	0.5
Provençale Vegetable Soups of the World, as sold KNORR	308	9	55.9	5.4	10.5
Red Pepper with Tomato Soup, blended HEINZ	51	0.8	5.2	2.9	0.7
Royal Game Soup BAXTERS	36	2.4	5.5	0.5	0.4
Scotch Broth					
BAXTERS	47	1.9	7.1	1.2	0.9
CAMPBELL'S	41	1.1	5.4	1.8	n/a
Scotch Vegetable Soup BAXTERS	43	1.9	7.4	0.6	1.3
Scottish Pea & Bacon Soups of the World KNORR	385	18.4	53.5	10	4
Scottish Vegetable Soup with Lentils & Beef HEINZ	52	3.4	8.2	0.7	1.2
Spicy Parsnip Soup					
BAXTERS	51	1.1	6.1	2.5	1.5
as sold KNORR	443	5.7	56.0	21.7	4
Spicy Tomato & Rice with Sweetcorn Soup BAXTERS	45	1.3	9.2	0.3	0.6

Calorie Counter

All amounts per 100g/100ml unless otherwise stated	Cal kcal	Pro g	Carb g	Fat g	Fibre g
Spicy Vegetable Cup-A-Soup Extra, per sachet BATCHELORS	109	2.9	22.3	1	1.2
Split Pea & Lentil Soup HEINZ WEIGHT WATCHERS	32	1.6	6	0.2	0.6
Spring Vegetable Soup					
CAMPBELL'S	21	0.5	4.5	0.1	n/a
HEINZ	31	0.8	6.2	0.4	0.7
Swedish Cauliflower & Broccoli Soups of the World, as sold KNORR	424	6.8	42	25.4	3.5
Tangy Tomato Cup-A-Soup Extra, per sachet BATCHELORS	137	3.4	25.8	2.2	1.1
Thai Chicken with Lemon Grass Cup-A-Soup Thick & Creamy, per sachet BATCHELORS	120	1.9	16.4	5.2	0.5
Thai Chicken with Noodles Soup BAXTERS	47	1.7	6.8	0.4	0.3
Thick Soups HEINZ					
Beef Broth	48	1.7	6.9	1.5	0.4
Beef & Vegetable	38	1.6	6.1	0.8	0.6
Country Vegetable with Ham	64	3	8.2	2	1
Pea & Ham	51	3.2	8.7	0.4	1
Potato & Leek	34	0.7	6.5	0.6	0.5
Scotch Broth	47	2.1	8.1	0.7	0.9

All amounts per 100g/100ml unless otherwise stated	Cal kcal	Pro g	Carb g	Fat g	Fibre g
Tomato Soup					
Cup-A-Soup, per sachet					
BATCHELORS	85	0.8	17.3	1.4	1.2
low calorie HEINZ WEIGHT					
WATCHERS	26	0.7	4.7	0.5	0.3
99% fat-free CAMPBELL'S	44	0.7	8	1	n/a
Tomato & Basil Cup-A-Soup Thick & Creamy, per sachet					
BATCHELORS	104	1.5	18.6	2.6	1.6
Tomato & Brown Lentil Soup					
BAXTERS	45	2.4	8.7	0.1	1.5
Tomato & Lentil Soup HEINZ	54	2.7	10.4	0.2	1
Tomato & Orange Soup BAXTERS	43	1.1	8.4	0.5	0.5
Tomato & Red Pepper Soup					
as sold KNORR	403	7.7	50.7	18.7	5.3
99% fat-free CAMPBELL'S	41	0.5	7.5	1	n/a
Tomato & Vegetable Soup					
Cup-A-Soup, per sachet					
BATCHELORS	109	2.6	18.6	2.7	1
organic BAXTERS	33	0.9	6.6	0.3	0.6
Tomato Rice Soup CAMPBELL'S	46	0.9	8.3	1	n/a

Calorie Counter

All amounts per 100g/100ml unless otherwise stated	Cal kcal	Pro g	Carb g	Fat g	Fibre g
Vegetable Soup					
CAMPBELL'S	35	0.8	6.2	0.8	n/a
canned HEINZ	47	1.4	8.4	0.9	1.1
canned HEINZ WEIGHT WATCHERS	31	1	5.9	0.3	0.9
Chunky Fresh BAXTERS	39	1.6	7.8	0.2	1.1
Country HEINZ	51	2.3	9.3	0.5	1.1
Country HEINZ WEIGHT WATCHERS	30	1.1	5.8	0.2	1
Hearty CAMPBELL'S	31	0.8	6	0.4	n/a
Vie Soups, chilled KNORR					
Carrot and Coriander	38	0.6	3.9	2.2	1.0
Country Vegetable	32	0.9	5.5	0.7	1.2
Red Pepper and Tomato	39	0.8	6.4	1.2	1.0
Smooth Autumn Vegetable	38	0.7	4.3	2.0	0.7
Smooth Leek and Potato	31	0.9	4.8	0.9	1.0
Tomato and Basil	29	0.8	5.5	0.4	0.9
Watercress Soup, as sold KNORR	414	11.1	51.1	18.5	1.7
Winter Vegetable Soup					
HEINZ	46	2.8	8.2	0.2	1.1
HEINZ WEIGHT WATCHERS	31	1.6	6	0.1	0.8
Woodland Mushroom Cup-A-Soup Thick & Creamy, per sachet					
BATCHELORS	123	1.8	16	5.3	1.3

SUGAR AND SWEETENERS

All amounts per 100g/100ml unless otherwise stated	Cal kcal	Pro g	Carb g	Fat g	Fibre g
Amber Sugar Crystals					
TATE & LYLE	398	Tr	99.9	0	0
Date Syrup MERIDIAN FOODS LTD	292	1.2	71.5	0.1	Tr
Golden Syrup	298	0.3	79	0	0
TATE & LYLE	325	0.5	80.5	0	0
Icing Sugar TATE & LYLE	398	0	99.5	0	0
Jaggery	367	0.5	97.2	0	0
Maple Syrup, organic					
MERIDIAN FOODS LTD	262	0	67.2	0.2	0
Molasses					
MERIDIAN FOODS LTD	321	0.2	80.1	0.1	0.1
organic MERIDIAN FOODS LTD	234	2.5	56	Tr	Tr
Sugar					
caster TATE & LYLE	400	0	99.9	0	0
dark brown, soft TATE & LYLE	378	0.4	94.5	0	0
Demerara, cane TATE & LYLE	400	Tr	99.2	0	Tr
granulated TATE & LYLE	400	0	99.9	0	0
light brown, soft TATE & LYLE	384	0.1	95.8	0	0
preserving TATE & LYLE	400	0	99.9	0	0
cube, white TATE & LYLE	400	0	99.9	0	0
Treacle					
black	257	1.2	67.2	0	0
black LYLE'S	290	1.7	64	0	0

SWEETS AND CHOCOLATE

All amounts per 100g/100ml unless otherwise stated	Cal kcal	Pro g	Carb g	Fat g	Fibre g
Aero NESTLÉ ROWNTREE					
milk chocolate	518	6.8	58.1	28.7	0.8
mint	529	5.5	61.4	29	0.4
snow	530	7.2	57.8	30	0.4
After Eight Mints NESTLÉ ROWNTREE					
original	417	2.5	72.9	12.8	1.1
White Chocolate	422	2.6	76.9	11.6	n/a
American Hard Gums TREBOR BASSETT	345	Tr	85.6	0	0
Apple Jack Chews TREBOR BASSETT	398	0.7	84	6.1	0
Barley Sugar TREBOR BASSETT	389	0	97.2	0	0
Black Jack Chews TREBOR BASSETT	399	0.7	85	6	0
Blue Riband NESTLÉ ROWNTREE	516	5.2	64	26.6	1
Bonbons					
buttermint CRAVENS	425	0.5	86.1	8.7	0
lemon TREBOR BASSETT	417	1.1	85.4	7.5	0
strawberry TREBOR BASSETT	415	1	85.5	7.5	0
toffee TREBOR BASSETT	430	1.4	81.7	10.8	0
Boost CADBURY	540	5.9	62.3	29.3	n/a
Bounty MARS					
dark	481	3.2	57.4	26.5	n/a
milk	485	4.6	56.4	26.8	n/a

Sweets and Chocolate

All amounts per 100g/100ml unless otherwise stated	Cal kcal	Pro g	Carb g	Fat g	Fibre g
Bournville CADBURY	495	4.6	59.6	26.7	n/a
Breakaway NESTLÉ ROWNTREE	496	6.8	59.7	25.5	2.5
Butter Mintoes CRAVENS	425	0.1	86.6	8.7	0
Buttermints TREBOR BASSETT	404	0.1	88.8	3.4	0
Butterscotch CRAVENS	411	0.1	89.9	5.7	0
Buttons CADBURY	525	7.8	56.8	29.4	n/a
Caramac NESTLÉ ROWNTREE	563	5.8	54.4	35.8	0
Caramac Breakaway NESTLÉ ROWNTREE	519	6.6	57.4	29.2	2
Caramel CADBURY	480	4.3	61.3	24.3	n/a
Caramels					
Grannymels ITONA	456	3.8	84.2	11.5	n/a
milk & plain chocolate CRAVENS	493	Tr	96.4	0	0
Chewing Gum WRIGLEY					
Airwaves, sugarfree	150	0	n/a	0	0
Doublemint	306	0	n/a	0	0
Extra Peppermint	165	0	N	0	0
Ice White, sugarfree	195	0	n/a	0	0
Juicy Fruit	295	0	N	0	0
Orbit, peppermint, sugarfree	195	0	N	0	0
Orbit, spearmint, sugarfree	190	0	N	0	0
PK, all flavours	353	0	N	0	0
Spearmint	281	0	N	0	0

Calorie Counter

All amounts per 100g/100ml unless otherwise stated	Cal kcal	Pro g	Carb g	Fat g	Fibre g
Chewits LEAF	392	0.4	90.8	3	0
Chocolate Caramel Creams TREBOR BASSETT	426	3.3	62.6	18	1.2
Chocolate Cream CADBURY	425	2.6	68.8	15.4	n/a
Chocolate Eclairs					
CRAVENS	479	2.8	71.9	20.1	0.5
TREBOR BASSETT	485	4.6	75	18.8	0
Chocolate Limes CRAVENS	406	0.6	90.9	4.5	0.3
Chocolate Mint Crisp CRAVENS	408	0.7	90.4	9.4	0.4
Chocolate Orange TERRY'S					
dark	511	4.3	56.9	29.3	6.2
milk	527	7.4	57.8	29.5	2.1
Chocolate Truffles ELIZABETH SHAW					
with Cointreau	475	3.8	63.2	22.3	0.3
with Irish Cream	477	3.9	63.4	22.8	0.3
with Tia Maria	477	3.8	63.5	22.5	0.3
Chocolate					
hazelnut & currant, organic					
GREEN & BLACK	528	7.7	49.7	34.5	0
milk	529	8.4	59.4	30.3	Tr
milk, organic GREEN & BLACK	541	9.3	56	31	0
mint, organic GREEN & BLACK	541	9.3	56	31	0
plain	525	4.7	64.8	29.2	N
plain, organic GREEN & BLACK	571	10	51	37	0

Sweets and Chocolate

All amounts per 100g/100ml unless otherwise stated	Cal kcal	Pro g	Carb g	Fat g	Fibre g
white	529	8	58.3	30.9	0
white, organic GREEN & BLACK	572	6	54	36.5	0
Chocolate, Maya Gold, organic GREEN & BLACK	556	7.5	53.1	34.8	0
Chomp CADBURY	465	3.6	67.8	19.9	n/a
Coolmints TREBOR BASSETT	237	0	98.7	0	0
Cough Candy					
CRAVENS	386	Tr	96.4	0	0
TREBOR BASSETT	383	0	95	0	0
Cream Toffees, assorted TREBOR BASSETT	433	3.7	73.3	13.8	0
Creme Egg CADBURY	445	3.3	71.6	16.2	n/a
Crunchie CADBURY	465	4	72	18.1	n/a
Curly Wurly CADBURY	450	3.9	69	17.8	n/a
Dairy Milk Chocolate CADBURY	530	7.8	57.1	29.9	n/a
Dairy Milk Tasters CADBURY	520	7.7	57	29.2	n/a
Dairy Toffee CRAVENS	472	1.8	75.3	18.3	0
Double Decker CADBURY	465	5	64.7	20.9	n/a
Drifter NESTLÉ ROWNTREE	478	3.7	67.3	21.5	0.8

Calorie Counter

All amounts per 100g/100ml unless otherwise stated	Cal kcal	Pro g	Carb g	Fat g	Fibre g
Energy Tablets LUCOZADE SPORT	361	0	89.2	0	n/a
orange	361	0	88.7	0	n/a
lemon	360	0	88.8	0	n/a
Everton Mints CRAVENS	413	0.6	89.8	5.7	0
Flake CADBURY	530	8.1	55.7	30.7	n/a
Fruit & Nut Chocolate CADBURY	490	8	55.7	26.3	n/a
Fruit & Nut Tasters CADBURY	505	9.3	52.1	29	n/a
Fruit Drops CRAVENS	386	2	70.3	22.7	0.5
Fruit Gums NESTLÉ ROWNTREE	342	4.7	80.8	0.2	0
Fruit Pastilles NESTLÉ ROWNTREE	351	4.4	83.7	0	0
Fruit Salad Chews TREBOR BASSETT	400	0.7	84.5	6.2	0
Fudge CADBURY	445	2.9	72	16.4	n/a
Fudge, Dairy TREBOR BASSETT	450	2.2	71.5	17.3	0
Fuse CADBURY	485	7.6	58.2	24.8	n/a
Galaxy chocolate MARS	532	9	56.6	30	n/a
caramel	488	5.3	60.1	25.1	n/a
double nut & raisin	534	8.4	55.7	30.8	n/a
hazelnut	572	7.7	48.5	38.6	n/a
praline	580	5.1	52	39.7	n/a
Galaxy Caramel Egg	465	5.5	61	22.1	n/a
Jellies, assorted TREBOR BASSETT	306	0	81.6	0	0

All amounts per 100g/100ml unless otherwise stated	Cal kcal	Pro g	Carb g	Fat g	Fibre g
Just Fruit Pastilles TREBOR BASSETT	344	4	81.2	Tr	Tr
Kit Kat NESTLÉ ROWNTREE					
4-finger	508	6	61.6	26.4	1.1
Chunky	516	5.6	61	27.7	0.9
Kola Chew Bar TREBOR BASSETT	398	0.7	84.3	6	Tr
Kola Cubes					
CRAVENS	386	Tr	96.4	0	0
TREBOR BASSETT	385	Tr	95.2	0	0
Liaison GALAXY	500	6.8	52.9	34.6	n/a
Lion Bar NESTLÉ ROWNTREE	489	4.7	67.6	22.2	n/a
Liquorice Allsorts BASSETT	352	2.3	75.5	4.5	1.6
Liquorice Torpedoes TREBOR BASSETT	370	3.5	88.3	0.4	1.1
Lockets MARS	383	0	95.8	0	n/a
M & Ms MARS					
chocolate	487	4.7	69.6	21.1	n/a
peanut	514	10.2	57.3	27.1	n/a
Maltesers MARS	494	10	61.4	23.1	n/a
Marble CADBURY	535	8.4	54.8	31.2	n/a
Mars Bar MARS	449	4.2	69	17.4	n/a

Calorie Counter

All amounts per 100g/100ml unless otherwise stated	Cal kcal	Pro g	Carb g	Fat g	Fibre g
Matchmakers, all varieties NESTLÉ ROWNTREE	475	4.3	69.7	19.9	0.9
Minstrels GALAXY	491	6	69.5	21	n/a
Milk Tray CADBURY	495	5.2	59.9	25.9	n/a
Milky Way MARS	451	4.5	71.6	16.7	n/a
Mint Assortment CRAVENS	414	0.3	89.4	6.1	0
Mint Crisp CADBURY	505	6.4	70.3	22.2	n/a
Mint Crisp Chocolates ELIZABETH SHAW	458	1.9	68	20.7	1.7
Mint Crisp Trio ELIZABETH SHAW	494	4.4	67.6	22.9	0.7
Mint Humbugs CRAVENS	413	0.6	89.7	5.8	0
Mint Imperials					
CRAVENS	387	0	96.3	0	0
TREBOR BASSETT	396	0.4	98.1	0.2	0
Mintetts G. PAYNE & CO	395	Tr	92.7	27	n/a
Mints, Best English CRAVENS	387	Tr	96.1	0.2	0
Minty Chews TREBOR BASSETT	395	0.8	84.2	6.1	0
Munchies NESTLÉ ROWNTREE	490	4.7	63.9	24	0.5
Mint	432	3.8	67.5	16.4	1.6
Murray Mints TREBOR BASSETT	409	0	90.3	5.3	0

All amounts per 100g/100ml unless otherwise stated	Cal kcal	Pro g	Carb g	Fat g	Fibre g
Nuts about Caramel CADBURY	495	5.5	58.1	26.7	n/a
Old Jamaica CADBURY	465	5.5	58.9	22.9	n/a
Orange Cream CADBURY	425	2.6	68.6	15.4	n/a
Orange Milk Chocolate CADBURY	525	7.8	56.8	29.7	n/a
Peanut Lion Bar NESTLÉ ROWNTREE	522	7.1	56.9	29.6	n/a
Pear Drops					
CRAVENS	386	Tr	96.4	0	0
TREBOR BASSETT	385	0	95.4	0	0
Peppermints	392	0.5	102.2	0.7	0
Peppermint Cream CADBURY	425	2.6	68.8	15.4	n/a
Picnic CADBURY	475	7.6	59.6	22.7	n/a
Pineapple Chunks TREBOR BASSETT	384	0	95.1	0	0
Polo Fruits NESTLÉ ROWNTREE	383	0	96	0	n/a
citrus sharp	393	0	96.6	1	n/a
super ojays	245	0	96	1.2	0
Polo Gummies NESTLÉ ROWNTREE	307	6.7	74.4	Tr	n/a
Polo Mints NESTLÉ ROWNTREE	402	0	98.2	1	n/a
sugar-free	238	0	99.1	0	0
supermints	236	0	97.3	0	0
Polo Smoothies NESTLÉ ROWNTREE	412	0.1	88.4	6.6	0
Pontefract Cakes TREBOR BASSETT	278	2.2	66.6	0.3	0.7

Calorie Counter

All amounts per 100g/100ml unless otherwise stated	Cal kcal	Pro g	Carb g	Fat g	Fibre g
Poppets G. PAYNE & CO					
peanut	544	16.4	37	37	n/a
peanut & raisin	460	10	53	24.5	n/a
raisins	409	4.8	66	14	n/a
white chocolate & raisins	286	5.9	63.6	16.6	n/a
Refreshers TREBOR BASSETT	375	0.1	90.2	0.3	0
Revels MARS	495	6.2	65.6	23.1	n/a
Ripple GALAXY	532	9	56.6	30	n/a
Rolo NESTLÉ ROWNTREE	471	3.2	68.5	20.5	0.3
Sherbet Fountain TREBOR BASSETT	352	0.6	84	0.1	0.2
Sherbet Fruits CRAVENS	423	Tr	89	7.4	0
Sherbet Lemons					
TREBOR BASSETT	382	0	93.9	0	0
CRAVENS	423	Tr	89	7.4	0
Skittles MARS	406	0.3	91.5	4.3	n/a
Mint	404	0	91.4	4.2	n/a
Snickers MARS	510	10.2	55.3	27.6	n/a
Soft Fruit Centres CRAVENS	386	Tr	96.4	0	0
Softfruits TREBOR BASSETT	366	0.1	88.1	1.2	0
Softmints TREBOR BASSETT	374	0.1	88.2	2.3	0

Sweets and Chocolate

All amounts per 100g/100ml unless otherwise stated	Cal kcal	Pro g	Carb g	Fat g	Fibre g
Spearmints, Extra Strong TREBOR BASSETT	396	0.4	98.7	Tr	0
Starbar CADBURY	540	9.1	55	31.6	n/a
Starburst MARS	411	0.3	85.3	7.6	n/a
Sourburst	307	4.2	72.6	0	n/a
Sugared Almonds CRAVENS	430	4.4	78.1	11.1	2.3
Sweet Peanuts TREBOR BASSETT	426	3.1	80	10.3	1.4
Sweets, boiled	327	Tr	87.3	Tr	0
Time Out CADBURY	540	5.4	61.8	29.9	n/a
Toblerone TERRY'S	525	5.4	59	29.5	2.2
Toffees, mixed	430	2.1	71.1	17.2	0
Grannymels Mint ITONA	465	3.8	84.2	1.5	n/a
Toffee Crisp NESTLÉ ROWNTREE	511	4.3	60.6	27.9	0.8
Toffo NESTLÉ ROWNTREE	452	2.2	69.9	18.2	n/a
Topic MARS	497	7.4	56.7	26.7	n/a
Trebor Mints TREBOR BASSETT	399	0.6	98	0.4	0
Tunes MARS	392	0	98.1	0	n/a
Turkish Delight					
CADBURY	365	2	73.3	7.2	n/a
TREBOR BASSETT	323	Tr	85.8	0	Tr
without nuts	295	0.6	77.9	0	0

Calorie Counter

All amounts per 100g/100ml unless otherwise stated	Cal kcal	Pro g	Carb g	Fat g	Fibre g
Twirl CADBURY	**525**	8.1	55.9	30.1	n/a
Twix MARS	**495**	5.8	63.5	24.2	n/a
Twixels MARS	**514**	4.9	64.2	2634	n/a
Vanilla Fudge CRAVENS	**469**	1.1	77.6	17.1	0
Walnut Whip, vanilla NESTLÉ ROWNTREE	**495**	5.9	60.8	25.4	0.6
Wholenut Chocolate CADBURY	**550**	9.3	48.8	35.2	n/a
Wholenut Tasters CADBURY	**555**	9.9	44.2	37.8	n/a
Wine Gums TREBOR BASSETT	**337**	6	76.7	0.1	0
Wispa CADBURY	**550**	6	55.3	34.1	n/a
Gold	**510**	4.8	57.9	28.6	n/a
Mint	**550**	6.1	56	33.6	n/a
Yorkie NESTLÉ ROWNTREE					
honeycomb	**509**	5.7	63.6	25.8	0.6
milk chocolate	**525**	6.5	58.6	29.4	0.7
raisin & biscuit	**487**	5.9	60.5	24.6	0.9

VEGETARIAN

All amounts per 100g/100ml unless otherwise stated	Cal kcal	Pro g	Carb g	Fat g	Fibre g
Baked Beans with Vegetable Sausages HEINZ	102	5.6	12.1	3.5	2.9
Bisto Vegetarian Gravy Granules, as sold CENTURA	367	2.6	59.5	13.2	1.3
Burgers, flame-grilled LINDA MCCARTNEY FOODS	134	22.6	2.9	3.6	1.6
Cauliflower Cheese BIRDS EYE	365	18	22	23	n/a
Cornish Pasties LINDA MCCARTNEY FOODS	228	5.6	27.2	11.5	1.6
Macaroni Cheese, each BIRDS EYE	375	13	47	15	n/a
Onions and Garlic Sauce, Chunky RAGU	58	2.3	9.2	1.3	n/a
OY PROVAMEL					
banana flavour soya milk	75	3.6	10.5	2.1	1.2
chocolate flavour soya milk	72	3.6	9.6	2.1	1.5
strawberry flavour soya milk	64	3.6	7.7	2.1	1.2
Pâté					
Herb TARTEX	196	7	6	16	n/a
Herb, per tub VESSEN	226	7	9	18	n/a
Herb & Garlic VESSEN	230	7	10	18	n/a
Mushroom TARTEX	200	7	7	16	n/a
Mushroom, per tub VESSEN	235	7	9	19	n/a

Calorie Counter

All amounts per 100g/100ml unless otherwise stated	Cal kcal	Pro g	Carb g	Fat g	Fibre g
Red & Green Pepper TARTEX	222	6	9	18	n/a
Red & Green Pepper VESSEN	222	6	9	18	n/a
Quorn, myco-protein	86	11.8	2	3.5	4.8
Ravioli in Tomato Sauce, meatfree HEINZ	75	2.4	14.4	0.8	0.5
Rice Dream IMAGINE FOODS	50	0.1	10.1	1	0.1
Rice Drink PROVAMEL					
calcium enriched	50	0.1	10	1.1	0
vanilla	49	0.1	10	1	0
Roast Vegetable & Tomato Pasta, 97% fat free, each BIRDS EYE	300	10	56	3.7	n/a
Sausage Rolls LINDA MCCARTNEY FOODS	260	10.9	23.1	14.5	1.6
Sausages LINDA MCCARTNEY FOODS	252	23.2	8.6	13.8	1.2
Soya Bean Curd: *see* **Tofu**					
Soya Chunks HOLLAND & BARRETT					
flavoured	345	50	35	1	4
unflavoured	345	50	35	1	4
Soya Curd: *see* **Tofu**					
Soya Dream PROVAMEL	178	3	1.7	17.7	1.1
Soya Flour					
full fat	447	36.8	23.5	23.5	11.2
low fat	352	45.3	28.2	7.2	13.5

Vegetarian

All amounts per 100g/100ml unless otherwise stated	Cal kcal	Pro g	Carb g	Fat g	Fibre g
Soya Milk					
sweetened	43	3.1	2.5	2.4	Tr
sweetened, organic PROVAMEL	45	3.7	2.8	2.1	0.3
unsweetened	26	2.4	0.5	1.6	0.2
unsweetened HOLLAND & BARRETT	36	3.6	0.6	2.1	1
unsweetened, organic PROVAMEL	36	3.7	0.4	2.1	0.3
vanilla flavoured, organic PROVAMEL	61	3.8	6.5	2.1	0.3
Soya Mince HOLLAND & BARRETT					
flavoured	345	50	35	1	4
unflavoured	345	50	35	1	4
Spaghetti Bolognese, meatfree HEINZ	86	3.1	13.1	2.4	0.7
Sweet Pepper Sauce, Chunky RAGU	54	1.7	6	2.6	2.3
Tofu (soya bean curd)					
steamed	73	8.1	0.7	4.2	N
steamed, fried	261	23.5	2	17.7	N
Vegetable Biryani, each BIRDS EYE	690	12	74	38	n/a
Vegetable Burgers, organic LINDA MCCARTNEY FOODS	238	3.1	27.7	12.7	2.3

Calorie Counter

All amounts per 100g/100ml unless otherwise stated	Cal kcal	Pro g	Carb g	Fat g	Fibre g
Vegetable Granulated Stock KNORR	199	8.4	39.8	1	0.9
Vegetable Gravy Granules, as sold OXO	316	8.4	59.5	4.9	0.9
Vegetable Oxo Cubes OXO	253	11.2	41.9	4.5	1.7
Vegetable Sauce, Chunky RAGU	59	2	7	2.6	2.5
Vegetable Stock VECON	171	25	17.5	1.5	3.5
Vegetable Stock Cubes KNORR	308	11.9	21.7	19.3	1.3
organic	284	6.4	19.8	19.9	1
Vegetarian Double Gloucester Cheese HOLLAND & BARRETT	405	24.6	0.1	34	0
Vegetarian Mild Cheddar Cheese HOLLAND & BARRETT	412	25.5	0.1	34.4	0
Vegetarian Red Leicester Cheese HOLLAND & BARRETT	401	24.3	0.1	33.7	0
Vegetarian Tandoori Vegetable Pasty HOLLAND & BARRETT	188	4.4	29.9	5.7	1.8
Yofu, organic, each PROVAMEL					
peach & mango	128	4.8	20.5	2.8	1.5
red cherry	125	4.8	20.1	2.8	1.5
strawberry	135	4.8	19.5	4	0.3

FAST FOOD

All amounts per 100g/100ml unless otherwise stated	Cal kcal	Pro g	Carb g	Fat g	Fibre g
McDONALD'S					
Big Breakfast, each	591	26.2	39.8	36.3	4
Big Mac, each	493	26.7	44	22.9	5.3
Cheeseburger, each	299	15.8	33.1	11.5	2.5
Chicken McNuggets (6)	253	18.6	11.5	14.8	2.1
Filet-O-Fish, each	389	16.6	40.8	17.7	1.2
French Fries, regular, per portion	206	2.9	28.3	9	2.8
Hamburger, each	253	13.1	32.8	7.7	2.5
Hash Browns	138	1.4	15.8	7.7	1.7
McChicken Sandwich, each	375	16.5	38.6	17.2	3.8
Milkshake, vanilla, regular, each	383	10.8	62.7	10.1	0
Quarter Pounder, each	423	25.7	37.1	19	3.7
with cheese	516	31.2	37.5	26.7	3.7
WIMPY					
All day breakfast	710	31.4	46.2	44.3	3.8
Bacon and egg in a bun	400	23.5	32.3	19.9	1.7
Bacon Classic Cheeseburger	455	26.2	33.3	23.1	2.4

Calorie Counter

All amounts per 100g/100ml unless otherwise stated	Cal kcal	Pro g	Carb g	Fat g	Fibre g
Turkish Delight	310	2	76	8	0.8
Vanilla Yogurt, virtually fat free, per pack	66	6.3	9.9	0.1	Tr

Calorie Counter

All amounts per 100g/100ml unless otherwise stated	Cal kcal	Pro g	Carb g	Fat g	Fibre g
Bacon in a bun	**290**	15	32.3	11.2	1.7
Bacon/Cheeseburger	**375**	21.4	32.3	18.1	1.7
BBQ Pork Rib in a Bun	**515**	25.1	68.9	16.2	3.4
Bender					
in a bun	**410**	18.8	33.5	22.4	2.2
in a bun with cheese	**455**	21.8	33.5	25.9	2.2
egg and chips	**490**	20.8	32.5	30.6	2.7
Cheeseburger	**315**	16.7	32.3	13.1	1.7
Chicken chunks and chips	**645**	21.4	68.3	31.6	4.2
Chicken in a bun	**435**	16.3	42	22.2	1.9
Chips	**295**	3.7	42.4	12.1	3.5
Classic Kingsize	**550**	36.2	33.3	30.3	2.4
Fish 'n' Chips	**465**	27.5	43.5	20.1	3.9
Fish in a bun	**510**	34.2	62.8	13.5	3.4
Halfpounder	**840**	51.2	42.3	51.5	6.7
Hamburger	**270**	13.7	32.3	9.6	1.7
Hot 'n' Spicy Chicken in a bun	**430**	18.5	45.7	19.7	2.4
International grill	**770**	36.7	46.4	49.1	3.9

All amounts per 100g/100ml unless otherwise stated	Cal kcal	Pro g	Carb g	Fat g	Fibre g
International grill deluxe	**970**	50.4	46.4	63.5	3.9
Quarterpounder	**550**	28.2	42.3	30	6.7 ·
with cheese	**595**	31.2	42.3	33.5	6.7
Spicy Beanburger	**535**	16.1	68.7	22	15.9
Toasted Tea Cake and butter	**250**	5.8	35.3	909	1.2
Wimpy Classic	**340**	19.6	33.3	14.5	2.4
special grill	**820**	39.2	46.2	53.3	3.7
with cheese	**385**	22.6	33.3	18	2.4
Wimpy special grill	**690**	30.2	46.2	42.7	3.7

BURGER KING

	Cal kcal	Pro g	Carb g	Fat g	Fibre g
Cheeseburger	**331**	19.6	30.1	14.2	1.8
Chicken Whopper	**548**	39.4	45	23.4	2.5
Chicken Whopper Lite	**289**	25	28.9	7.5	1.7
Hamburger	**290**	17.2	30	10.8	1.8
Regular King Fries	**400**	3	43	16	2.9
Veggie Burger	**432**	14.7	55.4	16.9	7.6
Whopper	**646**	30.6	47.6	37.9	3.6

Calorie Counter

All amounts per 100g/100ml unless otherwise stated	Cal kcal	Pro g	Carb g	Fat g	Fibre g
PIZZA HUT					
BBQ Dip, portion	31	2.8	7.3	0	n/a
Cheesy Bites					
Cheddar	319	8.5	28.7	18.9	n/a
Tomato and Cheddar	308	8.2	26.9	18.6	n/a
Chicken Wings (Take Away), portion	466	40	3	32.7	2.3
Dippin' Chicken, portion	329	24.2	26.3	14.3	0
Garlic and Herb Dip, portion	280	1.29	6.21	27.75	n/a
Garlic Bread with Cheese, portion	618	25.6	49.5	35.3	3.3
Garlic Bread, portion	386	8	44.3	19.6	2.5
Garlic Mushrooms, portion	215	6.6	22.1	11.1	3.8
Hawaiian Medium Pan, per slice	241	12.1	28	8.9	1.3
Jacket Skins, portion	570	7.6	51.4	37.1	4.7
Lasagne, portion	669	39.4	62.4	29.2	9.3
Margherita Medium Pan, per slice	238	10.7	26.3	10	1.8
Meat Feast Medium Pan, per slice	324	16.6	27.8	16.2	1

300

All amounts per 100g/100ml unless otherwise stated	Cal kcal	Pro g	Carb g	Fat g	Fibre g
Ranch Dip, portion	**489**	3.2	3.8	51	n/a
Spicy Chicken Bake, portion	**499**	18.5	80.7	12.4	0
Stuffed Crust Original Margherita, per slice	**328**	18.7	35.7	12.3	1.3
Supreme Medium Pan, per slice	**291**	26.5	14.6	1.3	0.5
Tangy Tomato Bake, portion	**653**	27.1	92.9	21.6	5.5
The Edge, per slice					
Meaty	**206**	10.6	14.9	11.6	n/a
The Veggie	**136**	6.9	14.8	5.6	n/a
The Works	**161**	8.25	14.1	8	n/a
The Italian Medium, per slice					
Ham and Mushroom	**269**	13	34	10.2	n/a
Margherita	**291**	14.4	37.5	10.2	n/a
Meat Feast	**324**	16.6	27.8	16.2	n/a
Supreme	**297**	13.7	26.5	14.6	n/a
Tomato and Herb, portion	**154**	1.1	38.4	0.1	n/a
Twisted Crust					
Margherita	**256**	13.5	31.5	8.5	n/a
Meat Feast	**266**	13	28	11.3	n/a
Supreme	**257**	13.1	29.6	9.6	n/a
Vegetarian Original Medium Pan, per slice	**225**	10.5	26.2	8.8	1.8

Calorie Counter

All amounts per 100g/100ml unless otherwise stated	Cal kcal	Pro g	Carb g	Fat g	Fibre g
DOMINO'S PIZZA					
Cheese and Tomato 9.5˝, per slice	**126**	6.7	18.2	2.9	1.7
Chicken Dunkers	**220**	23.5	1.5	13.3	0.5
Chicken Strippers	**219**	23.3	13.4	8	1
Deluxe 9.5˝, per slice	**171**	8.4	19.2	6.7	1.6
Full House 9.5˝, per slice	**183**	9.3	18.9	7.8	1.3
Garlic Pizza Bread, per slice	**117**	4.7	16.4	3.6	0.9
Mighty Meaty 9.5˝, per slice	**177**	9.9	18.1	7.2	2
Mixed Grill 9.5˝, per slice	**177**	9	19.6	6.9	1.7
Pepperoni Passion 9.5˝, per slice	**187**	9	20.6	7.6	1.4
Tandoori Hot 9.5˝, per slice	**138**	8.2	18.7	3.5	1.9
Vegetarian Supreme 9.5˝, per slice	**140**	7.7	19.3	3.3	1.7
PIZZA EXPRESS					
American	**753**	35.3	87.3	32.4	n/a
American Hot	**758**	35.9	87.4	32.6	n/a
Cannelloni, per portion	**556**	20.9	38.7	35.4	n/a

All amounts per 100g/100ml unless otherwise stated	Cal kcal	Pro g	Carb g	Fat g	Fibre g
Fiorentina	740	38.22	88.4	27.5	n/a
La Reine	665	34.9	87.4	22.8	n/a
Lasagne Pasticciate, per portion	579	26.4	29.9	39.5	n/a
Margherita	621	29.3	87.5	20.4	n/a
Mushroom	627	30.1	87.5	20.6	n/a
Pollo, per portion	573	41.1	32.5	31.8	n/a
Quattro Formaggi	636	29.4	87.2	22.1	n/a
Salade Nicoise, per portion	729	40	65	37	n/a
Sloppy Giuseppe	783	41	97	33	n/a
Tortellini, per portion	1116	26.9	91.9	71.3	n/a

FISH AND CHIPS

Cod, in batter, fried	247	16.1	11.7	15.4	0.5
Plaice, in batter, fried	257	15.2	12	16.8	0.5
Rock Salmon/Dogfish, in batter, fried	295	14.7	10.3	21.9	0.4
Skate, in batter, fried	168	14.7	4.9	10.1	0.2
Chips, fried in oil	239	3.2	30.5	12.4	2.2

Calorie Counter

All amounts per 100g/100ml unless otherwise stated	Cal kcal	Pro g	Carb g	Fat g	Fibre g
BOOTS SHAPERS					
American Style BBQ Waffles, very low fat	476	4.5	65	22	3.7
Apricot Custard Style Yogurt, per pack	82	5.9	12	1.2	0.3
Blackcurrant & Apple Drink, per pack	9	Tr	1	Tr	Tr
Boysenberry Still Water, per pack	5	Tr	Tr	Tr	Tr
Caramel Bar	352	3.7	74	11	1
Chargrilled Chicken Crisps	482	6.6	60	24	4
Chargrilled Chicken Sandwiches, per pack	295	23	38	5.7	5.9
Chargrilled Vegetables & Tomato Pasta, per pack	214	5.6	34	6.2	0.8
Cheese & Onion Crisps	482	6.6	60	24	4
Cheese & Pickle Sandwiches, per pack	341	16	51	8.1	3.8
Cheese Puffs	523	6.4	59	29	1.6
Cheese, Tomato & Spring Onion Sandwiches, per pack	306	21	43	5.5	3.6

All amounts per 100g/100ml unless otherwise stated	Cal kcal	Pro g	Carb g	Fat g	Fibre g
Chicken & Ham Sandwiches, per pack	**294**	25	34	6.4	3.2
Chicken Fajita Salad Wrap, per pack	**307**	18	46	5.7	3.2
Chicken Triple Sandwiches, per pack	**414**	29	58	7.3	5.3
Chicken, Egg & Cheese Triple Sandwiches, per pack	**434**	31	55	10	6.7
Chicken, Prawn & BLT Sandwiches, per pack	**412**	27	49	12	5.1
Chocolate & Orange Cereal Bar, per pack	**374**	4	73	11	1
Cloudy Lemonade, per pack	**13**	Tr	1	Tr	Tr
Cranberry & Apple Cereal Bar	**391**	4.2	76	11	2.2
Crispy Caramel Bar	**400**	3.9	67	17	0.4
Egg Mayonnaise & Cress Sandwiches, per pack	**305**	15	39	9.9	4.2
Egg Salad Sandwiches, per pack	**304**	13	44	8.4	2

Calorie Counter

All amounts per 100g/100ml unless otherwise stated	Cal kcal	Pro g	Carb g	Fat g	Fibre g
Flatbread					
chicken tikka	**172**	11	24	3.6	1.4
fajita	**138**	9	20	2.4	2.6
feta cheese	**172**	n/a	n/a	n/a	n/a
Italian chicken	**191**	11	21	7	1.7
Moroccan chicken	**176**	9.6	26	3.7	1.7
Peking duck	**169**	7.4	29	2.6	1.9
spicy Mexican	**156**	7	23	4	3.7
Thai chicken	**178**	10	22	5.4	4.3
tuna	**123**	8.8	19	1.3	1.3
Fruit Selection Pack, per pack	**66**	0.8	15	0.3	1.3
Gooseberry Custard Style Yogurt, per pack	**75**	6	10	1.2	0.3
Ham & Double Gloucester Sandwich, per pack	**307**	20	35	9.7	4.5
Ham, Cheese & Pickle Sandwiches, per pack	**296**	22	33	8.4	5
Ham, Cream Cheese & Chive Bagel, per pack	**319**	19	45	7	2.4
Herb & Tomato Twists	**468**	3.7	66	21	3.9
Honey & Mustard & Chicken Pasta Salad, per pack	**304**	17	46	5.8	4.1

All amounts per 100g/100ml unless otherwise stated	Cal kcal	Pro g	Carb g	Fat g	Fibre g
Just Fruit Medley, per pack	**55**	1	12	0.3	1.5
Just Fruit, per pack	**61**	0.8	14	0.2	2.1
Just Salad Wrap, per pack	**289**	10	43	8.6	3.7
Kiwi & Lime Sparkling Water, per pack	**5**	Tr	Tr	Tr	Tr
Lemon & Lime Yogurt Mousse, per pack	**89**	3.8	9.9	3.8	0.1
Lemon Chicken Sandwiches, per pack	**315**	14	40	11	2.6
Mini Sushi Selection, per pack	**293**	9.6	53	4.7	4.1
Mint Bar	**378**	2.9	75	14	2.5
New York Style Salted Pretzels, very low fat	**391**	11	81	2.5	3.8
Orange Drink, per pack	**10**	Tr	1	Tr	Tr
Oriental Chicken Triple Sandwiches, per pack	**440**	30	53	12	5.3
Paprika Chicken Sandwiches, per pack	**297**	20	35	8.6	4.3
Peppercorn Chicken Pasta, per pack	**316**	16	36	12	3.4

Calorie Counter

All amounts per 100g/100ml unless otherwise stated	Cal kcal	Pro g	Carb g	Fat g	Fibre g
Pineapple & Grape Drink, per pack	10	Tr	1	Tr	Tr
Prawn Cocktail Salad Sandwiches, per pack	296	17	30	12	4.9
Prawn Mayonnaise Sandwiches, per pack	320	16	37	12	5.1
Prawn Pasta Salad, per pack	250	10	35	7.8	1
Prawn Shells	469	6.6	68	19	1.6
Prawn, Salmon & Ocean Triple Sandwiches, per pack	404	21	53	12	5.7
Pure Apple Juice, per pack	121	0.3	30	Tr	Tr
Raspberry & Mango Drink, still, per pack	5	Tr	Tr	Tr	Tr
Red Apple Drink, still, per pack	5	Tr	Tr	Tr	Tr
Roast Chicken Salad Sandwiches, per pack	284	21	37	5.8	4.4
Roast Chicken Sandwiches, per pack	288	24	31	7.5	2.4
Salmon & Cucumber Sandwiches, per pack	327	18	39	11	3.5
Salt & Vinegar Crunchy Sticks	456	5.5	68	18	2.6

All amounts per 100g/100ml unless otherwise stated	Cal kcal	Pro g	Carb g	Fat g	Fibre g
Sea Salt & Black Pepper Crisps	482	6.6	60	24	4
Snack Pack	183	5	31	4.3	3.1
Sour Cream & Chives Crisps	482	6.6	60	24	4
Sparkling Forest Fruit Drink, per pack	5	Tr	Tr	Tr	Tr
Sparkling Peach Drink, per pack	5	Tr	Tr	Tr	Tr
Strawberry Bar	374	2.5	79	12	0.2
Strawberry Custard-Style Yogurt, per pack	83	6	12	1.2	0.2
Strawberry Yogurt Mousse, per pack	88	3.7	9.9	3.7	0.1
Thai Lemon Lanterns	454	4.4	64	20	3.8
Toffee Yogurt, virtually fat free, per pack	67	6.4	10	0.1	Tr
Tuna & Cucumber Sandwiches, per pack	323	20	43	7.9	3
Tuna & Sweetcorn Sandwiches, per pack	317	19	48	5.4	3.4
Tuna Melt Swedish Sandwiches, per pack	258	21	33	4.7	2.6

KIDS' FOOD

All amounts per 100g/100ml unless otherwise stated	Cal kcal	Pro g	Carb g	Fat g	Fibre g

SOFT DRINKS

Apple Juice, ready to drink					
ROBINSONS	46	Tr	11	Tr	n/a
Apple & Blackcurrant Special R,					
ready to drink carton ROBINSONS	4.2	Tr	0.7	Tr	n/a
Banana Nesquik NESTLÉ					
as sold	395	0	97.3	0.5	0
made up with whole milk	168	6.8	18.9	7.8	n/a
ready to drink	168	3.2	10.2	1.6	0
with semi-skimmed	155	6.8	24.9	3.4	0
Blackcurrant Juice Drink,					
ready to drink RIBENA	59	Tr	15.6	n/a	n/a
Blackcurrant Juice, ready to drink					
carton ROBINSONS	59	Tr	14.4	Tr	n/a
Capri-Sun Juice Drink COCA COLA					
orange	45	1	11	1	n/a
tropical	46	1	11	1	n/a
wild berries	46	1	11	1	n/a
blackcurrant	55	1	13	1	n/a
strawberry	54	1	13	1	n/a
Chocolate Nesquik NESTLÉ					
as sold	370	0	97.3	0.5	0
made with whole milk	168	6.8	18.9	7.8	0

Calorie Counter

All amounts per 100g/100ml unless otherwise stated	Cal kcal	Pro g	Carb g	Fat g	Fibre g
ready to drink, each	187	8.5	29	4.3	0.4
with semi-skimmed milk	155	6.8	24.9	3.4	0

Crusha BURGESS

banana	104	0.2	25.3	Tr	Tr
black cherry	153	0	37.1	0	0
chocolate	175	0	41.8	0	0
lime	95	0	22	0	0
pineapple	101	Tr	24.4	0	0
raspberry	103	Tr	24.7	0	0
strawberry	101	Tr	24.6	0	0
vanilla	161	0	39.7	0	0

Frijj Extreme Milkshakes, each DAIRY CREST

milk chocolate	85	3.9	12.7	2.1	n/a
white chocolate	85	3.6	12.9	2.1	n/a
banana	62	3.4	10.1	0.8	n/a
milk chocolate	69	3.5	11.6	1	0
strawberry	62	3.5	10.1	0.8	0

Fruit Shoots each ROBINSONS

blackcurrant & apple	58	0.1	14	Tr	Tr
blackcurrant & apple, no added sugar	5	0.1	0.8	Tr	Tr
orange & peach	58	0.1	14	Tr	Tr
orange & peach, no added sugar	5	0.1	0.8	Tr	Tr

All amounts per 100g/100ml unless otherwise stated	Cal kcal	Pro g	Carb g	Fat g	Fibre g
Orange C-Vit, Ready to Drink, each SMITHKLINE BEECHAM	42	Tr	10.1	0	n/a
Orange Special R, ready to drink, each ROBINSONS	5.6	0.1	1	Tr	n/a
Splat Milkshakes, each AMBROSIA					
banana	72	2.6	12.6	1.2	0
milk chocolate	80	2.8	14.2	1.3	0.4
strawberry	71	2.6	12.5	1.2	0
Strawberry Nesquik NESTLÉ					
as sold	390	0	96.7	0.5	0
made up with whole milk	168	6.8	18.9	7.8	0
ready to drink, each	170	8	25.5	4	0
with semi-skimmed milk	155	6.8	24.9	3.4	0
Sunny Delight Drink, each PROCTER & GAMBLE					
apple and kiwi kick	7.4	Tr	1.3	Tr	Tr
blackcurrant blast	10	Tr	1.7	0.1	Tr
Californian style	43	Tr	10	0.2	n/a
Florida style	40	Tr	9	0.2	n/a
orange outburst	10	Tr	1.3	0.2	Tr
tropical tornado	10	Tr	1.5	0.2	Tr
Um Bongo Fruit Drink, each LIBBY	43	Tr	10.7	Tr	Tr

See also: **DRINKS (NON-ALCOHOLIC)**

Calorie Counter

All amounts per 100g/100ml unless otherwise stated	Cal kcal	Pro g	Carb g	Fat g	Fibre g
DAIRY					
Babybel Cheese, mini FROMAGERIES BEL	308	23	0	24	n/a
Disney Fromage Frais, monsters NESTLÉ	120	7.4	15.7	2.8	1.8
Junior Yofu PROVAMEL					
Peach & Pear	84	3.8	12.4	2.2	1.2
Strawberry & Banana	85	3.8	12.7	2.2	1.2
Laughing Cow Cheese FROMAGERIES BEL	269	10	6.5	23	n/a
Milky Bar Fromage Frais NESTLÉ	200	3.3	22.4	11	0
Munch Bunch Mega Pot Shots Fromage Frais EDEN VALE	124	7	15	4	n/a
Petits Filous Fromage Frais DAIRY CREST	127	6.6	14.5	4.7	n/a
Petits Filous Frubes DAIRY CREST	128	7.6	13.7	4.8	n/a
Teletubbies Tubby Custard Style Yogurt ST IVEL	113	5.4	15	3	0
Wildlife Choobs DAIRY CREST	125	6.5	14.1	4.7	n/a
Wildlife Fromage Frais DAIRY CREST	97	7.2	14	1.3	n/a

All amounts per 100g/100ml unless otherwise stated	Cal kcal	Pro g	Carb g	Fat g	Fibre g
Winnie the Pooh Fruit Fromage					
Frais NESTLÉ	130	7.1	18.9	2.7	Tr
Yop Strawberry Yogurt Drink					
DAIRY CREST	81	2.9	15	1	n/a

See also: **DAIRY PRODUCTS**

DESSERTS

Banana Nesquik Dessert, as sold NESTLÉ	450	3.7	74.6	15	0.3
Disney Mousse, Buzz Light Year NESTLÉ	180	3.89	24.8	7.1	0.9
Fruitini Mixed Fruit Pieces, each DEL MONTE					
in Custardy Banana Sauce	72	1.2	15.7	0.9	n/a
in Orange Jelly	67	0.3	15.8	0.1	n/a
in Strawberry Jelly	65	0.3	15.3	0.1	n/a
in Juice	55	0.4	13	0.1	n/a
Jelly Pots, Rowntree, ready to eat NESTLÉ					
Blackcurrant	80	Tr	18.9	0	0
Orange	80	Tr	18.9	0	0
Strawberry	76	Tr	18.8	0	0

Calorie Counter

All amounts per 100g/100ml unless otherwise stated	Cal kcal	Pro g	Carb g	Fat g	Fibre g
Splat Custard Dessert Pot AMBROSIA					
banana flavour	104	2.7	16.6	3	0
milk chocolate flavour	119	3	20	3	0.7
strawberry flavour	104	2.7	16.6	3	0
vanilla flavour	105	2.7	16.7	3	0
toffee flavour	105	2.7	16.9	3	0

ICE CREAM

	Cal kcal	Pro g	Carb g	Fat g	Fibre g
Calippo, each WALLS					
Orange	100	0.1	25	Tr	n/a
Strawberry	95	Tr	24	Tr	n/a
Chupster, each WALLS	80	1.2	11.1	3.4	n/a
Fab, each NESTLÉ	83	0.5	13.7	2.8	n/a
Fruit Fives on a Stick, each WALLS	40	0.1	9.4	0.1	n/a
Fruit Pastille Lolly, each NESTLÉ	57	0	13.5	0	n/a
King Banana, each LYONS MAID	140	0.8	12	9.9	n/a
Lip Smacker, each LYONS MAID	77	0	19.4	0	n/a
Mickey, each LYONS MAID	98	2.2	11.7	4.7	n/a
Milkybar Ice Cream, each NESTLÉ	114	2	9.6	7.5	n/a

All amounts per 100g/100ml unless otherwise stated	Cal kcal	Pro g	Carb g	Fat g	Fibre g
Mini Fruit, each WALLS					
apple	35	Tr	8.3	Tr	n/a
orange	35	0	8.7	Tr	n/a
raspberry	35	0.1	8.7	Tr	n/a
chocolate	30	1.3	6.1	1	n/a
Mini Milk, each WALLS					
strawberry	35	1.3	6.1	1	n/a
vanilla	35	1.3	6.1	1	n/a
Mivi, each LYONS MAID					
pineapple & cream	85	1	13.8	2.8	n/a
raspberry & cream	84	1.2	13.5	2.8	n/a
strawberry & cream	83	1	13.4	2.7	n/a
Mr Men, each LYONS MAID					
orange	28	0	7	0	n/a
strawberry	28	0	7	0	n/a
vanilla	52	1.2	8.8	1.4	n/a
Nobbly Bobbly, each LYONS MAID	147	1.4	22	5.9	n/a
Orange Maid, each LYONS MAID	78	0.3	19.1	0	n/a
Tom & Jerry, each WALLS	40	Tr	9.6	Tr	n/a
Twister, each WALLS	90	0.6	17.4	1.8	n/a
Zoom, each LYONS MAID	46	0.3	10	0.5	n/a

See also: **DESSERTS AND PUDDINGS**

Calorie Counter

All amounts per 100g/100ml unless otherwise stated	Cal kcal	Pro g	Carb g	Fat g	Fibre g

BISCUITS

	Cal kcal	Pro g	Carb g	Fat g	Fibre g
BN Biscuit McVities					
chocolate	460	6	73	16	2.2
strawberry	395	5.8	78	6.8	1.3
vanilla	470	5.9	74	17	1.2
Happy Faces Biscuits, jam and cream Jacobs	484	4.8	66.1	22	1.5
Iced Gem Jacob's	403	5.4	88.5	5.4	1.5
Jammie Dodger Burton's Foods	488	5	75	14	n/a
Jam Rings Crawford's	470	5.5	73	17	1.9
Party Ring Biscuits Fox's	459	5.1	75.8	15	n/a
Pink Wafers Crawford's	525	3.8	70.5	25	1.2
Wagon Wheels Burton's Foods					
original	426	5.6	66.5	15.2	1.9
jammie	419	5.2	66.9	14.3	1.9

See also: BAKERY

SWEETS

	Cal kcal	Pro g	Carb g	Fat g	Fibre g
Freddo Cadbury	530	7.8	57.1	30	n/a
Fruit Pastilles, body parts Nestlé Rowntree	348	4.3	82.9	0	0

All amounts per 100g/100ml unless otherwise stated	Cal kcal	Pro g	Carb g	Fat g	Fibre g
Hubba Bubba Bubble Gum, all flavours WRIGLEY	280	0	n/a	0	0
Jelly Babies	334	5.2	78	0	0
Jellytots NESTLÉ ROWNTREE	346	0.1	86.5	0	0
Milky Bar/Buttons NESTLÉ ROWNTREE	542	7.6	57.5	31	0
Milky Way Magic Stars MARS	522	6.9	58.5	29	n/a
Orbit Chewing Gum, sugarfree, for children WRIGLEY	160	0	N	0	0
Postman Pat Chew TREBOR BASSETT	396	0.7	83.8	6.1	0
Pretzel Flipz NESTLÉ ROWNTREE	470	7.9	66.4	19	n/a
Smarties NESTLÉ ROWNTREE	458	4.1	73.5	16	0
giant	477	5.3	69	20	n/a
mini	455	4.2	71.5	17	0
Starburst Joosters MARS	356	0	88.8	0.1	n/a
Starburst Juicy Gums MARS	309	5.9	71	4.1	n/a
Taz CADBURY	485	4.8	62	24	n/a
Wildlife CADBURY	520	7.8	56.8	29	n/a
Winders, Real Fruit KELLOGG'S	380	0.1	80	7	1.5

See also: **SWEETS AND CHOCOLATE**

Calorie Counter

All amounts per 100g/100ml unless otherwise stated	Cal kcal	Pro g	Carb g	Fat g	Fibre g
TINNED PASTA					
Pasta Shapes					
Action Man, in tomato sauce HEINZ	59	1.9	12	0.4	0.6
Barney HP	68	1.8	14.3	0.4	0.7
Bob the Builder HP	69	1.4	12.7	1.4	0.4
Scooby Doo, in tomato sauce HP	69	1.4	12.7	1.4	0.4
Teletubbies, in tomato sauce HEINZ	61	2	12.3	0.4	0.6
Thomas the Tank Engine HEINZ	62	2.1	12.6	0.4	0.7
Thunderbirds, in tomato sauce HP	68	1.8	14.3	0.4	0.7
Tweenies HEINZ	59	1.9	12	0.4	0.6
Pasta shapes with sausages HEINZ					
Teletubbies, in tomato sauce	91	3.7	11.5	3.3	0.5
Thomas the Tank Engine	92	3.7	11.5	3.4	0.5
Pizzaghetti, cheese and tomato HEINZ	75	2.6	13.2	1.3	0.6
Spaghetti Shapes, Postman Pat, in tomato sauce HP	58	1.8	14.3	0.4	0.7

See also: **PASTA**

All amounts per 100g/100ml unless otherwise stated	Cal kcal	Pro g	Carb g	Fat g	Fibre g

POTATO PRODUCTS

	Cal kcal	Pro g	Carb g	Fat g	Fibre g
Alphabites BIRDS EYE	134	2	19.5	5.3	1.4
Dinosaur Bites McCAIN	189	3.5	27.5	7.2	n/a
Potato Smiles McCAIN	190	3.2	26.8	7.8	n/a

See also: **CHIPS, FRIES AND SHAPED POTATO PRODUCTS**

DIPS

	Cal kcal	Pro g	Carb g	Fat g	Fibre g
Dairylea Dunkers KRAFT	280	8.6	27.5	15	0.9
Salt and Vinegar	310	17.1	24.5	21	1.2
Smokey Bacon	300	7.3	24	20	n/a
Dairylea Dunkers Jumbo Chipsticks KRAFT	300	7.2	26.5	19	1.2

See also: **DIPS AND PRE-DRESSED SALADS**

READY MEALS

	Cal kcal	Pro g	Carb g	Fat g	Fibre g
Captain Chicksticks BIRDS EYE	274	14.4	13.3	18	0.8
Captain Coins Mini Fish Cakes BIRDS EYE	188	9.5	18.7	8.3	1.1
Chicken Dippers BIRDS EYE	280	12.5	12.9	20	0.2
Chicken Nuggets	295	12	19	19	0.7

Calorie Counter

All amounts per 100g/100ml unless otherwise stated	Cal kcal	Pro g	Carb g	Fat g	Fibre g
Chicken O's BIRDS EYE	**260**	13.1	14.6	17	0.7
Crispy Pancakes FINDUS					
cheddar cheese	**185**	6.4	23.5	7.5	0.8
chicken & bacon	**165**	6.4	23.3	4.9	0.9
chicken & mushroom	**165**	5.7	23.4	5.5	0.9
chicken korma	**170**	6.9	22.8	5.9	1
minced beef	**170**	6.1	22.8	5.8	0.9
southern style chicken	**100**	5.6	23.9	4.8	1.1
Dairylea Lunchable Fun Pack, each KRAFT					
chicken,	**430**	15.5	47	17	2.4
harvest ham	**445**	13.5	48.5	20	2.4
hotdog	**450**	13	47.5	21	2.3
tender turkey	**450**	14.5	48.5	19	2.7
Fish Fingers, oven crispy BIRDS EYE	**226**	10.7	15.5	13	0.5
Haddock Fillet Fish Fingers BIRDS EYE	**185**	12.5	15.6	8.1	0.7
Turkey Dinosaurs BERNARD MATHEWS	**151**	5.7	9.2	10	n/a
Turkey Jetters BERNARD MATHEWS	**75**	2.9	5.6	4.5	n/a
Twizzlers BERNARD MATHEWS	**285**	9.1	14.2	21	n/a

See also: **SNACK MEALS, READY MEALS**

All amounts per 100g/100ml unless otherwise stated	Cal kcal	Pro g	Carb g	Fat g	Fibre g
CRISPS/SNACKS					
Cheesy Nibbles, per 10p pack	77	0.9	7.2	4.9	0.4
Footballs, per pack, (23g) WALKERS					
Bacon	122	1.3	13.6	6.9	0.3
Cheese	122	1.4	13.1	7.1	0.3
French Fries, per pack, (22g)					
Cheese & Onion	94	1.2	14.1	3.5	0.9
Ready Salted	95	1.1	14.1	3.7	1
Salt & Vinegar	92	1.1	13.9	3.5	1
Worcester Sauce	92	1.1	14.1	1.8	0.9
Hula Hoops, per pack, (27g) UNITED BISCUITS					
Original	140	0.9	14.9	8.5	0.6
Barbecue Beef	139	1	14.6	8.5	0.6
Salt & Vinegar	137	0.8	14.4	8.5	0.6
Krunchie Onion Rings, per 10p pack	69	0.9	8.4	3.5	0.4
Krunchie Sticks, per 10p pack	66	1.1	8.3	3.2	0.3
Monster Munch, per pack, (25g) WALKERS					
Flamin' Hot	123	1.8	15	6.3	0.4
Pickled Onion	124	1.5	15.5	6.3	0.4
Pickled Onion Mystery	124	1.5	15.5	6.3	0.4
Roast Beef	119	1.7	14.5	6	0.4

Calorie Counter

All amounts per 100g/100ml unless otherwise stated	Cal kcal	Pro g	Carb g	Fat g	Fibre g
Oinks, per 10p pack	70	1.1	7.8	3.8	0.5
Petrified Prawns, per 10p pack	70	1	8.5	3.5	0.2
Quarterbacks, per 10p pack	72	0.9	7.6	4.2	0.5
Skips, per pack, (17g) UNITED BISCUITS					
Prawn Cocktail	88	0.6	10.2	5	0.2
Tangy Toms, per 10p pack	70	1	8.2	3.6	0.3
Transform A, per 10p pack					
Cheese & Onion	73	0.9	7.8	4.2	0.4
Pickled Onion	69	0.9	7.3	4	0.5
Spicy	63	1	8.6	2.7	0.3
Wotsits, per pack, (21g) GOLDEN WONDER					
Cheesey	114	1.8	10.6	7.1	0.2
Barbecue Beef	110	1.5	11.7	6.3	0.3
Prawn Cocktail	111	1.4	11.8	6.4	0.2

FAMILY FAVOURITES AND RECIPES

Calorie Counter

BEANBURGER, SOYA, FRIED IN VEGETABLE OIL

120g chopped onion	1 tsp mixed herbs
10g vegetable oil	20g soya sauce
320g boiled soya beans	35g tomato purée
75g porridge oats	1 egg
10g chopped fresh parsley	vegetable oil absorbed on frying (20g)

Fry onion in oil until brown. Mix beans and onions together with remaining ingredients. Form into 6–8 shapes approximately 1cm thick. Fry for 3 minutes either side.

Values per 100g: Cal 193, Pro 10.6, Carb 13.7, Fat 11.0, Fibre 4.7

BEEF BOURGUIGNONNE

1 tbsp vegetable oil	150g button mushrooms
100g button onions	5g tomato purée
1 clove garlic, crushed	1 tsp dried mixed herbs
500g stewing beef, diced	250ml red wine
50g streaky bacon rashers, chopped	250ml stock
	$1/2$ tsp salt
15g flour	$1/4$ tsp pepper

Brown the onions, garlic, meat and bacon in oil. Stir in flour, tomato purée, mixed herbs, wine, stock and seasoning. Bring to the boil, cover and simmer for 1 hour, stirring occasionally. Add mushrooms and cook for a further 30 minutes.

Values per 100g: Cal 105, Pro 14.3, Carb 2.5, Fat 4.3, Fibre 0.4

BEEF STEW

500g stewing beef, diced	500ml stock
150g onions, chopped	150g carrots, chopped
1 tbsp vegetable oil	½ tsp salt
30g flour	¼ tsp pepper

Brown the meat and onions in oil, add flour and cook for
1 minute. Blend in the stock, add carrots and seasoning,
transfer to a dish, cover and cook in the oven for 2 hours at
180°C/mark 4.

Values per 100g: Cal 107, Pro 12.0, Carb 4.7, Fat 4.6, Fibre 0.7

BOLOGNESE SAUCE

1 clove garlic, crushed	397g canned tomatoes
60g onions, chopped finely	250ml stock
500g minced beef	2 tsp vegetable oil
40g carrots, chopped finely	½ tsp salt
30g celery, chopped finely	¼ tsp pepper
10g tomato purée	¼ tsp dried mixed herbs

Brown the garlic, onions and mince in oil, add carrots and
celery. Stir in the other ingredients and simmer for 40 minutes
with the lid on.

Values per 100g: Cal 161, Pro 11.8, Carb 2.5, Fat 11.6, Fibre 0.6

BREAD PUDDING

225g white bread
275ml milk
50g melted butter
75g demerara sugar

4g mixed spice
1 beaten egg
175g dried fruit

Break bread into pieces, cover with milk and leave for
30 minutes. Add remaining ingredients, mix well and bake
for 1¼ hours at 180°C/mark 4.

Values per 100g: Cal 289, Pro 5.9, Carb 48, Fat 9.5, Fibre 1.2

CAULIFLOWER CHEESE

100g grated cheese
1 small cauliflower (700g)
100ml cauliflower water
½ level tsp salt

25g margarine
25g flour
250ml semi-skimmed milk
pepper

Boil cauliflower until just tender, break into florets. Drain
saving 100ml water, place in a dish and keep warm. Make a
white sauce from the margarine, flour, milk and cauliflower
water. Add 75g cheese and season. Pour over the cauliflower
and sprinkle with the remaining cheese. Brown under a grill
or in a hot oven, 220°C/mark 7.

Values per 100g: Cal 102, Pro 6.0, Carb 5.1, Fat 6.5, Fibre 1.3

CASSEROLE, SAUSAGE

400g diced pork
150g onions, chopped
200g streaky bacon rashers,
  chopped
1 tbsp vegetable oil
200g pork sausage,
  chopped

227g baked beans,
  in tomato sauce, canned
1 bay leaf
1 tsp dried mixed herbs
300ml stock
$^1/_2$ tsp salt
$^1/_4$ tsp pepper

Brown the pork, onions and bacon in the oil, add the
remaining ingredients and bake, uncovered, for 1$^1/_2$ hours at
170°C/mark 3.

Values per 100g: Cal 165, Pro 11.9, Carb 5.1, Fat 10.9, Fibre 0.9

CASSEROLE, VEGETABLE

240g diced potato
120g sliced carrot
120g diced onion
120g diced swede
120g diced parsnip

90g canned sweetcorn
90g frozen peas
90g chopped tomatoes
450g canned tomatoes
1 tsp marmite

Place all ingredients in a casserole and stir. Cover and cook
for approximately 1 hour at 190°C/mark 5.

Values per 100g: Cal 52, Pro 2.2, Carb 10.6, Fat 0.4, Fibre 2.1

CHILLI CON CARNE

500g minced beef	15ml vinegar
150g onions, chopped	1 tsp sugar
100g green peppers, chopped	30g tomato purée
1 tbsp vegetable oil	397g canned tomatoes
1 tsp salt	150ml stock
1/4 tsp pepper	115g red kidney beans, canned, drained

Brown the mince, onions and peppers in oil. Blend the other ingredients and stir into the meat. Cover and simmer gently for 40 minutes. Add the kidney beans and continue cooking for a further 10 minutes.

Values per 100g: Cal 121, Pro 9.2, Carb 4.4, Fat 7.5, Fibre 1.1

COQ AU VIN

100g back bacon rashers, chopped	1/2 tsp salt
1000g chicken leg quarters (weighed with bone)	1/4 tsp pepper
	100g shallots
50g butter	1 tsp dried mixed herbs
50g flour	100g button mushrooms
	600ml red wine

Brown the bacon and chicken coated in seasonal flour, in butter. Add the shallots, mixed herbs and red wine, cover and simmer for 35–45 minutes. Add the mushrooms and cook for another 20 minutes.

Values per 100g: Cal 155, Pro 11.1, Carb 3.2, Fat 11, Fibre 0.3

CRUMBLE, FRUIT, PLAIN OR WHOLEMEAL

400g prepared fruit
50g margarine

100g plain or wholemeal flour
100g sugar

Prepare fruit. Arrange in a dish and sprinkle with sugar. Rub together the other ingredients and pile on top. Bake for 40 minutes at 190°C/mark 5.

Values per 100g: Cal 195, Pro 2.6, Carb 31.6, Fat 7.4, Fibre 2.7

CURRY, BEEF

1 clove garlic, crushed
60g onions, chopped
500g lean braising steak, diced
1 tbsp vegetable oil
1 tbsp ground coriander
1 tsp chilli powder

$^1/_2$ tsp ground cumin
$^1/_2$ tsp ground turmeric
8g root ginger, ground
300ml water
$^1/_2$ tsp salt
5ml lemon juice
1 tsp garam masala

Brown the garlic, onions and meat in oil. Add spices and ginger. Stir in water, salt and lemon juice, cover and bring to the boil. Cook for $1^1/_2$ hours stirring occasionally. Add garam masala.

Values per 100g: Cal 143, Pro 18.8, Carb 1, Fat 7.1, Fibre 0.2

CURRY, CHICK PEA DAHL

225g dry chick pea dahl
220ml water absorbed
  on soaking
28g vegetable oil
60g chopped onion
2g crushed garlic

1 tsp chilli powder
1/2 tsp garam masala
7g chopped green chilli
100g chopped tomato
415ml water

Soak the chick pea dahl overnight. Fry the onion and garlic
until brown. Add a little water together with spices and
tomatoes. Stir and cook until dry. Add dahl and water,
simmer until cooked.

Values per 100g: Cal 154, Pro 7.9, Carb 17.9, Fat 6.1, Fibre N

CURRY, LAMB, MADE WITH CANNED CURRY SAUCE

500g stewing lamb, diced   385g curry sauce, canned
1 tbsp vegetable oil

Brown the lamb in oil. Add the sauce, cover and simmer for
45 minutes.

Values per 100g: Cal 249, Pro 11, Carb 3.6, Fat 13.4, Fibre N

FISH PIE

200g cooked cod
400g mashed potato

Sauce:
150ml milk
15g margarine
15g flour
$^1/_2$ level tsp salt

Flake the fish and mix with the white sauce. Pipe a potato border round a dish, pour in the fish mixture. Brown in the oven, 200°C/mark 6, for 30 minutes.

Values per 100g: Cal 102, Pro 8, Carb 12.3, Fat 3.0, Fibre 0.7

FRENCH DRESSING

25ml vinegar
75g olive oil

$^1/_2$ level tsp salt
$^1/_2$ level tsp pepper

Shake the ingredients together in a screw-topped jar or bottle.

Values per 100g: Cal 462, Pro 0.1, Carb 4.5, Fat 49.4, Fibre 0

FRUIT CAKE, RICH

200g margarine	250g flour
200g brown sugar	¼ tsp salt
4 eggs	750g mixed fruit
20g black treacle	150g mixed glacé fruit,
20ml brandy	chopped
	1 tsp mixed spice

Cream the fat and sugar. Beat the eggs, treacle and brandy. Fold in the sifted flour and spices and mix in the fruit. Turn into a 20cm cake tin. Bake for 4 hours at 150°C/mark 2.

Values per 100g: Cal 343, Pro 3.9, Carb 59.9, Fat 11.4, Fibre 1.5

FRUIT PIE, PASTRY TOP AND BOTTOM

450g raw shortcrust	450g fruit (eg. apple,
pastry	gooseberry, rhubarb, plum)
	80g sugar

Line a pie dish with half the pastry. Fill with prepared fruit and sugar and cover with remaining pastry. Bake for 10–15 minutes at 220°C/mark 7 to set pastry, then for about 20–30 minutes at 180°C/mark 4 to cook the fruit.

Values per 100g: Cal 260, Pro 3, Carb 34, Fat 13, Fibre 1.8

FRUIT SALAD

400g eating apples
113g grapes
320g oranges
40ml lemon juice

200g bananas
120g kiwi fruit
113g strawberries

Syrup
57g caster sugar

114ml water

Dissolve the sugar in the water in a pan over a low heat.
Bring to the boil and simmer for a minute, then remove from
the heat and allow to cool. Prepare fruit and sprinkle with
lemon juice. Mix fruit with the cool syrup and refrigerate.

Values per 100g: Cal 60, Pro 0.7, Carb 14.8, Fat 0.1, Fibre 1.3

GARLIC MUSHROOMS

250g mushrooms
2g garlic
40g butter

Clean mushrooms and remove stems. Crush the garlic and
sauté in butter. Fill mushroom caps with the garlic butter
mixture and grill for 5–7 minutes.

Values per 100g: Cal 140, Pro 2.1, Carb 0.7, Fat 14.4, Fibre 1.2

IRISH STEW

500g lamb neck fillet, diced	1 tsp dried mixed herbs
150g onions, sliced	15g flour
200g carrots, sliced	1/2 tsp salt
500g potatoes, sliced	1/4 tsp pepper
1 tbsp fresh parsley, chopped	300ml stock

Make layers of meat, vegetables, herbs, flour and seasoning in a casserole dish, ending with a top layer of potatoes. Pour in stock and cover. Bake for 1 hour at 170°C/mark 3, remove lid and cook for a further 30 minutes.

Values per 100g: Cal 107, Pro 7.7, Carb 8.6, Fat 4.9, Fibre 1

KEDGEREE

200g smoked haddock, cooked	2 eggs
	25g margarine
100g boiled white rice	1/2 tsp salt

Hard boil one egg. Melt the margarine and stir in the haddock, rice, salt and one beaten egg. Stir in chopped hard boiled egg and heat thoroughly.

Values per 100g: Cal 176, Pro 16, Carb 8, Fat 9.1, Fibre 0

LANCASHIRE HOTPOT

500g stewing lamb, diced
1/2 tsp salt
1/4 tsp pepper
100g carrots, sliced
100g turnip, chopped

100g onions, sliced
500g potatoes, sliced
300ml stock
2 tsp vegetable oil

Season the meat and mix with carrots, turnip and onions.
Layer this with the potatoes in a casserole, beginning and
ending with potatoes. Add stock and brush the top with oil.
Cover and bake for 2 hours at 150°C/mark 2. Remove lid to
brown the potatoes for the last 30 minutes.

Values per 100g: Cal 119, Pro 7.4, Carb 7.4, Fat 6.9, Fibre 0.9

LASAGNE

Meat sauce:
1 tbsp vegetable oil
50g streaky bacon rashers, chopped
50g onions, chopped
50g carrots, chopped
30g celery, chopped
300g minced beef
220g canned tomatoes
375ml stock
1 clove garlic, crushed
$1/2$ tsp salt
$1/4$ tsp pepper
$1/2$ tsp marjoram
1 bay leaf
50g mushrooms, sliced

Cheese sauce:
30g margarine
30g flour
400ml milk
75g cheese, grated

200g lasagne, raw

To top:
25g cheese, grated

Brown the bacon, onions, carrots, celery and mince in the oil. Stir in the remaining ingredients for the meat sauce and simmer for 15 minutes. For the cheese sauce, melt the margarine, add flour and cook for a few minutes, stir in the milk and cheese and cook gently until mixture thickens. In a dish, add alternative layers of lasagne, meat and cheese sauce ending with a layer of lasagne and cheese sauce. Sprinkle with cheese and bake for 1 hour at 190°C/mark 5.

Values per 100g: Cal 191, Pro 9.8, Carb 14.6, Fat 10.8, Fibre 0.8

MACARONI CHEESE

280g cooked macaroni	25g flour
350ml milk	100g grated cheese
25g margarine	½ tsp salt

Boil the macaroni and drain well. Make a white sauce from the margarine, flour and milk. Add 75g of the cheese and season. Add the macaroni and put in a pie dish. Sprinkle with remaining cheese and brown under grill or in a hot oven at 220°C/mark 7.

Values per 100g: Cal 162, Pro 6.7, Carb 12.2, Fat 9.9, Fibre 0.5

MILK PUDDING (RICE, SAGO, SEMOLINA OR TAPIOCA)

500ml whole milk	50g rice, sago, semolina
25g sugar	or tapioca

Simmer until cooked or bake in a moderate oven at 180°C/mark 4.

Values per 100g: Cal 130, Pro 4.1, Carb 19.6, Fat 4.3, Fibre 0.1

NUT ROAST

90g chopped onion
11g vegetable oil
20g flour
140ml water

225g chopped mixed nuts
115g wholemeal
  breadcrumbs
1 tsp marmite
1 tsp mixed herbs

Fry onion in the oil. Add flour and water and thicken. Mix in nuts, breadcrumbs, marmite and herbs. Pack into a loaf tin and cover with foil. Bake at 190°C/mark 5 for 35–45 minutes.

Values per 100g: Cal 333, Pro 13.2, Carb 18.4, Fat 23.5, Fibre 4.1

OMELETTE

2 eggs
10ml water
10g butter

$^1/_2$ tsp salt
pepper

Beat eggs with salt and water. Heat butter in an omelette pan. Pour in the mixture and stir until it begins to thicken evenly. While still creamy, fold the omelette and serve.

Values per 100g: Cal 195, Pro 10.9, Carb Tr, Fat 16.8, Fibre 0

OMELETTE, CHEESE

115g omelette, cooked
60g Cheddar cheese

Proportions are derived from recipe review.

Values per 100g: Cal 271, Pro 15.9, Carb Tr, Fat 23, Fibre 0

PANCAKES, SAVOURY

112g flour   56g lard (for pan)
300ml whole milk   ¼ tsp salt
1 egg

Method as for sweet pancakes.

Values per 100g: Cal 255, Pro 6.4, Carb 23.9, Fat 15.5, Fibre 0.8

PANCAKES, SWEET

100g flour   50g lard (for pan)
250ml whole milk   50g sugar
1 egg

Sieve the flour into a basin, add the egg and about 100ml of
the milk, stirring until smooth. Add the rest of the milk and
beat to a smooth batter. Heat a little of the lard in a frying pan
and pour in enough batter to cover the bottom. Cook both sides
and turn onto sugared paper. Dredge lightly with sugar.
Repeat until all the batter is used, to give about 10 pancakes.

Values per 100g: Cal 302, Pro 6, Carb 34.9, Fat 16.3, Fibre 0.8

PASTRY, Shortcrust

200g flour	½ tsp salt
50g margarine	30ml water
50g lard	

Rub the fat into the flour, mix to a stiff dough with the water, roll out and bake at 200°C/mark 6.

Values per 100g: Cal 524, Pro 6.6, Carb 54.3, Fat 32.6, Fibre 2.2

PIZZA, Cheese and Tomato

Dough:

200g flour
1 tsp salt
1 tsp sugar
150ml warm water
15g fresh yeast or
  2 tsp dried yeast

Topping:

200g tomatoes
150g cheese
8 black olives (40g)
20g oil

Make the dough, proving once. Knead and roll out shape. Leave for 10 minutes. Arrange sliced or pulped tomatoes on top, then cheese and olives. Brush with oil. Bake for 30 minutes at 230°C/mark 8.

Values per 100g: Cal 234, Pro 9.4, Carb 24.8, Fat 11.5, Fibre n/a

QUICHE, Cheese and Egg, Plain or Wholemeal

200g raw plain or wholemeal   150g milk
  shortcrust pastry   3 eggs
150g cheese

Line a 20cm flan ring with the shortcrust pastry. Fill with grated cheese. Beat eggs in the warmed milk and pour into pastry case. Bake for 10 minutes at 200°C/mark 6 and then 30 minutes at 180°C/mark 4.

Values per 100g: Cal 315, Pro 12.4, Carb 17.1, Fat 22.3, Fibre 0.6

QUICHE LORRAINE

200g raw shortcrust pastry   100g streaky bacon
2 eggs   100g cheese
200ml milk

Line a 20cm flan ring with shortcrust pastry. Fill with the fried, chopped bacon and grated cheese. Beat the eggs in warmed milk and pour into the pastry case. Bake for 10 minutes at 200°C/mark 6, then for 30 minutes at 180°C/mark 4.

Values per 100g: Cal 358, Pro 13.7, Carb 19.6, Fat 25.5, Fibre 0.7

RICE, EGG FRIED

35g vegetable oil
45g chopped onion

1½ beaten eggs
350g cooked white rice

Heat oil, add egg and remaining ingredients. Cook, turning mixture over, for 3 minutes.

Values per 100g: Cal 208, Pro 4.2, Carb 25.7, Fat 10.6, Fibre 0.4

RICE, FRIED WHITE

550g boiled rice
168g chopped onion
2 tbsp vegetable oil
21g garlic

2g salt
¼ tsp pepper
1g spices

Fry onion and garlic until soft. Add boiled rice and seasoning. Fry until oil has been absorbed and rice is fully coated.

Values per 100g: Cal 144, Pro 2.5, Carb 25.9, Fat 4.1, Fibre 0.5

RICE PUDDING *see* MILK PUDDING

SALAD, GREEN

150g shredded lettuce
230g sliced cucumber

160g sliced green pepper
30g sliced celery

Toss all ingredients together.

Values per 100g: Cal 12, Pro 0.7, Carb 1.8, Fat 0.3, Fibre 1.0

SAGO PUDDING *see* **MILK PUDDING**

SAUCE, CHEESE

350ml whole or semi- skimmed milk	25g flour
75g cheese	25g margarine
½ level tsp salt	cayenne pepper

Melt the fat in a pan, add flour and cook gently for a few
minutes stirring all the time. Add milk and cook until
mixture thickens, stirring continually. Add grated cheese and
seasoning. Reheat to soften the cheese, serve immediately.

Values per 100ml:
(whole milk)   Cal 198, Pro 8.1, Carb 8.7, Fat 14.8, Fibre 0.2
(semi-skimmed) Cal 181, Pro 8.2, Carb 8.8, Fat 12.8, Fibre 0.2

SAUCE, WHITE SAVOURY

350ml whole or semi- skimmed milk	½ level tsp salt
25g flour	25g margarine

Melt fat in a pan. Add flour and cook for a few minutes
stirring constantly. Add milk and salt, and cook gently until
mixture thickens.

Values per 100ml:
(whole milk)   Cal 151, Pro 4.2, Carb 10.6, Fat 10.3, Fibre 0.2
(semi-skimmed) Cal 130, Pro 4.4, Carb 10.7, Fat 8,   Fibre 0.2

SAUCE, WHITE SWEET

350ml whole or semi-
  skimmed milk
25g flour

25g margarine
30g sugar

As savoury white sauce except adding sugar and omitting salt.

Values per 100ml:
(whole milk)   Cal 171, Pro 3.9, Carb 18.3, Fat 9.5, Fibre 0.2
(semi-skimmed) Cal 152, Pro 4,   Carb 18.5, Fat 7.4, Fibre 0.2

SCONES, PLAIN

200g flour
4 tsp baking powder
1/4 tsp salt

50g margarine
10g sugar
125ml milk

Sift the flour, sugar and baking powder and rub in fat. Mix
in the milk. Roll out and cut into rounds. Bake in a hot oven
at 220°C/mark 7 for about 10 minutes.

Values per 100g: Cal 364, Pro 7.2, Carb 53.7, Fat 14.8, Fibre 1.8

SCRAMBLED EGGS WITH MILK

2 eggs
15ml milk

20g butter
1/2 level tsp salt

Melt butter in pan, stir in beaten egg, milk and seasoning.
Cook over gentle heat until mixture thickens.

Values per 100g: Cal 257, Pro 10.9, Carb 0.7, Fat 23.4, Fibre 0

SEMOLINA PUDDING *see* MILK PUDDING

SHEPHERD'S PIE

350g cooked minced beef	150ml water
100g onion boiled and	50ml milk
chopped	20g margarine
500g boiled potatoes	2 level tsp salt; pepper

Mix the beef and onion, moisten with water and add seasoning. Place in a pie dish. Mash the potato with the milk and margarine. Pile on top of the meat and bake in the oven for 25 minutes to brown, 190°C/mark 5.

Values per 100g: Cal 118, Pro 8, Carb 8.2, Fat 6.2, Fibre 0.6

SHORTBREAD

200g flour	100g butter
50g caster sugar	

Beat the butter and sugar to a cream. Mix in the flour and knead until smooth. Press into a flat tin to about 2cms thick. Bake for about 45 minutes at 170°C/mark 3.

Values per 100g: Cal 498, Pro 5.9, Carb 63.9, Fat 26.1, Fibre 1.9

SPONGE CAKE

150g flour
1 tsp baking powder
150g margarine

150g caster sugar
3 eggs

Cream the fat and sugar until light and fluffy. Add the beaten egg a little at a time and beat well. Fold in the sifted flour and baking powder. Bake for about 20 minutes at 190°C/mark 5.

Values per 100g: Cal 467, Pro 6.3, Carb 52.4, Fat 27.2, Fibre 0.9

TAPIOCA PUDDING *see* MILK PUDDING

VEGETABLE PIE

100g chopped onion
100g sliced carrot
100g sliced courgettes
60g chopped celery
50g sliced mushrooms
80g chopped red pepper
100g potatoes

200g canned tomatoes
100ml water
2 tsp cornflour
1 tsp mixed herbs
1 tsp marmite
300g raw shortcrust pastry

Place vegetables in a pan, together with herbs and marmite. Bring to the boil and simmer for 20–25 minutes. Make cornflour into a paste, add to pan, boil and stir until mixture thickens. Pour into pie dish and leave to cool. Roll pastry to fit dish size. Cut an additional 1 inch strip from remaining pastry, wet and place around the edge of the dish. Cover with pastry top and seal edges. Bake at 200°C/mark 6 for 30–40 minutes.

Values per 100g: Cal 159, Pro 3, Carb 18.8, Fat 8.4, Fibre 1.5

Calorie Counter

All amounts per 100g/100ml unless otherwise stated	Cal kcal	Pro g	Carb g	Fat g	Fibre g

All amounts per 100g/100ml unless otherwise stated	Cal kcal	Pro g	Carb g	Fat g	Fibre g

Calorie Counter

All amounts per 100g/100ml unless otherwise stated	Cal kcal	Pro g	Carb g	Fat g	Fibre g